THE PSYCHOTHERAPEUTIC IMPASSE

THE PSYCHOTHERAPEUTIC IMPASSE

Myron F. Weiner, M.D.

THE FREE PRESS
A Division of Macmillan Publishing Co., Inc.
NEW YORK

Collier Macmillan Publishers
LONDON

The Free Press
A Division of Macmillan Publishing Co., Inc.
866 Third Avenue, New York, N. Y. 10022

Collier Macmillan Canada, Inc.

Library of Congress Catalog Card Number: 81-68848

Printed in the United States of America

printing number

1 2 3 4 5 6 7 8 9 10

Library of Congress Cataloging in Publications Data

Weiner: Myron F.
The psychotherapeutic impasse.

Bibliography: p.
Includes index.
1. Impasse (Psychotherapy) I. Title
RC489.I45W44 616.89'14 81-68848
ISBN 0-02-934620-7 AACR2

To Jeanette

For your love and hard work

Contents

	Acknowledgments	ix
	Introduction	1
1	Diagnosis and Management of Impasse: General Principles	8
2	Contract-Related	42
3	Process-Related	61
4	Stage of Psychotherapy	84
5	The Therapist's Life Cycle	110
6	Repressive Therapy: Dealing with Ego Deficit	128
7	Ego-Supportive Therapy: Treating Adolescents	155
8	Group Psychotherapy	171
9	Couple and Family Therapy	193
10	Summary	212
	References	221
	Index	235

Acknowledgments

The original impetus for this work came from David Fuller, teacher, colleague, and friend. David used to say that one learns the most from one's most difficult cases. I used to reply that I never had any easy ones. Many ideas came from the work of Bob Beavers and Jerry Lewis on healthy families and on the parallels between communication in healthy families and the teaching of clear communication in psychotherapy. Zane Liff's paper on impasse helped to round out my discussion of the creative aspects of impasse. I am also grateful to Keith Johansen, Director of Professional Education at Timberlawn Psychiatric Center, for allowing me to present my material on contracts in a series of lectures to his residents.

Much of the material in this book was developed over nearly 18 years of teaching and supervising residents in the Department of Psychiatry at Southwestern Medical School. Serving as book review editor of the *International Journal of Group Psychotherapy* has given me access to many of the newly published works in research and practice of psychotherapy.

Early portions of the manuscript were typed by Sandi Love. The bulk of the manuscript was typed by Lisa Jackson, who has been responsible for the orderly flow of material that evolved from many preliminary states of disorganization.

My wife Jeanette listened patiently to every word of the first draft and helped to clarify my thinking, correct my grammar, and shorten my sentences. Gary Weiner functioned as editor and helped to keep me on the track. Kitty Moore of the Free Press came to the right place at the right time.

Writing is a lonely business. Thanks to all of you who kept me company.

Introduction

Why do psychotherapists with adequate skills and knowledge make errors in the type, timing, or dosage of their interventions? Why are patients damaged at some times and not at others? These are the questions I attempt to answer.

It is my intention to counter the presumption that applying an appropriate psychotherapeutic technique at an appropriate time will deal effectively with the entire spectrum of human psychological difficulties that present for treatment. There are many problems that are beyond the reach of psychotherapeutic intervention. They may indicate hospitalization, drugs, or environmental changes, and there is much that we do not know. Our knowledge is sufficient, however, to catalogue and describe the pitfalls of psychotherapy that cause significant slowing of therapy or that disrupt therapy and cost lives or many years of unnecessary suffering.

I hope also to demonstrate that all is not lost because an impasse has been reached in psychotherapy. In such a complicated endeavor as psychotherapy, it is a tribute to the practicing psychotherapist that impasses do not occur more frequently than they do. Many impasses can be resolved by management of the situation based on adequate diagnosis of the impasse, and some impasses call forth unsuspected resources in the patient and the therapist as both realize their contributions to the stalemate and their need to change.

It is more difficult to determine the proportion of patients who are harmed by psychotherapy or who fail to improve than to estimate what proportion improves significantly. No single outcome measure, such as patient satisfaction, is universally applicable. In fact, different outcome measures must be applied to different patient populations. A positive outcome measure for a group of delinquents, such as a reduction in unplanned behavior, might be a negative outcome variable for a group of shy, socially inhibited people.

Recent documentation of harm by psychotherapy does not surprise the observant psychotherapist.* All psychotherapists, like all health care practitioners, do some damage during their professional careers. The issue we must face is not whether patients are damaged or fail to be helped, but what can be done to minimize damage to patients and to prevent, detect, and correct therapeutic stalemates.

Truax and Carkhuff (1967) have held that the most helpful aspects of the psychotherapeutic relationship are the therapist-offered conditions of accurate empathy, nonpossessive warmth, and genuineness. By logical extension, one would expect the opposites of these qualities—that is, lack of empathy, lack of warmth, and failure to respond authentically—to be antitherapeutic. My own experience and more recent research suggest that there is more to helping or harming a patient than the presence or absence of these three qualities (Mitchell, Bozarth, & Krauft, 1977).

Psychotherapy is a type of communicative interaction that aims to heighten self-esteem, increase coping ability, and help people to cooperate constructively with one another. Many com-

*The accumulation of statistical evidence that determines the degree of harm to patients began with Eysenck (1952) and has recently been summarized by Lambert, Bergin, and Collins (1977). There is strong evidence that even brief contact in a quasitherapy setting can be harmful. Lieberman, Yalom, and Miles (1973) found that 16 persons in a population of 209 members of short-term encounter groups led by experienced professionals suffered emotional setbacks.

municative interactions, with or without therapeutic interest, undermine self-esteem, interfere with coping, and make cooperation with others difficult. Communication of this sort has been described in mothers of schizophrenics (Beavers et al., 1965) and in severely dysfunctional families (Henry, 1965; Lewis et al., 1976). It is so obvious to the lay person that many of the types of pathological communications have been described in lay literature. Most important is that communication that is harmful to the patient has also been observed in interactions between psychotherapists and their patients (Bergin, 1971; Weiner, 1978).

If psychotherapy is only one type of life-enhancing communication, we might study naturally occurring situations in which communication has positive or negative effects in order to ascertain which interpersonal communications have salutary effects and which have detrimental effects. This information is available from studies of healthy and dysfunctional families. If we examine the data, we find specific differences between well-functioning families and families that cope poorly with life events (Beavers, 1977). Severely disturbed families influence a member's behavior by coercion. By contrast, healthy families cooperate for the good of the family as a whole. Goals are dictated or imposed in dysfunctional families. In healthy families, they are negotiated and mutually agreed upon to a degree commensurate with each family member's maturity and ability to understand. Obedience is demanded by parents in dysfunctional families, regardless of the reasonableness of the request. Thinking for one's self is discouraged. Healthy families cultivate appropriate interdependence and autonomy. Others' thoughts and needs are presumed in unhealthy families. In healthy families they are determined by asking. Members of unhealthy families blame others for what they do. Dysfunctional families act as if the world and the people in it were always the same. For them, the present is the same as the past. They are closed to new information and therefore have stereotyped responses. Healthy families are open to new information, and their members are flexible in their responses and their roles. Finally, perhaps because they view the world as hostile, dysfunctional families evidence little altruism, while altruism and a positive view of the world are common in healthy families.

The above qualities of families associated with optimal function and dysfunction in natural settings carry over into the psychotherapeutic setting. Psychonoxious therapists (Bergin, 1971) are coercive and unwilling to negotiate, are unwilling to recognize their patients as individuals, and tend to perceive only their own needs in the therapeutic relationship. They assess the patients' needs by presumption, and tolerate neither the patients' dependence nor autonomy. They blame the patients when things go wrong, take the credit when they go right, entertain no new ideas about their patients, and do not change their responses to the patients. They see the patients as a means to fulfill their own needs and view the patients and patients' world negatively. Impasse or damage results.

No psychotherapist behaves in these ways all of the time, but we do attempt to force our frame of reference onto certain patients. We attempt to force some patients to accept treatment because we feel their lives are in danger; we are unwilling to negotiate because of our appraisal of the risks involved. We lump our patients into diagnostic categories. We avoid patients who cause us discomfort. We make educated guesses, based on inadequate information, about patients' needs, and berate patients for their clinging or for their unwillingness to depend on us. When things go wrong, we say the patient was poorly motivated or was acting out. We refuse to listen to the patients who tell us that they find insight of little use and we refuse to change our therapeutic goal to one that better suits the patients' abilities. We become upset when our patients refuse to meet our omnipotent need for them to get well on our terms and we impugn their malignant marital situations or their unconscious resistances.

Obviously, there are times to coerce, to maintain a firm position, to make diagnoses, to avoid certain patients, to make educated guesses, to be intolerant of certain behaviors, to hold the patient responsible, to be convinced of the correctness of one's judgment, and to recognize negative aspects of the patient and his life situation. None of the qualities of the dysfunctional family is negative in an absolute sense, and, by the same token, no quality of a healthy family is positive in an absolute sense. Instead, paraphrasing Paul (1967), we must ask *what* behavior or attitude by *what* therapist is most effective for *this* individual with *that* specific problem and under *which* circumstances.

It is clear that people are more vulnerable in their personal lives and in the treatment situation at certain times than at others. Interpersonal vulnerability is not static. There are often certain critical points in therapy that we can aptly term as nodal points. Nodal points in therapy occur when a specific vulnerability of the patients enters the interaction between therapists and patients and must be dealt with. It may be dramatic or subtle. When nodal points do arise, the experience of interacting with the therapists is, for the moment, the primary vehicle of treatment. Seen from one point of view, the patients are exposed and vulnerable. From another viewpoint, they have an opportunity to rework feelings, attitudes, and ways of behaving in the world. Whether they change in a positive way or whether they are wounded is the therapists' technical problem and therapeutic responsibility. If the patients change in a self-enhancing way through an encounter of this sort, they have had what Alexander (1946) called corrective emotional experiences. If the patients are unchanged or damaged, and if the same process is repeated when similar nodal points in therapy recur, a state of impasse exists.

Therapists cannot tell which patients will have dramatic or crucial nodal points in therapy. This depends more on the specific interaction between therapists and patients than on any specific quality of either one. Therapists must be prepared to deal with nodal points when they arise and to decide, on the spot, to open the patients to new ways of looking at themselves and the world or to reinforce aspects of the patients' current ideas and behavior because of the patients' inability to deal with the anxiety they must tolerate in working toward a new view of the world. Not all psychotherapy can promote emotional growth. With certain patients, one is thankful to maintain the status quo. Maintaining the status quo of a person who has the capacity for profound regression can in no way be considered a therapeutic impasse. It is a fact of life in the treatment of people whose adjustment is tenuous at best. Therapists, through training and experience, become able to spot the patients for whom the nodal experiences in a growth-promoting approach would threaten psychological equilibrium or might lead to irreversible damage or prolonged suffering. Therapists must be able to tell the difference between extracting a psychological splinter and pulling the props out from under a person.

Eysenck's (1952) study that showed equal rates of remission in patients treated psychotherapeutically and applicants to a clinic who were placed on a waiting list has been restudied, and, when viewed in the light of more recent research, shows that patients treated psychotherapeutically have a wider range of outcomes than the untreated group. This suggests that much of the positive outcome of psychotherapy is statistically obscured by the fact that many patients are harmed or made worse by psychotherapy (Bergin, 1963). Bergin (1966) coined the term "deterioration effect" to describe the tendency for controlled outcome studies to show an increase in outcome score variability after treatment.

There can be disagreement as to whether or not a patient is really worse. It can be argued, for example, that patients who become psychotic during the course of psychotherapy have not been harmed and that they are only experiencing a temporary regression while seeking a more satisfactory resolution of their intrapsychic conflicts. I disagree. One episode of psychosis increases the likelihood of a second psychotic break. Even if this were not true, the regression costs the patients months away from work and family. It can also be argued that psychotherapy patients who attempt suicide are only attempting to manipulate the therapists. This may be partly true, but the patients have compounded their psychological difficulties by placing their physical well-being at risk. We must ask ourselves if there are means to avoid such disruptive and dangerous reactions to psychotherapy.

By studying situations in which treatment has been ineffective or in which harm has been done, we may learn to avoid harming patients and we may reach a better understanding of the factors that promote symptomatic improvement and emotional growth.

Mistakes are common in psychotherapy, as they are in any complex undertaking in which there is substantial freedom of action for each of the parties involved. Untrained psychotherapists bite off more than they can chew. Experienced psychotherapists become jaded and opinionated. Therapists can become so enamored of their techniques that they lose sight of their patients' needs, and they may become so concerned with meeting their own or their patients' personal needs that they lose sight of the therapeutic process and their professional responsibility.

Everyone readily acknowledges that to err is human. Professionals buy malpractice insurance not only to defend against rapacious patients and their lawyers, but to compensate the victims of their more serious mistakes. Courts recognize that treatment of any kind is based on trial and error and that we can never eliminate some element of trial and error (Pope, Simpson, & Weiner, 1978). People and the interactions between them are so complex that not all therapists can treat every patient, and virtually every patient requires some modification of any treatment approach. Therapists must avoid getting lost in the individuality of each patient and must keep in mind the general principles of the treatment they are attempting to implement.

It has been said that one learns more from one's mistakes than from one's successes. In some respects, this book is a catalogue of mistakes. I hope to show the common elements of these mistakes, and I hope that this will contribute to the recognition, alleviation, and prevention of further mistakes, thereby contributing to the education of psychotherapists and to the well-being of their patients.

1 Diagnosis and Management of Impasse: General Principles

Different types of psychotherapy are better suited to some problems than to others, and psychotherapy must often be combined with biological and environmental measures. Well-conducted or effective psychotherapy does not follow a smooth upward course. Even the best-conducted psychotherapeutic experience periodically stalls and has other moments of rapid progress. Indeed, plateaus are frequent and temporary regressions common.

An impasse is an acute or long-term failure of treatment in which the patients' presenting problems and their overall level of coping with themselves and their world are not improved or significantly worsen. Its result is unnecessarily prolonged emotional discomfort or impairment of function.

It is not difficult to diagnose an impasse after patients have made suicide attempts, required hospitalization, or precipitously terminated treatment, but earlier recognition is obviously desirable.

Oftentimes impasses occur early in psychotherapy, and result in failure to continue psychotherapy (Garfield, 1980). Garfield and Kurz (1952) reviewed 560 cases in a psychoanalytically oriented VA outpatient clinic whose staff saw itself as doing intensive psychotherapy. In this series, 43 percent of the patients dropped out before the fifth interview, 50 percent terminated prematurely before the sixth interview, and only 8.8 percent remained for 25 or more therapy sessions. Similarly, the National Center for Health Statistics (1966) reported an average of 4.7 visits per patient to psychiatrists during a 12-month period. In studies conducted in urban mental health clinics, Fiester and Rudestam (1975) reported that 37 to 45 percent of the patients dropped out after the first or second interview; Craig and Huffine (1976) found that 43 percent terminated before the fourth interview.

Studies of the age, sex, and psychiatric diagnosis of patients who drop out prematurely have shed no light on the subject, nor have psychological tests or appraisals of motivation (Garfield, 1980). The cause of premature dropouts is evidently not to be found in the patient, but in the interaction of the patient with the treating person or environment.

A study by Garfield and Wolpin (1963) does shed some light in this area. They asked 70 patients to complete a questionnaire before assignment to treatment. In this group, whose median education was 12 years, psychotherapy was selected from a list of other therapies as the preferred treatment by 88 percent of the patients. A majority indicated that emotional factors were of some importance in their difficulties, and they also indicated that self-understanding would help improve their lot. This apparent positive attitude toward psychotherapy and toward dealing with psychological issues contrasted with other responses to the questionnaire and with the views held by their therapists. Over one-third of the group thought that therapy sessions would be 30 minutes or less, 73 percent expected improvement by the fifth session, and 70 percent expected psychotherapy to be successfully concluded in ten sessions or less!

Heine and Trosman (1960) found that terminators sought medication or diagnostic information and passive cooperation while remainers were more likely to stress collaboration and help in changing behavior. In another study, Heine (1962) found that terminators more frequently expected advice in the first session. Overall and Aronson (1962) found that patients whose expectations of therapy were less congruent with those of their therapists were more likely to terminate prematurely.

Rosenzweig and Folman (1974) found that ratings made by therapists after their patients' second group psychotherapy sessions, including their ability to empathize with the patient, their positive feelings toward the patient, and their evaluation of the patient's ability to form a therapeutic relationship, were all related to continuation in psychotherapy. Shapiro (1974) found that therapists' positive feelings toward their patients were related to continuation in therapy.

Even the question of patients' motivation must be examined from an interactional point of view because therapists usually assess patients' motivation in terms of the treatment that the therapist offers. To an insight-oriented therapist, motivation is willingness to engage in self-exploration, to face the negative aspects of one's personality, and to deal with emotionally painful aspects of one's past life that influence one's present-day thinking and behavior. To therapists with this orientation, the wish for quick, easy answers is seen as lack of motivation, and they may respond by demonstrating their lack of motivation for dealing with emotional problems in this way.

The material presented thus far suggests that incongruent therapist and patient expectations are probably frequent causes of premature termination from treatment, and that serious impasses may occur in the treatment of nearly half the people who seek help with their emotional problems.

Sources of Impasse

For the untrained psychotherapist, errors in diagnosis and technical errors in treatment are the most common causes of impasse in psychotherapy (Chessick, 1971). The most common diagnostic error is the overestimation of ego strength and capacity for self-examination. The most common technical error is the application of an inefficient or inappropriate therapeutic technique, usually a result of the therapist's treatment bias or naiveté. For the experienced psychotherapist, resistance and noncompliance are the most important patient variables leading to impasse in psychotherapy. Resistance is the patient's unconscious obstruction of the conduct or course of psychotherapy. Noncompliance is the patient's conscious failure to cooperate with the treatment process. Both resistance and noncompliance occur to some degree in every therapeutic encounter.

Resistance

The formal study of resistance began with Breuer and Freud (1895), who found that if certain forgotten thoughts and feelings were remembered, patients with hysterical complaints were relieved of their symptoms. After his initial success with this method, which involved strong elements of suggestion, Freud found that something in the minds of his patients actively opposed their remembering significant events, thoughts, and feelings. He called this opposing force resistance and termed its mechanism repression (Freud, 1910). The depository of repressed memories, thoughts, and feelings was named the unconscious. At first Freud considered resistance a nuisance, an obstacle to curative insight and abreaction. He later concluded that working through resistance is the basic work of psychoanalysis and that repression is only one part of the process of resistance (Freud, 1940).

Further light was shed on resistance by Anna Freud (1946), who delineated the ego's defenses against painful memories, thoughts, and feelings. She found that the resistances encountered in psychoanalysis are part of the normal functioning of the psychic apparatus. Further work has shown that, except in the treatment of traumatic conditions that arise from overwhelming psychological traumata, recovery of material from the unconscious is therapeutically ineffective unless the defenses and coping mechanisms that miscarried and resulted in the patient's symptoms are partially reworked.

Sigmund Freud found that resistance had intrapsychic and interpersonal elements, manifested in the transference and its acting out. He claimed, however, that psychopathology is in the patient, that it is to be studied in the patient, and that it is best dealt with by interpreting the patient's thoughts, feelings, and behavior toward the analyst as repetitive attempts to master or to recreate certain aspects of his or her childhood.

Freud (1912) was also aware that analysts may suffer distortions in their relationships with patients based on their own unconscious wishes, the phenomenon now known as countertransference. He went so far as to suggest "psychoanalytic purification" for the analyst to minimize the countertransference. Again, the emphasis was on the analyst as an individual. But there is more to the emotional relationship between therapist and patient than transference and countertransference. The latter term, incidentally, is often broadened to include all of the therapist's feelings toward the patient (Singer & Luborsky, 1977). A substantial number of the factors that affect the therapeutic relationship are based on neither transference nor countertransference, and much of what has been regarded as transference and countertransference is based on accurate perceptions and appropriate emotional reactions of therapist and patient alike.

In the contemporary practice of psychotherapy, resistance is the obstruction of the therapeutic process by mental activities of which the patients are unaware, and from which they are conscious of no gain. It results in part from the ego's attempts to maintain repression of unacceptable drives and threatening memories. Resistance can also stem from the ego's wish to maintain the secondary gain which results from the symptoms. For example, the pension awarded for a disability can reduce a person's motivation to return to work, especially if the work is unpleasant or dangerous. The therapy of compensation cases is often delayed until after the compensation award has been made. After the award is made, the symptom is no longer reinforced by the need to appear disabled so as to ensure adequate compensation (Sternbach, 1974).

Experience with combat-related emotional problems during two world wars suggests that acute anxiety disorders arising in combat are best treated at the front lines. Return of the emotional casualty to a distant convalescent site reinforces anxiety as a means to avoid combat (Kardiner, 1959).

Resistance can result from the superego's insistence that one suffer for past or present misdeeds through psychologically painful symptoms. Id resistances also occur. Neurotic symptoms involve disguised, symbolic discharge of id impulses that would be curtailed if the neurotic symptoms were abandoned. In addition, the transference, whether positive or negative, can be a source of resistance. Positive transference becomes a resistance when the patient waits expectantly for the beloved, omnipotent therapist magically to remove symptoms. Resistance that stems from negative transference can arise. Patients may sulk over the therapist's failure to gratify their expectations for the treatment or for the patient-therapist relationship. Transference as a resistance is illustrated by the following vignette.

> Mrs. A.K.'s sessions had been dull and boring for several months. She brought up little of psychological interest, and confined herself to discussing daily events without dealing with their emotional significance. Since all else failed, the therapist eventually suggested reducing visits from twice a week to once a week. After a few once-a-week sessions her anxiety level rose, and she revealed the transference resistance that had developed. She had learned from a friend that there was a serious illness in the therapist's family. She had been trying not to burden the therapist further by raising any issues that might prove difficult. The therapist told her that he appreciated her trying to spare him. They jointly concluded that the tedious sessions they had been spending together were doing neither of them any good, and they agreed to investigate further her motivation for stopping work on herself. The issue boiled down to her idea that if she protected him from stress and strain, the therapist would not desert her as her father had deserted her and her mother. As they worked through the transference issue, she began to express the negative feelings toward him that she had withheld during the previous months and began to resolve her wish for him to be as dependent on her as she felt on him. This bit of transference behavior was tied to her feeling that if she had been more attentive to her father, he would not have deserted her and her mother. Resolving the transference issue left her more free to establish other relationships. As she became more comfortable with negative feelings toward the therapist, her feelings toward her father, her mother, and her religion all became more positive.

In the course of insight-oriented therapies, resistances may be allowed to stand, may be reinforced, may be dealt with by showing that they are inappropriate, or may be dealt with by interpreting their unconscious significance. Resistances are left untouched when they are irrelevant to the current focus of inquiry. For example, one does not begin therapy by dealing with minor phobic symptoms in a person whose chief difficulty is a painful relationship with a spouse.

The therapist reinforces resistances when he or she senses

that disruptive levels of anxiety will be stimulated if the patient's ego is not generally shored up while its defenses are assailed in the area of primary therapeutic inquiry. For example, a patient's avoidance of a feared activity may be temporarily reinforced while the therapist explores the guilt-provoking aspects of his or her dependent needs, as illustrated by the following case.

> Miss N. was a 17-year-old diabetic high school senior with a school avoidance problem that had begun in the eighth grade. Her family blamed this behavior on her diabetes. Her internist thought differently, and referred her for management of her emotional difficulties.
>
> The source of Miss N.'s difficulty was clear. She and her mother had an unpleasant, but mutually reassuring symbiotic relationship that centered on the girl's diabetes. Their mutual tie helped both to deal with their sense of inadequacy and helped Miss N. to deal with her tenuous impulse control by restricting her activities. When Miss N. was anxious, she overate at night. Her blood sugar rose, and in the morning she felt too nauseated and uncomfortable to go to school.
>
> She had been on a homebound instruction program for several months, but insisted that she was ready to face school again at the beginning of the next quarter. She resumed school, but felt too ill after the Christmas break to return. At this point, the therapist urged her not to return to school because he felt that daily concern over her returning to school would make it impossible to deal with the underlying issues which had to be faced first—her interdependence with her mother and her fear of her own impulses.
>
> By staying home and by having to deal with her mother each day, she became aware of her own clinging and of the ways in which she increased her mother's tendency to hold on. She also became aware that her clinging to her mother cost her self-esteem. Starting from this more regressed point, it was easier for her to see what she was doing and it was also easier for her to begin acquiring new skills, such as sewing, that enabled her to feel better about and more in control of herself. She did not return to high school. She finished her course work by correspondence and began attending a junior college in the fall. Siding with her resistance enabled her to develop the skills necessary to take her next major step.

Patients can be shown that they are inappropriately angry with their therapists or inappropriately loving toward them. Or, therapists may interpret the resistance in terms of the patient's early object relations in the hope of providing an understanding that will forestall the reemergence of such resistances in the future and that will allow the patient to see his or her present interpersonal relationships with less contamination by the past.

Dealing with resistance by showing its inappropriateness or by interpretation requires many repetitions. In addition to grinding away at the resistance by repetition, the therapist also encourages the development of coping mechanisms which are less crippling to the patient's ego. The best course of action when an intervention fails to resolve a resistance is to repeat the same intervention. Continued failure of the intervention to alter a patient's patterns of thinking or emotional reaction suggests that an impasse may have been reached, and calls for a reassessment of the situation.

Noncompliance

Patients have the right to dismiss the recommendations of professional helpers. They often do so because of their value systems, their personalities and intrapsychic tensions, their current living situations, or because of factors arising in their dealings with the professional helper, including transference and countertransference. Noncompliance is the patient's conscious, deliberate refusal to follow the therapist's suggestions. Usually, the patient refuses to discuss significant issues, refuses to act on insights developed in therapy, fails to keep appointments, or fails to pay the bill.

Some problems of compliance are determined by the context of treatment, as we see in the following vignette.

> A voyeur, detected by his wife, came for treatment. He enjoyed his peeping habit, but he needed to propitiate his wife, and he felt a certain amount of guilt and uncertainty about his ability to control himself. The anxiety stimulated by the prospect of dealing with his inner feelings, however, was much more discomforting than his guilt or his concern over his ability to control himself. He therefore managed to space out his visits to the therapist and managed to confine the conversation to progress reports. The therapist's knowledge of the peeping habit served to ease the voyeur's guilt, and the therapist's presence, at a distance, helped temporarily to reinforce the voyeur's self-control.

Compliance-related issues are usually greatest in the first contacts between therapist and patient. It is then that one deals with most of the patients who come for treatment because of someone else's discomfort with their behavior or thinking. The noncompliance of the unmotivated patient may be subtle, a failure to cooperate with the spirit of therapy instead of an outright refusal to talk. For the unmotivated patient, such as an apprehended shoplifter, talking to a psychiatrist is the lesser of two punishments and is not part of a wish to change. Noncompliance in this case results from well-rationalized resistance; nobody is really hurt by a small theft from a big store.

The response of therapists to resistance is ordinarily different from their response to noncompliance. They tolerate "I can't" much better than they tolerate "I won't." They resent conscious duplicity more than unconscious efforts at evasion, perhaps because they feel that only the patients are duped by their unconscious efforts to avoid seeing themselves, and perhaps because therapists enjoy their sense of being able to see through defenses. But the primary difference between resistant cooperative patients and uncooperative patients is the aspect (conscious or unconscious) of their personalities involved in defensive maneuvering, and not the degree of defensiveness. In one case, the patients know they are resisting. In the other case, they do not. Unconscious resistance often cannot be resolved and is often more difficult to deal with than conscious refusal to cooperate, as the following interaction with a neurotic patient illustrates.

> Mrs. A.P., a married woman in her late twenties, had become increasingly disabled over seven years by muscular pain, fatigue, and weakness for which no organic cause could be found. Her history and psychiatric examination strongly suggested that hypnosis might be a good means to ameliorate her physical symptoms. She enthusiastically agreed and scheduled her next visit for the soonest possible hour, saying that she would do anything to obtain relief.
>
> After she left, she became panicky. Fearing that hypnosis might be a means for the devil to enter her life, she checked with her minister, who reassured her that she was safe in the hands of a reputable physician. Nevertheless, she called to ask if her husband might attend her next visit. It was agreed that she would be tested for hypnotizability with her husband present.

> In the preliminary discussion with her and her husband, he stated that she had been taken advantage of sexually by a physician who had performed an abortion on her in the latter days of her first marriage. She rejoined that she had not been taken advantage of. They had had an affair. At this juncture, she was willing to undergo trance induction, and a slight level of trance was induced with her eyes open. She called before the next scheduled session to cancel her treatment, saying that she intended to seek further help from a "Christian" psychiatrist.

The largest part of this woman's resistance was unconscious, and was rationalized by her wish to see a Christian psychiatrist who would be certain that the devil did not enter her life. This woman was massively resistant to the idea of self-examination, in spite of her professed wish for cure. Continuing with her symptoms was decidedly preferable to facing the fact that the devil was already in her, in the form of her drives, wishes, and fantasies. This patient's massive unconscious resistance was sustained by repression, denial, projection, somatization, and rationalization, and culminated in refusal to continue treatment.

Relatively small resistances in other patients may be compounded into noncompliance by the therapist who makes unrealistic demands in relation to the patient's character or defense mechanisms, or who refuses to deal with the problem for which the patient sought help. For example, insisting that sexually inhibited people discuss their sexual fantasies on a first visit ensures that there will be no second visit. The patient's reticence, coupled with realistic anger over the therapist's inappropriate intrusiveness will cause him or her to terminate therapy before it begins, and may well preclude seeking further help.

Other Sources of Impasse

There are many other sources of impasse. A common denominator of many forms of impasse is failure of adequate communication between patient and therapist. The therapist and the patient fail to understand each other in ways that block their further communication and work together. The simplified schema below is presented as a structure on which the following chapters will be based. Two general types of impasse will be considered:

contractual impasses, which arise in the establishment of the therapeutic relationship, and process impasses, which arise during ongoing therapy for which an adequate plan had been established. Contractual impasses are due to reality factors, an unclear therapeutic contract, an invalid therapeutic contract, an inappropriate context for therapy, or an inappropriate therapist. Process impasses arise from an inadequate therapeutic alliance, an antitherapeutic alliance, adverse transference reactions, countertransference problems, inappropriate transference gratification, and technical errors in treatment.

Impasses which arise from reality factors are relatively uncommon in a private practice but are common in public mental health facilities. They have to do with the patient's real inability to comply with the demands of the treatment, such as inability to meet regularly with the therapist owing to job demands or financial limitations. An unclear therapeutic contract is common in all treatment settings. It does not adequately specify what is expected of whom, so that therapist or patient agree to engage in an activity to which they would not have agreed had they more fully understood. An invalid therapeutic contract is an agreement to work in a manner which is not possible for the therapist or patient or is an agreement to work toward a goal which is impossible. This happens with therapists who have a stong emotional commitment to certain treatment goals or to one type of therapy. Invalid therapeutic contracts arise from the largest single source of impasse, misdiagnosis. Misdiagnosis may result from error in judgment or from an inadequate evaluation. The therapist may miss the proper descriptive diagnosis but even more important, may fail to appreciate a patient's overall ego strength, his or her chief coping and defense mechanisms, interpersonal assets and liabilities, and environmental supports. This may lead to an inadequate therapeutic alliance, a failure to develop sufficient empathy between therapist and patient for the relationship to withstand the ordinary strains of a joint endeavor. Or, it may cause an antitherapeutic alliance, an agreement between therapist and patient to work in a way or toward a goal that is not in the patient's best interest. Inappropriate context for therapy refers to implementing a theoretically sound plan in a setting in which it cannot succeed. This often occurs when a therapist tries to treat people who have been caught shoplifting or driving vehicles when intoxicated and seek treatment as a means to avoid conviction and punishment. An inappropriate therapist is one whose values and attitudes will significantly frustrate a particular patient's efforts toward ameliorating his or her difficulties. The following case example illustrates many of these types of impasse.

> A 14-year-old girl had been hospitalized by her internist, who was treating her for a syndrome resembling anorexia nervosa. She had been in psychotherapy in another city and had asked to continue in therapy. After several months of therapy with a psychiatric colleague, she demanded to see another therapist. Her internist and a colleague of the therapist referred her for consultation.
>
> Miss O. was a tiny, wiry, emotionally intense girl with much insight into her own conflicts and into her family dynamics. She complained that her psychiatrist was too liberal. He used four-letter words and wasn't bothered by the possibility that her father's affair with another woman might have aggravated her mother's drinking problem and contributed to her parents' separation and divorce. Talking with her was like talking to a tiny 30-year-old woman who had spent years in therapy. She and her psychiatrist were trying to deal with issues that would have required an intact adult ego. Her primary concern in therapy had been to discover whether or not her father had really had the affair of which her mother accused him.
>
> Toward the end of the session she said that she liked the therapist and would like to continue therapy with him. He said he would be happy to work with her. He told her he would watch his language, but said that if they were to work together, they would need to talk about a 14-year-old's issues and not about adult issues. They would talk instead about going to school, girlfriends, boyfriends, and her daily activities. He told her that he felt her father's sex life and her mother's alcoholism could not be primary concerns for her because she could do nothing about either one, and had her own problems to deal with.
>
> She agreed. They worked together at this level while she remained in the hospital, where she began eating regularly enough to gain weight, and at infrequent visits after she left the hospital for her home over a hundred miles away. Her therapeutic impasse had been resolved and she began to struggle with age-appropriate issues.
>
> The therapist felt that this impasse arose originally from a

misdiagnosis of this girl's ego strength and her stage of development. She was first treated as a neurotic adult. The therapist treated her as a child who was trying to avoid the problems of childhood by plunging herself into adult issues. He did not feel that she had sufficient maturity to deal with her oedipal difficulties and to face the tasks of adolescence simultaneously. The original misdiagnosis resulted in an invalid therapeutic contract to explore her oedipal problems. An inadequate alliance with her immature ego and the therapist's colleague's misassessment of her emotional strength led eventually to an antitherapeutic alliance in which she was treated as an adult and from which she fled.

Errors in treatment are the therapist's ordinary mistakes. Most therapists' chief mistake is the application of an overall treatment method that does not fulfill the patient's treatment needs, and may be based on a bias toward a particular kind of therapy or the unavailability of a more suitable therapy. This idea is supported by Yalom's (1966) study of group therapy dropouts in which he discovered that 40 percent of these people subsequently improved in other forms of therapy. Adverse transference reactions, countertransference problems, and inappropriate transference gratification result from therapists' acute or chronic unawareness of themselves and of the patient's psychological operations, and manifest in a distorted, nonhelpful relationship between the therapist and his patient.

Diagnosing Impending Impasse

It is obviously better to recognize and to deal with an impending impasse than with a fully developed impasse. One clue to potential impasse is if the therapist makes a far different therapeutic contract from the contracts he or she ordinarily makes, such as a drastic fee reduction, or an agreement to work psychotherapeutically with a person with whom he or she has an ongoing social or professional relationship.

Recognition of impending impasse requires that the therapist have formulated (usually in conjunction with the patient) a goal for treatment and the means by which he or she and the patient hope to reach that goal. For example, patient and therapist may contract to work on the patient's relationship problems with the other sex. They agree to scrutinize the patient's thoughts, feelings, and behavior in dating relationships to find means to alter the self-defeating aspects of the patient's behavior. Therapist and patient may agree at the beginning of the treatment that they will deal with the patient's self-defeating behavior by advice, by the therapist's demonstration of more appropriate behavior, or through insight into the irrational elements of the patient's behavior, as reflected in his or her thoughts and feelings, and as they manifest in the therapeutic relationship.

If the patient experiences no positive change, reexamination of the therapeutic contract may reveal that neither patient nor therapist is working in the manner in which both initially agreed to work, and that neither is working toward their agreed-upon goal. If they cannot bring themselves into line with their therapeutic contract, they have reached an impasse in relation to that contract, and may need to negotiate a different therapeutic contract. Therapist and patient may agree to work directly on a phobic symptom, but each time they meet, the discussion may deal with important intrapsychic and interpersonal problems that are related tangentially to the presenting symptom. They may then decide to change their priorities for therapy and agree to see if the phobic symptoms resolve during the course of a more general exploration and, if not, to return to their direct treatment at a later date.

On the other hand, working in the agreed-upon manner toward a mutually accepted goal can also lead to impasse. For example, therapist and patient may find that working toward insight into intrapsychic and early environmental factors may increase a patient's anxiety and further disrupt his or her functioning. This occurred in the following case.

> A 19-year-old man, hospitalized because of increasing suicidal preoccupation, encouraged his therapist to explore his intrapsychic life in the hope of working out of his depression through insight. The therapist agreed to a trial of "digging in," as the patient put it. After following the therapist's suggestion for a short period of time, both were able to see that he was coping less well and they agreed to focus temporarily on his reaction to his immediate hospital environment instead of his relationship to the important people in his past. As they did so, the patient began to improve, and they agreed that they had taken the wiser course of action.

When no clear goals have been established and when no means has been agreed upon to accomplish these goals, patients and therapist have other means to detect an impasse. The therapist's emotional reactions to the patient and behavior with the patient may tell part of the story. Therapists may note that they are bored, restless, indifferent, or hostile to a patient, they dread a patient's visits, or that they are overly eager for their appointments. They may find themselves preoccupied with a patient away from their hours together, or may find that they are totally unable to recall their conversations from one visit to the next. They may find that they feel a patient's situation is hopeless or that they have difficulty understanding what a patient tells them. In terms of their own behavior, therapists may be chronically early or late for a particular patient, may too readily or too reluctantly cancel appointments with a patient, or may be too stringent or too lenient with a patient about paying the bill or in working with a patient after hours.

Patients may become visibly uncomfortable in the therapeutic relationship. They may become anxious, hostile, defensive, or obsequious. They may be aware that nothing positive is happening or that their emotional state is worsening. They may miss appointments or may become very uncomfortable if they have to miss an appointment. The therapist may become aware of an increase of primary process thinking by the patient, profound mood changes, or an increase in self-damaging activity. In all of these situations, it is imperative that therapists be aware that they are not bystanders observing the natural course of the patient's illness, and that they may be doing something wrong.

Kepecs (1979) has devised a system for detecting therapist errors in insight-oriented therapy that may be useful in preventing and resolving impasses. He employs typescripts of ten-minute segments of psychotherapy sessions and examines them for tracking errors, which are statements by the therapist that get the patient off his track. Tracking errors stand in contrast to correct statements, which facilitate the patient's understanding and encourage him or her to open up to the therapist. Kepecs finds that tracking errors are most likely to have been made when the patient disagrees with the therapist's statement, when the patient's remarks after the therapist's interventions become confused or confusing, when the patient's associations are blocked or when he or she begins to ramble, when the flow of speech becomes choppy, or when therapists begin to contradict themselves or to oversell their point or therapeutic approach.

Other devices for detecting therapist errors are listening to brief segments of audiotapes, viewing videotapes, consultation with peers, and supervision. Audiotape recorders are readily introduced into therapy sessions with the therapists' explanation that they are trying to attend more closely to their interaction with the patient. Indeed, both can listen to understand where matters are going awry. The same is true for videotaping, but it incurs greater expense and requires more cumbersome equipment. Audiotapes, and especially videotapes, can produce startling insight into the patient-therapist interactions (Berger, 1970; Alger, 1972): I have found little resistance from patients to such procedures. The greatest resistance stems from the therapists' avoidance of facing themselves.

I find that it is not necessary to examine large segments of therapist-patient interaction to find the difficulties in their relationship. A five- or ten-minute videotaped or audiotaped segment from a portion of the session that the therapist recognized as difficult for him or herself or the patient will usually yield significant information. The first portion of a recorded session for a therapist-patient pair who do not ordinarily record is a period of adaptation and reaction to the intrusion of the recording medium into their relationship. Noting the means by which each deals with this intrusion can be as useful as the information from later in the session when therapist and patient become more involved with each other. One can see if the therapist glosses over the intrusion, if he or she allows patients to deal with the intrusion and the situation which has necessitated it, and in what way the therapist allows patients to express themselves. In this way, one can examine the therapist's defenses and coping style as well as the patient's and can see in what areas they are compatible with the patient's needs and in what ways they are detrimental to a constructive working relationship.

Problems Secondary to Impasse

Impasses should be prevented not only because the patients' discomfort and poor management of their lives are continued or worsened, but because the impasse itself creates further problems. The problems secondary to an impasse are the reactions of the patient, the therapist, and the patient's world to the impasse.

An impasse can be seen as both a victory and a defeat. It is a victory for the forces within the patient that brought about his or her emotional difficulties, and occasionally during an impasse one sees a wry smile or the gallows laugh described by Berne (1972) that says, "I deserve what I'm getting." An impasse is also a defeat that confirms the patients' feeling that their problem is the result of inexorable forces. Their will to struggle against themselves is diminished and their acceptance of their social difficulties and their psychopathology is reinforced.

Patients at impasse are frequently compassionate toward their therapists and will often say that the therapists are doing the best they can, and that they shouldn't be blamed for the patients' own lack of progress. A patient's understanding attitude gives a clue to the fact that the therapist has been playing into a resistance and has unwittingly contracted to be impotent. The therapist may, unfortunately, feel that the patient's compassion is a healthy response to the therapist's failure. It is not. The most appropriate reactions are feelings of frustration, helplessness, and anger. In fact, the patient may become depressed as he or she assumes the blame for the failure of therapeutic effort.

The therapist will feel angry, guilty, and impotent at times of impasse. The anger of the therapist in response to this impotence frequently manifests indirectly, through lateness, missed appointments, sarcasm, coldness, and other behaviors that compound the patient's own hostility. The therapist's guilt may cause him or her to cease appropriately insisting that the patient bear some responsibility for the therapy and may further undermine his or her therapeutic leverage.

Impasses also significantly heighten family resistance to supporting the treatment of the identified patient. Skeptical family members are given ammunition to undermine the identified patient's self-confidence and confidence in the therapist. An impasse can also reinforce designation of the patient as sick, bad, or uncooperative, and can give the family a further excuse to discharge its hostility toward him or her or to reinforce the patient's dependence on the family. Prolonged impasses can produce sufficient marital tension to stimulate separation or divorce, and to impair child-parent relationships significantly.

For these reasons, the family may need to be told of a prolonged impasse, and the feelings of family members may need to be heard and considered. For example, working with a chronically suicidal or psychotic person outside of a hospital may so strain the family's emotional resources that it cannot emotionally support the identified patient. It may be wise to hospitalize some patients before their families' emotional resources are so taxed that their families align against them and discount or extrude them.

When one does not detect a significant family reaction to an impasse, one should wonder about the importance of the patient's symptomatology for the family. It may be, in spite of the identified patient's discomfort, that his or her behavior helps to maintain an important balance in family relationships.

For all of the above reasons, it is frequently useful for the therapist to become acquainted with significant family members at the beginning of therapy and to open a channel of communication between them and the therapist or an appropriate intermediary.

Dealing with Impasse and Impasse-Related Problems

There are general principles for determining the nature of an impasse and for resolving it. When at a point of suspected impasse, but uncertain of its etiology, the therapist has four alternatives: observe the therapeutic process more closely; obtain consultation; transfer the patient to another therapist; or suggest a vacation from therapy to the patient.

Enlisting the Patient in Resolving the Impasse

The therapist must decide whether or not to enlist the cooperation of the patient in understanding and in resolving an impasse. This decision will depend partly on the therapist's ability to ascertain the nature of the impasse and to resolve it without the patient's help and partly on the therapeutic usefulness of including the patient. It also depends on the therapist's ability to admit a mistake to a patient, or to this particular patient, and whether he or she will compound the errors committed by his or her own defensiveness or embarrassment. In these instances, therapists are better off seeking supervision or therapy for themselves in the hope of discovering and ameliorating the cause of the impasse.

I prefer to include the patient when I suspect an impasse. Including the patient in diagnosing the impasse and in deciding what to do about it can further engage the patient in the therapy. By asking the patient, the therapist clearly states that both participants share the responsibility for the outcome of the therapeutic endeavor. The decision to include or exclude the patient also depends on the patient's ability to explore collaboratively, and on the patient's need to depend on the therapist's judgment instead of using his or her own. Specifics of this will be dealt with in later chapters.

Including the patient can have negative effects. Talking about impasse will usually increase the guilt and self-blame of ruminative, depressed people, and one must weigh the possible long-term gain against the possibility of worsening the patients' condition by including them in a process that they cannot yet manage. The discussion of impasse may reinforce the patients' view of themselves as hopeless. It must also be weighed against the patients' impulsiveness and their tendency to turn their aggression toward themselves, as well as their tendency to act out. Patients may attempt suicide, may precipitously leave therapy, or may seek out relationships that will help them gratify their sexual, dependent, or other needs without facing the issues that brought them into therapy.

If the therapist feels that the best means to diagnose and resolve the impasse is objective observation of the therapeutic relationship, the patient must be involved. The need to use a one-way mirror, videotape recording, or a consultant in the room during the therapeutic hour must be explained to the patient and consent must be obtained.

The process of including the patient in ascertaining the origin of an impasse and in determining how to correct it starts by the therapist asking the patients for their perception of how therapy is going, reminding them of their mutual goals and of their agreement to assess their progress toward these goals periodically. In the unusual event that patients report that all is going well, the therapist can ask what the patients mean, and explore the difference between his or her perception of the situation and the patients' perceptions. It may lead the therapist to become aware that he or she has unstated goals for patients that were not part of the original therapeutic contract. The therapist must then explore within himself or herself the possible roots of his or her incongruent expectations of the patient.

If patients feel that the therapy is not going well, the therapist must again follow up by asking in what way, and can ask patients for their ideas for remedying the situation. The therapist may gain sufficient enlightenment from patients that the impasse can be resolved without taking further steps. If exploration of the patients' point of view does not suggest alternatives, there are further options.

They can explore their conscious reactions to each other from the beginning of therapy to the point of impasse. They can also state their perceptions of one another, and indicate the ways in which their perceptions have changed. In this way, both parties will be helped to see the unconscious biases in these perceptions and the unconscious aspects of their behavior toward one another. If this also fails, psychological testing or consultation is indicated.

Psychological Testing

Psychological testing is, of course, a form of consultation for therapists who do not routinely incorporate testing in their evaluation of their patients. When possible, it should always include direct verbal communication between therapists and psychologists to discuss the reason for referral and the test results. Often, more is gained from their discussion of the testing than from the testing itself. Psychological testing can be helpful in the prediction, diagnosis, and resolution of many impasses. Cognitive and intellectual testing can detect persons whose level of intellectual function impairs their capacity for abstract thinking, and can detect persons with organic deficits that make it impossible to attain the level of integration necessary for verbal psychotherapy.

Projective testing can identify persons with poor impulse control and impaired reality testing, and can alert the therapist to the need for a repressive or an ego-supportive approach instead of an evocative approach, thus averting a potential impasse.

Projective psychological testing of the patient can be especially useful when therapists experience intense emotional reactions to their patients' communications and behavior. A sense of confusion or despair, massive anxiety, or a wish to retaliate against or withdraw from patients may signal that therapists are dealing with an unsuspected borderline personality and that they need to modify their approach along the lines suggested in Chapter 4. The diagnosis of a borderline personality can be readily confirmed on psychological testing by a basically intact WAIS (Wechsler Adult Intelligence Scale) coupled with glaringly deviant Rorschach responses (Gorney & Weinstock, 1980).

Consultation

The process of deciding whether or not to obtain another form of consultation by another therapist and the type of consultation that is agreed upon give important clues about the nature of the difficulty between therapist and patient. Unwillingness of the patient to obtain consultation may denote unwillingness to engage significantly with the therapist, and may point to a lack of motivation for therapy or for a type of therapy in which dealing with the significance of therapist and patient for each other is important. It may also signify fear of abandonment, and the therapist must make it clear that he or she is not attempting to be rid of the patient by using the subterfuge of consultation.

On occasion, patients will request consultation. After mutually ascertaining if the consultation is indicated, therapists must ask how they would like to go about obtaining consultation. Most commonly, patients will ask therapists to designate a consultant. While therapists cannot control whom their patients see as a consultant, they have a right and a professional obligation to tell patients who they feel to be an appropriate consultant. They also have a right and an obligation to express their opinion of a consultant whom a patient suggests. If therapists feel strongly about whom the patient should consult and under what circumstances, they must ask themselves whether they have an inappropriate need to control their patients, or whether this is what the patients require.

The patient or the therapist can see the consultant, or both can see the consultant, singly or together. Therapist and patient can explore these options and can decide unilaterally or bilaterally.

Consultants work out an evaluation contract with the person who consults with them. If it is the therapist, they agree that the consultant will evaluate the treatment and advise the therapist. If a consultant sees the patient, two evaluation contracts are needed: one with the therapist, and the other with the patient. The patient and consultant agree that the patient has come for help in dealing with an impasse and agree that the consultant will exchange information with the therapist as well as the patient. Consultants use professional judgment to decide at what point they want input from the therapist: before seeing a patient, after seeing a patient, or during a series of interviews. Consultants also ascertain which of their conclusions should be transmitted to the patient, and in what way. When consultants do present their conclusions to the patient, they must allow for interchange, and also need to help the patient with his or her feelings about the need for the consultation and the consultation itself.

After the consultation, therapist and patient review the consultant's findings as they both understand them, deal with the consultant's recommendations or formulations, and decide how to proceed.

In consulting with therapists at loggerheads with patients, I find sometimes that the behaviors of therapist and patient toward one another have become so stereotyped or that therapist and patient have become so defensive toward one another that transfer to another therapist is necessary to work out the problem (sometimes unrelated to the patient's main emotional problem) created in the patient-therapist relationship. This can be explained to the patient and therapist in a nonpejorative way. Usually, both sigh with relief.

Transfer

Patients may resist consultation with or transfer to another therapist because they wish to maintain their current therapist in his or her present idealized or debased position, depending on the nature of their transference needs. Suggesting that the patient start with a consultation and with no commitment to transfer is often the best way to initiate a transfer, and is the way in which many transfers come about. The fact that many transfers occur as the result of visits with a consultant suggests that, in many instances, the patient's transference needs had blocked their ability to deal with their problems. And, in many instances, transferring to the consultant is the patient's way of getting out of the therapist's life before he or she is forced out.

Transfer of the patient is appropriate when therapist and patient become aware that the therapist does not offer the kind of treatment the patient needs or when the quality or context of their interaction blocks effective working together.

If transfers are arranged without the use of a consultant, or patients are to be transferred to someone they do not know, it is wise, when feasible, for patients to have preliminary visits with the proposed therapist to be reasonably certain that they can work together. This is less necessary when patients are to be transferred on an emergency basis to an institution, but preliminary visits to a proposed institutional treatment facility are also useful to help patients work through the separation from their original therapist and to establish a new tie.

Working through the loss of the old therapist and making the attachment to the new therapist is the responsibility of both therapists. The transferring therapist needs to deal with the patients' feelings about their separation, whether they be a sense of abandonment or a feeling of relief. He or she also needs to deal as much as possible with the patients' negative feelings toward him or her and toward the transfer so that the new relationship will not be undermined from the outset. The receiving therapist must deal with the same issues, bringing negative feelings to the surface as quickly as possible, or recognizing that much of the negative feelings directed toward him or her are displaced from the former therapist and are also reactions to frustration, a sense of failure, and feelings of desertion. At this stage of the relationship, the patients' feelings are dealt with as reactions to their real situation and not as transference, because transference interpretations will be seen as discounting the patients' current reality and their right to their feelings.

An alternative to transferring patients who require medical measures is multiple treatment, with a physician supplying supervision of medications and the nonmedical therapist continuing psychological treatment. In a sense, multiple treatment reduces the complexity of the issues for each of the therapists, but it also offers the opportunity for therapy to be confounded when each has a different explanation of what is going on with the patient. Unless carried out in an institutional or agency setting in which the two treating persons have frequent contact, multiple treatment is difficult to work out.

Termination of Therapy or Vacation from Therapy

Raising the question of termination or setting a date for termination has long been used as a means to deal with impasse (Freud, 1937). From my own experience with weekend group therapy workshops, I feel that a time limit gets people down to business, and that a patient's knowledge that therapy can last many years can help to postpone facing important issues.

Raising the possibility of termination should not be used to stir things up when therapy is dragging. The question of termination of treatment should be raised only when the therapist feels that actual termination may be the only way to break up a specific type of impasse. When used as a manipulation, the threat of termination reinforces a lifestyle of manipulation and countermanipulation. When it is a realistic alternative to a dilemma that the therapist is presently helpless to resolve, it enlists the patient in a joint effort to see what recourse they have other than parting company. It is a statement by the therapist that he or she can do no more without the patient's active assistance and guidance.

The therapist can raise the question of termination by pointing out to the patient that all of the efforts they have jointly undertaken no longer produce any tangible gain for the patient, which leaves the alternatives of continuing to do what they are doing together, consultation, transfer to another therapist who may work better with the patient, or vacation for the patient away from therapy.

The dangers of raising these questions with patients are the same as the dangers of telling them that the therapist is at an impasse. Patients may act impulsively against themselves or others, may establish substitute relationships, may feel even more demoralized, or may quit therapy abruptly, abandoning the therapist before they can be abandoned.

Suggesting a vacation from therapy is often a good way to propose termination. It has less finality and raises less of a note of hopelessness than suggesting a final and complete termination. Vacation from therapy suggests that in time circumstances in the patient's internal and external life which now mitigate against change may alter. The same can also be said of the therapist, but usually isn't. It also indicates that the therapist is not rejecting the patient as a person, and that he or she is willing to try again should the patient wish to do so.

Even when raising the question of termination helps patients get down to business, eventual termination must still be kept in mind and must be actively planned by the patients and the therapist. Otherwise, patients lose their impetus to deal with issues. In a sense, the threat of termination is only useful as long as the threat of losing the relationship with the therapist is more disturbing than the fear of losing symptoms.

Dealing with Reactions to Impasse

As indicated earlier in this chapter, patients and therapists have strong emotional reactions to impasse. In dealing with retroflexed anger related to failure of treatment, the therapist must help direct patients' anger away from themselves and onto the therapist, if appropriate, making it clear that the anger will not disrupt the therapeutic relationship. Working out the reactions to the impasse itself can be a valuable experience for a patient whose previous relationships have been based on mutual blame instead of mutual responsibility. Modeling appropriate behavior is often helpful. For example, the therapist may express surprise at the patient's lack of anger and say that he or she would be angry in similar circumstances, being careful to encourage appropriate expressions of anger and not to encourage a vindictive attack that will hurt both the patient and the therapist.

Just as the patient's anger can be turned to advantage by dealing with it directly, so can the patient's guilt and sense of helplessness and frustration. One deals with these feelings as a problem that has arisen within the therapist-patient relationship and *not* as an intrapsychic phenomenon. In other words, therapists use the impasse as an opportunity to insert themselves further into the patient's world, instead of standing to one side observing and criticizing the patient along with the part of the patient that observes and criticizes him or herself. The therapist emphasizes that he or she and the patient are in this quandary together. It is in this situation that the existential approach of being and staying (Havens, 1974) is the most useful to the patient. The impasse can be a shared dilemma that calls for a change in the therapist as well as the patient. The therapist makes an effort to be with the patient psychologically and to stay with him or her, to share his or her frustration and sense of helplessness, and to move together with the patient away from this position.

I have asserted elsewhere (Weiner, 1974b, 1974c) that this type of mutuality must be based on an adequate therapist-patient alliance and that it must not be used to seduce an unmotivated patient into therapy or to substitute for the patient's self-examination.

In other words, the existential approach to the patient in which each opens his or her world to the other and in which each changes as a result is not employed in every therapeutic relationship. It is reserved for those who need it and for the specific times at which it is needed. In this way, an impasse can be converted into a nodal point in therapy. It must be borne in mind that the problem worked out between the therapist and the patient may be unrelated to the patient's presenting complaint, but in general the experience of sharing a difficulty with another person and of establishing a rapprochement is helpful in diminishing the general sense of discouragement experienced by people with significant emotional complaints (Frank, 1973).

Therapists themselves have a wide range of reactions to impasse depending on their personalities, their life situations, and their relationships to particular patients. The therapist's reaction to the impasse must also be dealt with. A frequent reaction of the therapist to impasse is the direct or indirect expression of hostility. My guilt in relation to Mrs. L. (p. 69) was partly a cause and partly a result of the impasse. Other responses on my part have included overempathic smiling and overt indifference (Weiner, 1978).

Therapists frequently become defensive as impasses arise, and thereby compound the impasse by becoming less able to respond to the patient's communications. Instead, they diagnose the patient as an angry person, and look for the source of the patient's anger in past or present relationships outside the therapy hour. The harder therapists try to apply rational analysis, the greater the distance they place between themselves and the patient, and the more the patient feels out of contact and abandoned. Mistakenly, therapists focus on the patient's basic fear of loss instead of the tense, alienated atmosphere of the therapy session.

The therapist's defensiveness frequently leads to long explanations of the patient's behavior which give the patient the sense of being lectured to instead of listened to, a familiar scene from everyone's childhood that may be seized upon by the therapist as transference instead of the reality of the patient-therapist relationship.

Impasse and the Transference Neurosis

The development and resolution of the transference neurosis is the sine qua non of psychoanalysis (Greenson, 1967), but many people are able to dispel neurotic symptoms without developing or resolving a transference neurosis, and there is little evidence to suggest that other means of dealing with neurotic symptoms are less permanent than psychoanalysis (Bergin, 1971).

What, then, is the therapeutic value of the transference neurosis? The study of impasse suggests that the transference neurosis is but one kind of impasse. Its resolution has the same value as the resolution of any impasse, whether or not it is related to the presenting problem. Resolution of any impasse that develops between the patient and therapist can eventually contribute to the patient's general sense of competence and potency.

On the other hand, experiences with impasses indicate that one is better off avoiding an impasse if one can because of the risk of disrupting therapy or of demoralizing the patient. One must therefore ask if subjecting the ordinary patient to the risks involved in developing an impasse are worth the possible benefit of creating a nodal point in therapy which the patient may be able to use to advantage.

The answer, I think, is that the ordinary patient should not be subjected to the vicissitudes of the transference neurosis because most patients are unable to resolve an impasse of such magnitude. The development and resolution of a transference neurosis can be useful for patients with whom one must create a crisis in order to draw them into therapy, but with whom the crisis will not become life threatening in magnitude.

I suspect that in some cases the nonspecific esteem-enhancing effect of resolving the therapy-generated crisis accounts as much for the increased self-esteem following psychoanalysis or psychoanalytic psychotherapy as do the specific psychodynamic insights acquired during the course of the treatment.

Positive Aspects of Impasse

I have, thus far, defined a psychotherapeutic impasse as an acute or chronic failure of treatment in which the patients' presenting problems and overall level of coping with themselves are not ameliorated or significantly worsen in spite of the active efforts of the therapist and the patient working together. I have presented this negative view of impasse because most impasses are negative outcomes and because I want to avoid helping the naive, uninformed, or insensitive therapist to rationalize avoidable therapeutic stalemates. In the hope that I have sensitized the reader to impasse as a negative or destructive occurrence in psychotherapy, I will examine impasse from an entirely different perspective.

Liff (1970) defines an impasse as a situation in which more energy flows into sustaining the opposition than in trying to work out of it, and more value comes from opposition than its resolution. This definition raises the possibility that impasse can be a constructive force and raises the question of whether sustained opposition may in some cases be preferable to resolution of conflict.

There are at least three possibilities: an impasse can sustain an intrapsychic equilibrium; an impasse can maintain a relationship with a patient until events in the patient's external life allow him to change; and an impasse can be a nodal point in therapy. It can help develop a creative partnership between therapist and patient that leads to a solution that neither would have predicted.

An impasse can sustain an intrapsychic or interpersonal

equilibrium that, while unsatisfactory in many respects, is better than the solutions available at the time. An impasse may be better than a solution to a problem if the only apparent solutions are suicide, homicide, or psychosis. Given these alternatives, a non-progressive struggle with phobic, obsessive-compulsive, or other symptoms may be preferable to destructive action or decompensation into psychosis. The difficulty with this point of view is that one cannot predict with certainty which people will act destructively and which severely disabling symptoms will worsen if left untreated or if approached too vigorously unless the history strongly suggests such possible outcomes. Taking this point of view also blocks the possibility of attempting alternative psychotherapeutic approaches, as we will see in the example that follows.

> A 49-year-old man with a 25-year history of crippling obsessive-compulsive symptoms had been previously hospitalized several times and treated by chemical and physical measures. Previous psychosurgery had mildly relieved his compulsive showering and handwashing which occupied six hours each day to enable him to leave his apartment. Previous psychological testing showed minimal ego strengths and possible borderline psychosis.
>
> He sought behavior therapy for himself, but after a few months no progress had been made. He agreed to hospitalization where, with considerable support from the staff, he was exposed to a variety of psychological flooding techniques. As a result of three weeks of this type of inpatient therapy, his symptoms were considerably relieved. He only required an hour and a half to prepare himself in the morning, and his ability to resist his fear of contamination had increased to the point that he became able to work regularly for the first time in seven years.

Had the therapist said to himself that the stalemate which occurred in his outpatient therapy was helping the patient to defend against further decompensation, no further progress would have been made.

The next case demonstrates maintaining an intrapsychic equilibrium.

> A single woman in her fifties had been maintained by her therapist for several years in a moderately comfortable emotional equilibrium while she struggled unsuccessfully with her

difficulty establishing positive emotional relationships with men.

Earlier in her life, she had severely decompensated when she withdrew from romantic attachments with men. In her fifties, she became attached to a rigid, quarrelsome man who frequently had difficulties with potency. He and she had attempted sexual therapy as a couple, but experienced only minimal improvement in their relationship.

The therapist, based on his past experience with her and his knowledge of her psychodynamics, elected not to help her strive for a higher level of adaptation than the control-or-be-controlled relationship she had with her man friend. He instead saw the woman at widely spaced intervals and encouraged her to be more tolerant of her man friend. The therapist felt that her intrapsychic and interpersonal impasses were preferable to working toward resolution of her difficulties, which might result in her losing her man friend altogether. In this situation, the therapist decided that a bad psychological marriage was better for this woman than no marriage at all, because her previous severe decompensations had occurred when she experienced an emotional divorce.

An impasse can also be a means for the therapist to maintain a strong emotional tie with a patient until his life situation changes in a way that will allow him to change intrapsychically, for example, until the death of a dominating or dependent parent, or a chronically ill spouse. Why should the therapist choose to maintain an ongoing relationship under these circumstances? Why not discharge the patient from treatment with the suggestion that he or she return at a later date when circumstances are more conducive to change? The answer, I believe, lies in the patient's irrational reaction to being dismissed. The unfortunate conclusion reached by many patients is that the therapist does not care or thinks that the situation is hopeless.

Maintaining a therapist-patient relationship during these two types of impasse does not require frequent visits, and these situations are defined as impasses instead of supportive therapy because the therapist and patient are struggling toward a goal which, under the present psychological and interpersonal circumstances, cannot be reached.

In these situations, struggling with and against the therapist can help define the boundaries of the patient's ego and can help the patient to maintain internal integration and coherence. A controlled impasse also serves to ward off separation anxiety. It helps allay feelings of powerlessness through the sense of power that comes through stalemating the therapist. A persisting therapeutic impasse can be seen at one level as clinging, and at another level as an assertion of power and of one's individuality and intactness. Getting well is in this sense giving up one's identity and assuming another's values. Attempting to resolve certain impasses may cost the patient his or her reality testing or his or her life. Indeed, the frequent need for hospitalization of the borderline patient in intensive, insight-oriented therapy is a case in point. Aggressive intrusion into the patient's unconscious leads to action or psychological regression as the patient feels increasingly helpless to deal with himself. The countertransference which leads to this situation is the therapist's wish to avoid the narcissistic injury or despair that comes with impasse.

The inability of therapist and patient to resolve an impasse also has another potential positive aspect: the development of a creative solution that is outside the current repertoire of both the therapist and the patient. The therapist who says in genuine despair that he or she does not know what else to do may trigger a chain of events that leads to a creative solution by the patient, who finally understands that the therapist alone cannot supply the one insight or the one really potent behavioral technique that will lead to a breakthrough. It is important that the therapist emphasize that they are at impasse because of the therapist's inability to find the means to influence the patient's symptoms and not because of the patient's rottenness or unwillingness to cooperate. In short, the creative solution will not come if the therapist blames the patient. That will only increase the patient's despair further. It is also not useful for the therapist to blame himself. This stimulates the patient's guilt and pity, and distracts from the task at hand. With some patients, an impasse can be the stimulus for developing a real partnership by helping the patient to see that resolution of a particular problem is not to be found in following the lead of the therapist.

If the therapist can say, in a way that blames neither one, that he or she needs the patient's guidance, the way may be opened to the patient's creative mobilization of his or her own powers. This occurred in the treatment of the next patient to be described.

Mrs. A.K., a divorced woman in her mid-thirties, had been in therapy for eight years for symptoms of anxiety. During this period, she resolved crippling dependencies on two men who were father substitutes, and developed a positive relationship with her own father for the first time since her adolescence. The main problem remaining, as the therapist saw it, was to begin her social life again and to begin dating instead of spending evenings at home watching television with her son or playing bridge with other women who lived nearby. Much work had been done on her relationship with her son, and he was developing well.

For the bulk of Mrs. A.K.'s eight years of therapy, she had been seen twice a week. She and her therapist had tried to reduce the frequency of her sessions as they approached what seemed opportune times for their separation. On the several occasions that they tried, her anxiety increased and abated only when the twice-weekly sessions were reinstituted. Therapist and patient agreed, however, that a one-week cruise would be a reasonable way for the patient to try her wings toward the close of therapy. As the trip approached, her apprehension increased. Shortly after the cruise began, she had an altercation with another woman, experienced overwhelming anxiety, and withdrew to her cabin for the remainder of the trip. Frightened and angry, she called her therapist and both agreed that the trip had been a mistake, that her trying to become involved in the type of social life that her therapist thought best for her was not going to work. On her return, the therapist said that he didn't know what further psychological measures to pursue and told the patient that the decision about the future conduct of therapy needed to be hers, and that the direction of her life had to be hers as well. She agreed and said that from now on she was going to do what she felt was in her best interest instead of relying blindly on the therapist's advice. She proposed that her sessions be gradually spaced out to allow her to make her own decisions and to assume the responsibility for her own life. Over a period of time, she comfortably spaced out to visits every three months and maintained an adequate level of psychological comfort and function.

The transference issue that she resolved was her wish for dependence on an omnipotent father. The countertransference was the wish to be that omnipotent father. The only way it could have been resolved was through the therapist's admission of his limited ability and of his need to depend on her guidance for the conduct of the remainder of her therapy.

The three positive uses of impasse are rare events in psychotherapy and should be considered only after all other obstacles to the therapeutic process have been adequately ruled out. In the case of Mrs. A.K., the therapist and the patient had previously considered transfer to another therapist and had employed an outside consultant after her return from her cruise. The consultant felt it best that they work out the situation between themselves instead of transferring the patient to another therapist.

Summary

A degree of noncompliance and resistance occurs in all forms of psychotherapy with every patient. Minor degrees of noncompliance and resistance can usually be managed without damage to the patient or the therapeutic relationship if they are detected early enough. If undetected, or if allowed to develop unimpeded, ordinary noncompliance and small resistances can become impasses.

If an impasse cannot be avoided, it should be resolved quickly, not only because the patient's presenting problem is unresolved, but because the impasse itself can cause secondary difficulties which further complicate the patient's life and therapy.

Even if the impasse is unrelated to the patient's presenting problem, its successful resolution can contribute to the patient's overall sense of potency in dealing with his or her own feelings and with life events. This may even explain the therapeutic value of the development and resolution of the transference neurosis in psychoanalysis.

If therapists cannot resolve an impasse through their own efforts, there are alternatives. They may consult the patient, employ psychological testing, use a professional consultant, transfer the patient to another therapist, or terminate the therapy.

On occasions, an impasse can become an important nodal point in therapy from which great benefit derives. It can be the beginning of a creative partnership between therapist and patient which leads to totally unexpected positive solutions that neither patient nor therapist could have anticipated on the basis of the patient's past experience or the therapist's training. In this sense, every impasse is a creative opportunity as well as a potentially destructive event.

2

Contract-related

Contract making has received recent attention as a significant aspect of psychotherapy. It has been an important part of the treatment by therapists who practice behavior modification (Ayllon, 1975), and has been used in community mental health centers (Lombillo, Kirescik, & Sherman, 1973). It has been advised for patients by consumer advocates (Adams & Orgel, 1975) and by lawyers who deal with treatment relationships (Schwitzgebel, 1979).

Failure to deal with contractual issues is a significant source of impasse. If therapists do not specify what therapy is about and what is required of the patient, they cannot assess the patient's motivation for therapy and cannot obtain a realistic agreement by the patient to cooperate actively.

Failure to deal with contractual issues is also failure to use a potentially growth-promoting aspect of the patient-therapist relationship. Engaging patients in contract making can reduce the patients' sense of helplessness in dealing with their world and can also help them begin to assume responsibility for themselves.

Appropriate renegotiation of contracts helps patients learn flexibility of roles in relation to themselves and others.

As we will see, formal contract making is not appropriate for every patient, but when it is, it can help the therapist model healthy relatedness. Contract making helps to establish the need to make one's wishes and the needs of others known to them instead of expecting one's needs to be fulfilled by others who somehow, by virtue of caring or of special powers, know what is needed from them in a relationship.

Contracts

A therapist-patient contract is an explicit, mutually agreed upon, noncoercive statement of the tasks each is to perform and the ends to which those tasks are a means. The entire process of psychotherapy can be viewed as a series of contracts between therapist and patient.

A contract entered into under coercion is invalid, and at best can be considered a grudging consent. Contractual relationships, however, are rarely entered entirely of free will. People accept unsatisfactory jobs because they need to earn a living. They enter marital relationships because of loneliness or unmet sexual or dependent needs. They enter psychotherapy not by choice but because they are suffering and can find no other relief from their inner turmoil or the pressures from peers, loved ones, or the law.

Contracts In Psychotherapy

Contract making with patients can help initiate healthy mutuality, explicitness, assertiveness, and appropriate responsibility for one's self. Furthermore, it accords the patient overt power in defining the therapeutic relationship and its goals, an act which confirms and enhances his or her potency as a person.

The internal or external pressures which drive people into psychotherapy will frequently lead them to make a contract they do not understand or cannot fulfill, even though they might wish to do so. As a result, they are confused, damaged, or diverted from a more appropriate approach to their problem. The psychotherapist must be certain that the candidate for treatment has some genuine wish to enter into a psychotherapeutic contract, that it is mutually understood and agreed upon, and that the terms are explicit (Weiner, 1981).

The contract may be verbal, or it may be written out and signed by both parties, as suggested by Adams and Orgel (1975). Whether or not a formal, signed contract is made, the points agreed upon by the patient and therapist must be recorded to avoid retrospective falsification by the patient or the therapist.

Therapists themselves must be considered in establishing a contract for psychotherapy. Therapists must know themselves well enough to be able to deliver within reason what they promise. If they promise an outcome beyond their reasonable ability to predict, or promise to work in an uncomfortable or personally compromising style, they must consider the possibility that they are establishing an invalid psychotherapeutic contract based on their own emotional needs, and should investigate their motives (Langs, 1973).

In working toward a contractual relationship, the psychotherapist develops an awareness-in-action of the quality of the patient's interpersonal interactions that helps determine the level at which he or she must address the patient and that suggests interactional goals for the patient: for instance, becoming appropriately aggressive.

An impasse will occur if certain persons are pushed to enter a contractual relationship; for example, people who wish or require total dependence on authority and those who cannot or will not assert their own viewpoint. Psychotics who cannot manage their daily affairs and suicidally depressed persons are obviously in no position to negotiate a contract. Some of these severely impaired people may require involuntary treatment to prevent them from destroying themselves and their families.

Nonpsychotic persons under overwhelming stress must also be dealt with unilaterally to avoid an impasse. The therapist asks the patient to follow what is prescribed. When any patient appears able to negotiate constructively for himself, a tentative contract can be offered to test the patient's ability to deal effectively with choices, and to acknowledge his or her ability to participate in a mutual endeavor.

Two types of contracts can be offered by the psychotherapist: an evaluation contract and a therapeutic contract.

Evaluation Contracts

Some institutions use a formal evaluation procedure performed by a designated diagnostic team. The evaluee is told in advance that the evaluation team may not be the eventual treatment team. The evaluee knows that evaluation is the sole purpose of his or her contract with this group of people, and enters an evaluation contract (Schectman, DeLaTorre, Garza, 1979).

An evaluation contract is a commitment to exchange information. It involves no commitment to action by either party. The evaluee contracts to supply enough information for the evaluator to formulate a diagnosis and a treatment plan.

Clearly, individual practitioners will have more difficulty (not only with their potential patients, but within themselves) establishing an evaluation contract than an institution which has a formal evalution program. It is especially difficult to patients to retrace their steps and to reassess the whole question if the evaluee comes as a patient from another professional with a diagnosis and a recommendation for treatment. The individual practitioner is additionally handicapped by the fact that his or her referral source has not usually ascertained the evaluee's capacity to work psychotherapeutically, although he or she may have based the referral on an intuitive sense of fit between the person referred and the therapist.

When the potential patient is referred without an evaluation, the therapist can justifiably start at ground zero and give the evaluee a chance to convert a complaint into a diagnostic and treatment issue (Schectman et al., 1979).

Establishing an evaluation contract separate from the therapeutic contract can be of great help in avoiding an impasse. It helps avoid premature closure owing to failure to explore the psychological and interpersonal context in which the difficulty arose and in which it currently operates. It also helps avoid focusing too sharply on the chief complaint and thereby avoids premature action on an inapropriate therapeutic contract, as shown in the following case.

> A 52-year-old woman sought help for depression. Although her complaint was depression, she was not interested in talking about her feelings. Instead, she spent most of her first session

describing her relationship with her second husband and expressing misgivings about her third husband to whom she had been married for six weeks. At the end of the session, when the therapist suggested further interviews, she balked and pressed for immediate relief of her emotional discomfort. The therapist wrote her a prescription for an antidepressant only to find that she had already secured a prescription from another physician but had discontinued the medication because of its side-effects. In fact, she had recently consulted a number of people. She had told each a fragment of her story, had obtained an opinion, and then obtained another opinion from still another person. At the end of the visit, she pressed the therapist to tell her if she were justified in maintaining her relationship with her second husband in case her doubts about her third husband were justified.

At this point, the contractual difficulty between the woman and therapist became clear. She had been unwilling to put forth all the necessary facts at the outset. Ultimately, she made it clear that she wanted an answer that would alleviate her depression, enable her to cling to her ex-husband, alleviate her pangs of conscience, and demand no change in her modus operandi, which also included clinging to her children to the exclusion of her second and third husbands.

The therapist dealt with her by refusing to offer a treatment contract on her terms, which would certainly have led to a stalemate. Instead, he said that the situation was extremely complicated and required more thought, not a recommendation for immediate action or a sanction of her behavior. The problem faced by this woman, as she saw it, was which course of action to take. The problem, as the therapist saw it, was to help her look before she leaped again.

An evaluation contract is subject to abuse if taken too literally and if imposed under circumstances in which such an overt agreement is not in the evaluee's best interest. Talking about evaluation to a person who is preoccupied with possible desertion by the people important to him or her is tantamount to threatening desertion as the opening move of the therapeutic relationship. *Imposing* a contract negates the entire concept of a contractual relationship as a means to stimulate a person's potency in his or her interactions with people. Viewing psychotherapy as a contractual relationship merely provides a conceptual framework for the therapist. It is not a school of psychotherapy and does not require rigorous adherence to its precepts. It requires only thoughtful, judicious application when appropriate.

Psychotherapists understandably hesitate to make evaluation contracts. The person who seeks help with emotional problems wants concrete assistance, not just a description of his or her difficulties from the therapist's point of view. The therapist also wishes to help, and not merely to label a problem and to make recommendations. Failure to establish an evaluation contract, however, that is separate from the treatment contract is an unwitting agreement by the therapist to deal with the problem as the evaluee sees it, and on the evaluee's terms, frequently a setup for impasse. Sharply separating evaluation from treatment allows evaluators to define the problem in their terms, stating what they believe to be the primary problem, outlining secondary problems, and indicating the likelihood of amelioration of each. They then make recommendations for treatment.

Therapeutic Contracts

Therapeutic contracts are commitments to helpful actions. They commit the evaluee to the role of patient and the evaluator to the role of therapist. A delay in offering a therapeutic contract can be useful. It can stimulate healthy reflection, self-awareness, and self-control. It can also frustrate patients excessively and undermine the establishment of a therapeutic contract.

Let us examine several clinical problems in relation to therapeutic contracts.

A patient's primary complaint is sexual impotence. Thorough evaluation suggests that the impotence is a secondary feature of a depressive illness, and that symptomatic treatment of the impotence per se is not indicated at the beginning. Patient and therapist agree to work toward amelioration of the depression with the stipulation that the contract can be renegotiated if the impotence fails to clear along with the depression.

After indicating the problem toward which the therapy is to be directed, the therapist also specifies by what means the treatment will be carried out and who will be responsible for what aspect of the treatment.

The patient's responsibility in one treatment approach may

be to record certain thoughts and feelings, and how he or she deals with them (Beck et al., 1979). In another approach, the patient may be asked to free associate without attempting to draw conclusions about his or her mental productions until their patterns become clear.

After the therapist explains the patient's responsibilities, he or she asks if the patient understands the method proposed, and if he is willing to cooperate. In paying meticulous attention to establishing the therapeutic contract, the therapist has begun to educate the patient in his or her theory of the patient's problems and their treatment. In doing so, the therapist also begins to work out the type of therapeutic alliance that best meets the patient's treatment needs.

For some patients, obedience to authority or uncritical acceptance of suggestion is the preferred relationship. This approach is used when dealing with crises and when the patient's capacity for emotional maturation is limited.

With stable patients who have greater capacity for emotional growth, the therapist works toward an understanding cooperation with the treatment process that will serve as the nucleus for a mature therapeutic alliance.

Most patients initially view self-understanding as explanation by the therapist, a passive-receptive process in which the therapist observes, interprets, integrates, and gives the patient a finished product to swallow. This again sets the stage for an impasse. The therapist can assert that there is more to therapy than attempting to figure out why, and, when appropriate, that therapy will involve facing the consequence of acts as well as their probable cause, and that it will involve implementing actions based on the new view of the patient's self and his or her world that is acquired through insight. Phobic individuals, for example, must be told that at some point they will need actively to confront situations which were initially too frightening, but only at a mutually agreed-upon time and place.

Commonly, the therapist is seen as a commentator on interpersonal difficulties that arise outside the therapeutic hour. Patients are occasionally aware that interpersonal difficulties they experience in their outside lives may arise during therapy sessions, especially in group therapy, but they tend to deny or to be unaware that they may bring their interpersonal set into the relationship with the therapist. It is therefore important for the therapist to suggest that unconsciously motivated behavior may develop in the therapeutic relationship. If the therapist wishes to establish an interpersonal, here-and-now focus for the therapy, the therapist may state that he or she will supply feedback about the impact of the patient as a person in their relationship. If the therapist wishes to establish an intrapsychic focus, he or she may state that they will see the origins of behavior in the patient's past relationships and in his or her unconscious mind.

The patient is usually unaware of the transference potential of the relationship. The issue of transference can be raised by the therapist to help orient the patient. The therapist can inform the patient that many people recapitulate some aspects of former relationships with the therapist—relationships as patients felt they experienced them, or as they wished they had experienced them. One can also tell the patient that such occurrences are usually stimulated by some real aspect of the therapist or by some interaction that occurs between them.

The patient may be encouraged to report his or her perceptions of the therapist, especially if they change or if they produce intense emotional reactions. The patient may be told that transference is not only a useful source of insight, but may obstruct the course of therapy and therefore may require resolution.

Without an orientation to the level at which therapy will operate and the means by which therapist and patient will work, significant partial impasses may occur. The transference-developing aspect of therapy may flourish while the supportive aspect fails, leading to emotional decompensation. Or, the supportive aspect may succeed without the sufficient development of insight to prevent the reoccurrence of the same situation.

In spite of the sharp line I have drawn between the evaluation contract and the therapeutic contract, there is usually no abrupt change in the therapist-patient interaction. The evaluation is carried out in a comfortable, conversational manner, not as an interrogation. Patients are also supported in the transition from highly focused questioning to a more open-ended approach. They are not suddenly left high and dry with no cues to guide them.

Contracts are not always needed, even with patients who are

able to make them. In many cases, the therapist and patient never come to an explicit goal for therapy. The patient seeks treatment for vague, ill-defined unhappiness, discusses a number of issues in his or her life, and leaves feeling better. No explicit contract was established or required for the patient to reach the implicity agreed-upon goal of feeling better.

Most patients seek therapy to feel better. It is the therapist's job to ask, "Feel better about what?" Some patients would like to feel better about abusing others. A few would like to tolerate abuse better. Therapists must ascertain which of the patient's treatment goals are in his or her best interest, or in the best interest of the community at large. They must also ask if the patient's goals for him or herself are reasonable, and if not, must help set reasonable goals.

An explicit contract not only helps keep therapist and patient on the track toward reasonable goals, but also can be established so as to facilitate progress. Goals that are made small enough can be readily reached, and the patient's experience of success is encouraging. Each small goal reached also serves as a benchmark so that patient and therapist can assess progress. Failure to reach these goals in reasonable periods of time points to possible impasse.

Contracting for Therapeutic Level

The therapeutic contract agreed upon at the end of the evaluation period should establish the level at which the therapeutic process will operate: repressive, supportive, or evocative (Weiner, 1970). The terms repressive therapy and ego-supportive therapy are roughly equivalent to the terms expressive treatment and supportive treatment used by Kernberg et al. (1972). Evocative therapy includes all approaches that deal primarily with material from the unconscious.

The structure of a repressive therapy will be presented in detail in Chapter 4. The detailed structure of an ego-supportive therapy will be presented in Chapter 5. Psychoanalysis and psychoanalytic psychotherapy, the most widely practiced evocative techniques, will not be presented at length because they have been adequately elucidated elsewhere (Greenson, 1967; Langs, 1973, 1974).

Repressive Therapies

Repressive therapies maintain repression of unconscious material because it is irrelevant to the therapeutic task or because the therapist judges it too disruptive for the patient, even if the patient wants a gut-wrenching experience. Repressive therapies teach coping techniques, assure that certain thoughts are normal, foster identification with the therapist's values, and focus on the problems of daily living. A repressive approach is indicated for acute situational crises, for individuals with little ego strength, and for people with little motivation for understanding their unconscious mental processes.

In crises, when a patient's ego strength has been acutely depleted, therapists do not engage in elaborate contract making. They respond to the patient's cry for help with direct interventions based on their professional judgment. Contract making is, however, a useful exercise for the person with chronically low ego strength. It acknowledges him or her as a person and provides a healthy interpersonal relationship in which there are no covert power moves and in which responsibility is shared as equally as possible. It also establishes that the therapists do not think for the patient, and that they do not feel they know what is best without knowing the patient and without taking the patient's goals and wishes for him or herself into consideration. This helps establish the patient's individuality and reinforces his or her ego boundaries.

Where the chief complaint is marital discord, for instance, therapist and patient may agree to work toward understanding and amelioration of marital conflicts through exploring the patient's relationship with his or her spouse. Eventually, the contract may call for the alteration of certain behaviors, as illustrated in the following telescoped negotiation of a therapeutic contract. This example compresses the negotiations of many sessions into a single interchange.

PATIENT: I want a better relationship with my wife.

THERAPIST: What aspect of your relationship do you want to change?

PATIENT: I want to be more tolerant of her shortcomings.

THERAPIST: Shortcomings? Such as?

PATIENT: Such as not being able to manage the children. She's always coming to me for help, and it makes me mad.

THERAPIST: Then?

PATIENT: Then I criticize her and she gets upset.

THERAPIST: You mean that when she turns to you for help, she gets criticism instead.

PATIENT: (Embarrassed) Yes.

THERAPIST: Let's try to come to some agreement, then, about what you want changed.

PATIENT: Okay. I want to respond positively to my wife instead of criticizing her when she asks for my help with household chores or with the children.

THERAPIST: Agreed.

Such an agreement is not usually consummated during a patient's first session with his therapist. Few patients are able to pinpoint their problems with this degree of precision at the beginning of therapy. A more likely presenting complaint is generalized marital turmoil. It is the therapist's job to help the patient determine the specific area of conflict, to determine how conflict arises, and suggest means to diminish or to resolve the conflict. Failure to establish these ground rules sets the stage for impasse in a repressive therapy.

Ego-Supportive Therapies

Ego-supportive therapies require less structure than do repressive therapies. They reinforce or do not disturb repression in the areas the ego cannot deal with, but they do encourage the development of less crippling ego defenses in areas with which the ego can deal. Patients are confronted with their projection, their denial, and their rationalization. They are encouraged to take responsibility for their feelings but are not encouraged to explore the unconscious roots of these feelings. Perceptual distortions and self-defeating behaviors are corrected by feedback in the here-and-now relationship with the therapist. The patient identifies with the aspects of the therapist which he or she can constructively adopt. Ego-supportive therapies are indicated for people who are coping adequately on a day-to-day basis, and who have greater motivation and capacity for self-understanding than the candidate for repressive therapy, who may require hospitalization, medication, and other kinds of environmental measures to help him or her stabilize.

A contract for ego-supportive therapy stresses that the reactions of the patient to the therapist, and vice-versa, are important elements in the therapeutic process. In preparation for an ego-supportive group therapy experience, the therapist underscores the importance of dealing openly with the reactions of the group members to one another (Kadis et al., 1974). Patients are also helped to understand that the observations made about their interactions are only observations and not criticisms. They are encouraged to report any feelings of criticism that they may experience. This will indicate to the therapist the factors which mobilize the punitive aspects of the patients' superegos.

A contract for ego-supportive therapy is generally worked out over time. It calls for a shift in the traditional doctor-patient relationship that might produce an adverse reaction were it spelled out at the beginning. Establishing initial therapeutic contracts is easier in repressive and evocative therapies because they involve generally accepted relationships, that of traditional doctor to patient and of analyst to analysand.

At the beginning of an ego-supportive therapy, the contract is for self-understanding at an interpersonal level, to help patients become aware of the self-defeating behavior that causes interpersonal difficulties which are responsible for the individual's emotional discomfort. As therapy progresses, the therapist introduces him or herself as part of the patient's interpersonal world. He or she is an observer, a commentator, and a participant. As the patient's interactions with the therapist become part of his or her interpersonal world, the therapist asks him to take note.

PATIENT: I was very depressed all last week.
THERAPIST: Anything happen?
PATIENT: Not that I can think of.
THERAPIST: We missed our session, didn't we?
PATIENT: Yes. So?
THERAPIST: I think it may be useful to look at what happens between us, as well as what happens in your daily life and what happened in your past.
PATIENT: Sure.
THERAPIST: What about last week?
PATIENT: Nothing in particular. I did wonder why you cancelled at the last minute after being so sticky about me cancelling appointments at the last minute.

THERAPIST: How'd you feel about that?
PATIENT: I thought you probably had an emergency.

Even when the therapist asks the patient's cooperation and the patient agrees, the therapist must still deal with the patient's unconscious resistance, as illustrated by the patient's last reply.

Evocative Therapies

Evocative therapies allow or provoke emergence of material from the unconscious. In psychoanalysis this is accomplished by leaving the therapy hour unstructured, by frustrating the patient's object needs, by providing minimal interpersonal cues, and through use of free association. As a result, there is partial ego regression and the emergence in fantasy of the patient's instinctual drives, his or her infantile conflicts, and fixations, which blend together and are expressed in the relationship with the analyst as the transference neurosis.

Because of the extreme deprivation in an evocative technique, it is suitable only for patients who can tolerate frustration without resorting to action or without becoming overwhelmed by their feelings.

The therapeutic contract in an evocative therapy acknowledges the frustrating nature of the relationship and underscores the need for the patient's active participation and reflection. In turn, it offers greater understanding of unconscious mental processes and the hope that this understanding, as experienced in the transference relationship, will lead to more adaptive patterns of thinking and behavior.

The negotiations involving the therapeutic contract should also involve the patient's expectations of the therapist. The patient may say, for example, that he or she expects the therapist to be completely passive and that he himself expects to shoulder the entire responsibility for the therapy. Instead of contradicting the patient, as he or she would in negotiating a repressive or ego-supportive contract, the therapist needs to ask, "Why?" The reply may give an important clue about the patient's attitudes about parents and about designated helpers.

THERAPIST: We're agreed that your responsibility is to say what comes to your mind. What's mine?
PATIENT: (Hesitantly) Well . . . uh . . . I don't know. I guess it's to let me talk and to hear what's on my own mind.

THERAPIST: And what's my job?

PATIENT: I guess you prompt me if I don't think of anything to say.

THERAPIST: And then?

PATIENT: If I don't have anything to say, you just sit.

THERAPIST: So you expect me to keep some pressure on you to talk, but otherwise don't expect much from me.

PATIENT: Probably so.

THERAPIST: I want to raise a question, but I'm not looking for the complete answer right away. Why do you come to me for help, but expect virtually nothing from me?

The therapist has clarified the patient's expectation and notes that the patient is unilaterally deciding to do all the work. Instead of insisting on closure of the contract at this point, the therapist questions the unilateral decision, but allows it to stand until there is further evidence that the patient has contracted for an impotent therapist. By that time, of course, the real question of the therapist's potency will be well on the way toward an answer and the transference can be dealt with.

The actual establishment of a therapeutic contract in an evocative therapy is far less important than observing and commenting on how the patient makes and enters contracts. In theory, the stable neurotics and mild personality disorders who are amenable to evocative methods require less of the experience of negotiating than they do of observing how they negotiate.

When therapists fail to negotiate an adequate contract for the optimal level of psychotherapy for their patients, they risk two types of impasse, each destructive in its own way. Establishing a contract for an evocative therapy with a person for whom a repressive method is needed poses the danger of overwhelming his or her ego and also may stimulate unrealistic expectations that will make therapy interminable. Establishing a contract for a repressive therapy with a person who has the capacity for an ego-supportive or evocative approach is destructive in that it limits the patient's potential for growth.

The Spouse or Other Concerned Relative

Contracts may also be made with the spouses and other concerned relatives of adult patients. This is of particular importance when the identified patient's judgment is poor and when there is substantial need for others to provide information and to be prepared to take action. It is also important when the spouse or other relatives significantly affect the patient's emotional state and need to be seen regularly by the therapist or someone designated by him to help deal with issues in the relationship of the patient to them.

Brushing aside a spouse or a concerned relative can complicate the treatment of any patient. It gives them a real reason to be angry, and the anger is likely to be acted out against the patient in the form of derisive remarks or overt efforts to disrupt the therapeutic relationship.

Family members can be informed that direct contact with the therapist will not be frequent, will probably come about as the result of considerable stress or distress, and the patient will be informed regarding the contact. The provision that these contacts will be reported tends to minimize calls and keeps the therapist from having to referee family fights. If the therapist deems direct contact with the family to be inadvisable, he or she needs to offer an explanation and to suggest someone to whom the family can turn with their concern about the patient.

It is difficult to say when it is advisable for the same therapist directly to treat the identified patient and other involved persons simultaneously or jointly. These are common practices among counselors but are infrequent practices among psychiatrists and psychologists. The spouse and other relatives were kept away by the early analysts for fear of contaminating the transference. Since that time, it has become clear that analysis of the transference is less useful in many cases than breaking up the stranglehold that many family members have on one another.

A spouse or other concerned relative can be seen therapeutically by the identified patient's therapist if the identified patient has no objection and if the therapist's interactions with these people do not undermine the therapy of the designated patient. Greater specifics with regard to seeing a family will be discussed in Chapter 9, "Couple and Family Therapy."

Families must know whom they can contact at times of distress, and what kind of help they can receive. Failure to agree on the relationship between therapist and important persons in the patient's environment can be a significant cause of tension because they do not know what to expect of the therapist or what is expected of them. Anger and frustration displaced onto the patient by them may intensify the identified patient's distress and sense of alienation. The same anger and frustration expressed about the therapist to the patient may undermine the therapeutic relationship. An impasse reached with the patient's family may be just as destructive as an impasse with the patient himself.

Renegotiation

Therapeutic contracts are periodically renegotiated as the patient progresses or fails to progress, or as his or her view of the problem changes. People whose initial goal was symptom relief often become intrigued with the possibility of understanding themselves better. People whose initial goal was insight often find it sterile and unrewarding and opt for advice or behavioral measures. Ordinarily, the therapist can be flexible enough to renegotiate when indicated.

Situations arise in which therapist and patient are unable to renegotiate a contract. These cases usually involve a strong transference-countertransference bind in which the therapist, the patient, or both cannot shift. The best approach to such an impasse is to use a consultant, as was done in the following case.

> The treatment of Mrs. A.M., a 28-year-old woman with anorexia nervosa, had degenerated to a monotonous twice-a-week repetition of her feelings of depression and her unwillingness to deal with her self-induced vomiting which was not ameliorating her greatest problem: self-hatred.
>
> Viewed in perspective by a consultant, the therapeutic relationship had become a power struggle: the therapist insisting on seeing the patient twice a week to deal with her feelings, and the patient wanting to assert her autonomy by exerting control over the relationship.
>
> Treatment had begun four years earlier when the patient's husband became aware that she regularly induced herself to vomit her meals. She had been hosptialized twice because of excessive weight loss, had gained weight, but now weighed 82 pounds. She said that she felt her desire to be cured of her self-hatred was probably asking too much of anybody.
>
> The consultant spent several sessions clarifying the situation and suggested to the patient and her therapist that they negotiate to ignore her vomiting, to allow her to set the frequency of visits, and to work on her self-criticism as it

manifested in the here and now; or that she seek therapy with someone who could come to this agreement with her. To the consultant's surprise, the patient suggested a transfer to his care, having previously thought that nobody else would undertake the treatment of such a resistant person. They were able to negotiate successfully and the transfer was accomplished, to the patient's great pleasure, and with the effect of enhancing her self-esteem. The impasse was resolved by the consultant's refrainment from struggling with the patient over the goals and conduct of her therapy. Her resistance had been in large measure her demand for a voice in the structure of the therapeutic relationship.

Contracting for Fees

The fee is an important part of the contractual relationship between therapist and patient. The therapist is responsible for setting a fee, for indicating how it may be paid, and with what frequency payment will be expected if treatment continues. When a contract for ongoing therapy is negotiated, the therapist should deal with the issue of charges for missed appointments and the possibility of an eventual change in fee charged to all patients by the therapist.

Discussion of fees by the therapist early in the patient-therapist relationship allows the patient to express and deal with his or her feelings, and also allows the patient to deal with the fee and to set the frequency and length of visits in relation to the ability to pay. Failing to allow the patient to deal openly with the therapist about the fee may diminish his or her expectation of being allowed a voice in other important issues, and may establish the therapist-patient relationship as arbitrary and one-sided.

Therapists omit or sidestep discussion of fees for many reasons. Trainees often feel they are not worth it. Therapists who are employed by institutions express their negative feelings toward the institution in this way. Private practitioners may wish to reinforce the illusion that the therapist is a priest-healer, above such banalities as money. This attitude of the therapist can intensify the transference expectation of nurturance and may lead to acting out of the therapist's anger toward the patient when the unmentioned fee is unpaid. To pretend, by avoiding the subject, that money is not a consideration affronts some patients' reality testing and reinforces others' denial of reality. The therapist's unconcern about fees pleases people who want special considerations in life but will contribute to the development of an impasse when the patient is told that no special concessions are available in life. Failure to deal with fees also disturbs people who need to know the degree and nature of their indebtedness to others.

Charging for uncancelled appointments or for appointments cancelled with inadequate notice is another important aspect of fee negotiations. Charging fees for unkept appointments underscores the patient's responsibility to the therapist, where other aspects of the therapeutic contract largely deal with the patient's responsibility to himself. It emphasizes one of the real needs the therapist has of the patient and indicates the real consequences that will occur if the therapist's needs are not met.

If, in the discussion of fees with the patient, therapists do not enter a contract, they have set the stage for an impasse, as the next case shows.

> A young woman was referred for continuation of her treatment by a hospital psychiatrist because she had reached an impasse with her former psychotherapist. In the first interview, she disclosed that she had not paid a large portion of her former therapist's bill. The therapist told her that he would not tolerate nonpayment of his bill. She responded with a smile. Her unpaid bill eventually became the central issue in their relationship and resulted in the therapist temporarily interrupting their working relationship.
>
> She had responded to the therapist's ultimatum by asserting her own power. A contract about fee had never been entered into. The therapist had, instead, triggered a struggle in which she proved herself as powerful as he.

It is probably unwise to discuss fees with involuntarily hospitalized persons. A discussion of fees can intensify the anguish of a psychotically depressed person or a suicidal person. It is appropriately deferred until the severely decompensated person achieves a better psychological balance.

Therapists must also note their own willingness to negotiate their fees. Unwillingness or overwillingness to negotiate fees may point to significant potential difficulties in the therapeutic relationship.

Written Contracts

Written contracts have been employed in some situations and are useful means to detect impasse. Ayllon & Skirban (1973) have prepared a written contract with parents for the behavioral treatment of their children. Rutherford (1975) has created a behavioral contract for use with delinquent adolescents. Simons et al. (1979) use contracts in dealing with chronic pain patients. Adams and Orgel (1975) recommend that the consumer have a written contract with the therapist that includes the day, time, and length of the visits, three goals, the fee, the fee for missed sessions, the consumer's option if dissatisfied, a provision for renegotiation, and an agreement by the therapist to maintain confidentiality unless given written consent by the consumer.

The greatest merit of a written contract is that it helps ensure that the therapist and the potential patient review the important aspects of the therapeutic contract: what they will work on, how they will work on it, and what else is expected of each in the process. All therapists, whether or not they actually have a written contract with their patients, should ask themselves what contract they have established with their patients, should examine its adequacy, and if inadequate or if too stringent in some respects, should ask themselves why.

Summary

Contract making is an important part of psychotherapy. Failure to make an appropriate contract is an important source of impasse. Establishing a contract is a constant reminder to the therapist that the patient has a voice in the treatment and a constant reminder to the patient that he or she is potent. It reduces needless uncertainty and facilitates the patient and therapist working together toward mutually agreed-upon concrete goals instead of toward a vague state of mental well-being that cannot be adequately defined and that, therefore, can never be reached. Vague, unreachable goals provide an annuity for the therapist, and leave the patient who terminates therapy with a gnawing sense that something more could have been done had he or she but stayed in therapy longer.

3

Process-related

The largest single cause of impasse in my own treatment of persons with a good prognosis for psychotherapy is poor management of the emotional interaction between me and my patient. The problems fall into three categories: a poor match of personalities, transference, and countertransference. I find the same problems at the root of impasses with patients whom I see in consultation for experienced colleagues. This is quite different from the impasses I see with trainees, who miss the diagnosis, do not understand the patient's psychodynamics, or lack the technical expertise to deal effectively with a particular patient's difficulties.

Mismatch

A referring person often neglects to inform the patient that an evaluation by his prospective therapist will be necessary. With some patients, it can be stressed that the process is one of mutual evaluation. This does not mean that referring persons have no ability to make a match. It means that in spite of their knowledge of the patient and the proposed therapist, there can be a mismatch. In the case where the prospective patient and prospective therapist cannot establish rapport, it should be clear that each has the option to terminate the relationship in favor of a better alternative.

Along with the emphasis on individuality that has developed among therapists, there has also developed an assumption that the therapist's individuality can be as well accepted by patients as it is by colleagues, but such is not the case. There is much evidence that the therapist should be someone with whom the patient can establish a positive partial identification. The therapist must be prepared to deal with the patient's reaction to those aspects of his or her clothes and mannerisms that he or she knows to be highly idiosyncratic in a neutral, nondefensive manner just as he or she deals with any other potential obstruction to therapy.

Therapists usually develop conscious and unconscious means to screen from their practices the people whom they cannot help or with whom they cannot cope. We need not argue whether these limitations of the therapists are good or bad. There are few, if any, universally competent therapists. The average therapist need only recognize his or her limitations and avoid situations with which he or she deals poorly. It is, however, incumbent upon the therapist to do no damage to the patient's self-esteem while protecting the patient from the therapist's shortcomings. It is better for a therapist to tell a patient that more suitable or more effective treatment can be found elsewhere and to specify the person or institution that can supply it than to throw up one's hands and say, "I can't treat someone like you." This, of course, is part of the evaluation contract: to help the patient find the best possible help commensurate with the exigencies of his or her life.

When a technically competent therapist makes significant errors in treating a patient from the very outset, one suspects a misdiagnosis or an adverse reaction between the personality or values of the therapist and the personality or values of the patient. An impasse that results from adverse interactions between personalities and value systems may be termed a mismatch. Since therapists and patients do not readily change their fundamental values, mismatches are most commonly resolved by having the patient begin work with a more compatible therapist.

Will (1980) illustrates this poignantly. During the course of his work with a young man, the latter became fervently religious and tried to convert his therapist to his new religion. The therapist, growing increasingly frustrated, told the young man, "I don't want to be converted by you." The patient angrily rejoined, "I don't want to be converted by you, either!" and terminated therapy. As Will reflected on this event, he realized that he had planned college graduation, marriage, a steady job, a house, and children for his patient, a way of life that he valued highly but that his patient did not.

Therapists must be aware of their own personality and of the people with whom they function best and worst. Many therapists cannot tolerate clinging, dependent patients. Others do poorly with aggressive patients, whom they experience as hostile and threatening. Certain therapists do poorly with alcoholic patients or homosexual patients, or patients who express themselves through physical complaints. During his or her training, every psychotherapist must be exposed to persons with a wide variety of personality types, coping and defense mechanisms, and value systems. He or she should attempt, through supervision and through personal therapy, to work out his own personal difficulties in relation to the patients he encounters. In doing so, he will broaden his ability to deal with patients and will find those aspects of his personality and value systems that compromise his ability to function effectively with certain types of problems or certain types of people. He or she will also become sufficiently self-aware that he can predict the kinds of transference reactions certain patients will have toward him and can also develop some awareness of the countertransference problems that are likely to occur.

In most cases, neither the personality of the patient nor the personality of the therapist as such causes the impasse. It is the interaction of the two. A mild-mannered, effeminate boy may have enormous difficulty expressing himself to a robustly masculine therapist with whom a histrionic young woman might be very comfortable. A very aggressive woman might not be able to tolerate a male therapist whom she experiences as passive, but whom a schizoid person experiences as nonintrusive and nonthreatening. In all of these instances, the likelihood of impasse is more related to the interaction between the personalities of the therapist and the patient than to the patient's degree of psychopathology (Strupp, 1980).

The therapist's value systems play such a strong role in therapy that one can describe ideal psychotherapy patients. They are young, physically attractive, well educated, upper middle class, verbal, willing and able to discuss and to take responsibility for their problems, have good ego strength, and have no signs of gross psychopathology (Rabkin, 1977). Viewed from one standpoint, these people have the best prognosis for psychological treatment. From another standpoint, they are the most socially desirable, and are the persons whom the therapist can idealize and with whom he or she can most strongly identify in reality or in fantasy.

Value systems are also important in the evaluation of psychopathology because they blur the distinction between socially undesirable behavior and psychopathology. Thus, the inability of the therapist to see the patient's potential gain from psychotherapy may be based on the patient's socially undesirable behavior instead of the patient's inability to respond to psychological measures.

The state of psychological health for which therapists strive for their patients, and the value they attach to the means by which they strive are also important variables. For example, a therapist who sees autonomy as the sine qua non of mental health may have difficulty accepting a patient's strong tie to his or her parents. A therapist for whom a successful heterosexual love relationship is the hallmark of mental health may cause perpetual frustration for a schizoid person who is afraid of engulfment by the opposite sex.

It is also easy to value the means of treatment over the results of treatment and to insist, for example, that if a patient has not been cured by insight, he has not been cured at all. Insight is not feasible for all patients, and other means of treatment are no less potent, although considerably less esteemed. We need to be careful not to let our commitment to a particular type of psychotherapy blind us to the positive elements in all types of psychotherapy. We must not eschew suggestion, reinforcement, and education because they are less prestigious. We must meet our patients where they are and use the tools available to them. Impasses are a frequent result of misapplied ideology.

There are times when therapists' enthusiasm for their technique blinds them to its limitations and causes a mismatch of technique to patient, as will be described later in connection with the alexithymic and the "uptight" patient. Financial pressures may induce them to undertake the treatment of patients for whom their style or technique work poorly. It is difficult, under the pressure of having to pay the office rent each month, to put the patient first under all circumstances.

The specific vulnerabilities associated with crises in the therapist's life and with his or her personal and professional life cycles are discussed in Chapter 5, "The Therapist's Life Cycle."

Transference

Patients' transference reactions are a frequent source of impasse. Transference is a form of resistance. Resistance was originally a technical term in psychoanalysis and was applied to everything that prevents an analysand from producing material derived from the unconscious (Fenichel, 1945). Nowadays, the term resistance has been generalized to encompass anything that obstructs a psychotherapeutic endeavor, whether or not the goal of therapy is to bring unconscious material to the patient's awareness.

Fenichel (1945) states that understanding the content of the patient's unconscious is the analyst's least difficult task, and that handling the transference is the analyst's most difficult task. He defines the transference as the patient's misunderstanding of the present in terms of the past. Instead of remembering one's childhood, for example, an analysand strives unwittingly to relive it and to make it more satisfactory than it was when one actually lived it. In this way, one transfers past attitudes to the present.

The process of endlessly repeating aspects of one's past in order to master them is called the repetition compulsion. Clinical experience also suggests that another goal of the repetition compulsion, in addition to a more satisfactory reliving of the past, is to capture and maintain those aspects of the past that were most satisfying and were therefore most reluctantly abandoned, whether real or fantasied. The fact or fantasy of having been one's parents' favorite child can stimulate as much transference behavior as the fact or fantasy of having been the least loved child.

Transference is also a regressive process. In the portion of his or her mental operations that are affected by the transference, the patient may think and behave in ways that reflect the state of his or her cognitive and emotional processes at the stage of development from which the transference derives. For example, a patient who is experiencing transference love for his or her therapist may be totally willing to follow the therapist's judgment, as an adoring child with a beloved father. Knowledge of the regressive aspects of the transference now extends beyond therapeutic sessions into our courts of law, and mismanagement of the transference is now recognized as the basis for malpractice action (Pope et al., 1978). More than one malpractice suit has arisen from a transference-related impasse.

Transferences, while a resistance to remembering, often help to maintain the therapeutic relationship during its early stages. The calmness and compassion of the therapist stimulate the transference wish for an empathic parent and fantasies of the therapist's omnipotence. The patient endures information gathering at the beginning of therapy in the hope of becoming the passive recipient of caring and great knowledge.

Should the therapist wish to establish a more equal, cooperative relationship, the transference wishes that were useful in the early stages of therapy become obstacles and must be worked through before they become impasses. In certain types of psychotherapy these transference wishes are not dealt with. The therapist allows him or herself to be seen as all-knowing and the patient is encouraged to follow his or her orders and suggestions.

Because of the ubiquity of transference reactions, therapists of all persuasions must be prepared to recognize and deal with them when they obstruct the therapeutic process. Insight-oriented therapies which focus on the unconscious deal with them by bringing their unconscious meaning to light. In therapies which focus on here-and-now thinking and behavior such as Cognitive Therapy (Beck, 1976), Transactional Analysis (Berne, 1964), or Behavior Therapy (Meyer & Chesser, 1970), transferences may be dealt with by labeling them as irrational negative cognitions, as games, or as maladaptive learned behavior. These cognitions, games, and learned behaviors are dealt with by correcting negative cognitions, by abandoning interpersonally destructive games, and by learning new, more adaptive behaviors.

Transferences can be partially avoided by not fostering a climate in which they can easily flourish. Brief, highly structured interviews, short-term therapy, or infrequent sessions enhance a benevolent parental transference and lessen other transferences. Even under these circumstances, transference-based difficulties can arise and can result in sufficient failure to cooperate or to deal with important issues so that an impasse will occur.

The psychoanalytic means to stimulate and highlight the development of transference is the quietness and anonymity of the analyst in a relatively stimulus-free environment. People who seek out analysis expect to be frustrated and expect to free associate. People who come only for psychological help usually do not know what to expect. Extreme passivity and uncommunicativeness with an unprepared patient can give rise to a hostile impasse based partly on a transference reaction to the therapist as a depriving patient. In this circumstance, however, not all of the patient's hostility is transference-based. People have a right to know what is going to happen to them. Without adequate preparation for treatment, the patient readily rationalizes his or her negative transference reaction, and therapy may become stalemated.

Therefore, if one wishes to reduce the nontransference sources of the patient's anger or frustration, it is useful to give some brief description of the therapeutic technique one intends to employ and to be certain that the patient understands its rationale. Making such explanations helps the therapist as well as the patient. Both of them know where they are supposed to be going and how they are supposed to get there.

Stone (1961) points out that even the psychoanalyst cannot be completely neutral. Certainly, no face-to-face psychotherapy goes on without a palpable human relationship, but active attempts to draw the patient into a relationship with the therapist and to create a climate of mutual, intimate exchange can also lead to impasse, as we will see from the case below.

> Miss M., a 17-year-old high school junior, was referred after five months with another therapist, whom she had met while attending an interpersonal skills development class. As they became acquainted, Miss M. told of her chronic depression,

her suicidal ideas, and her mistrust of people. She was enticed into therapy by the older woman's caring attitude, had improved for a time, but had begun her suicidal threats again. Her former therapist had established a postitive, intimate relationship with Miss M. by expressing warm feelings through words and embraces, and through allowing the patient to enter her personal life. This therapist shared her experiences with her own children and discussed her own dating.

Miss M. was a slim young woman who walked, talked, and dressed like a boy. She was unwilling to socialize with boys because she knew they were only interested in sex and she feared that she might be raped. Miss M.'s transference wish was to be loved as a boy. She responded to her therapist with love and with increasing depression. She was unaware that her increasing depression and increasing thoughts of suicide were an outgrowth of her positive reaction to her therapist.

Miss M. had not wanted to leave her former therapist, and used the issue of their forcible separation by her parents and by another consultant as a means to block investigation of her intrapsychic conflicts. The transference impasse with her former therapist could have been avoided had the therapist been less eager to overcome Miss M.'s barriers to intimacy. The therapist's treatment approach was doubly damaging because it also impeded Miss M.'s establishment of a relationship with another therapist.

The transference reaction illustrated above was vigorously cultivated by a therapist who was unaware of unconscious dynamics, but adverse transference reactions can begin without strong stimulation by the therapist.

Mismanagement of the transference results from the therapist actively or passively joining with the patient in acting out aspects of the transference. The therapist fails to take into account that an apparent short-term gain in the patient-therapist relationship may eventually obstruct therapy. He or she creates a channel for the discharge of impulses that is difficult to close because it is reinforced by the patient's pathologic ego defenses and is acceptable to his or her superego and thereby creates an impasse. When the therapist finally decides to deal with the transference in some way, he or she will be faced by resistance from id, superego, and ego.

Mismanagement of the transference may result from the interaction of the therapist's personality with that of the patient, from situational factors to the therapist's life, from the therapist's incompetence, from a miscalculation or oversight, or from a conscious or unconscious exploitation of the patient.

All therapists have blind spots that render them vulnerable to certain kinds of transference behavior. These blind spots vary according to the changing events in therapists' interpersonal, professional, and intrapsychic lives, and can change at times from pinpoints to substantial scotomata, as we will see in the treatment of the following patient.

> Mrs. L., an attractive woman in her early thirties, was pushed into therapy by her husband, who hoped in this way to alleviate some of the tension between his wife and his mother.
>
> Mr. L. was not greatly concerned about her relationship with her mother-in-law, whom she did not regard highly and whose influence over her husband she disliked intensely. She instead wanted help with her chronic self-hatred, for which she was unable to see any cause.
>
> She had endured much abuse and deprivation by her parents, but had somehow managed to stay on an even keel, had graduated from high school and college, and had married a decent, tolerant man. Her husband was active in his church and had often urged her to join his faith. She was not interested. Nevertheless, one of the ministers at her husband's church told her that he would leave a specific time open each week, during which they might get together and discuss religious issues. She never came.
>
> Mrs. L. had little to say to her therapist after their first few sessions, during which they explored her developmental history. The therapist was unable to recognize that she was unwilling to cooperate further, and used every means he could think of to draw her out. Free association did not work, nor did increasing sessions to twice a week, letting her know how much she frustrated the therapist, and letting her know that the therapist found her attractive. Things went better for a while after the therapist sought consultation. The therapist then combined group therapy with her individual sessions, but they eventually were stalemated, and the therapist felt responsible and guilty.
>
> One day, in complete exasperation, the therapist asked if she felt she had any need of his services. When she said, "No," he suggested termination of treatment. She accepted the suggestion, but later became angry and attempted to incite her lawyer-husband to sue for malpractice because the therapist

had terminated her without adequate preparation. He was unable to find grounds to establish a suit. She entered therapy with his therapist, whom she had already consulted without her former therapist's knowledge.

The therapist colluded with Mrs. L.'s transference wish to act out her unconscious sadistic urges toward her parents in the form of passive obstructionism with him, as she had with her mother-in-law and her husband's minister. The therapist's blindness to her lack of cooperation was due to his guilt over his attraction to her, for which he compensated by assuming the entire responsibility for her treatment. When he was finally able to confront the issue that she was not using the sessions for self-examination, he faced the full fury of her id, superego, and ego—the impasse described above. Her id had been satisfied with the discharge of her sadistic impulses. Her superego and her ego were satisfied because her id impulses were adequately disguised by their passive means of expression. She was able to discharge her sadistic urges openly after termination because her ego and superego agreed that she was entitled to hurt the therapist for terminating her in a manner she saw as unfair.

The most dramatic examples of transference mismanagement are found in malpractice suits based on sexual exploitation of patients. One of the best-known suits was filed only after the therapist refused to continue having sexual relations with his patient, which suggests that the therapist was not the only one exploiting the sexual aspects of the relationship (*Roy* v. *Hartogs*, 1975). In his defense, Hartogs stated that he was physically unable to engage in sexual relations. Unfortunately for him, several other ex-patients testified that they had found him able to perform during the time he claimed impotence.

In another case of sexual exploitation, the judge based his finding of malpractice on the conclusion that the therapist had "mishandled the transference phenomenon, which is a reaction the psychiatrists anticipate and which must be handled properly" (*Zipkin* v. *Freeman*, 1968).

Many cases in which the therapist exploits the erotic transference have not stimulated malpractice suits, only impasses which have left the patients feeling bewildered, frustrated, and guilty. One can reasonably argue that not all of a patient's erotic feelings toward a therapist are transference-based. The sexual attractiveness of many therapists does not require invoking transference to explain their patients' sexual interest, and the opposite holds as well. Robertiello (1975), however, suggests that the evidence for strong transference elements is that many patients who have entered such relationships show very good judgment in their extratherapeutic relationships, and he cites case after case in which well-functioning people allowed themselves to be swayed by the specialness of the psychotherapist-patient relationship.

In the cases I have seen, a variety of transference wishes and ordinary social wishes were being gratified: the wish to be attractive, especially to a powerful or attractive person, the wish to please, the wish to continue using sexual means to discharge emotional tensions and to avoid interpersonal and intrapsychic conflict, and the wish for a substitute relationship after an important loss.

Barnhouse (1978) and Dahlberg (1970) agree that sexual contact between therapist and patient undermines the patient's ability to establish a trusting relationship. Most striking, and again confirming the role of transference, is Chesler's (1971) finding that women who were actively seduced by their therapists held themselves to blame and did not feel entitled to redress in spite of the fact that the sexual exploitation was falsely presented as therapy!

Should a sexually exploited patient ever reach another therapist for help, therapist and patient face the complex task of sorting out the original presenting problem from the former therapist-patient interaction. They also face the difficult task of ascertaining at what point in the former treatment sexuality intervened and therapy stopped (Ulanov, 1979). The point at which the patient's (and therapist's) sexual fantasy became real and impasse developed is the point at which the transference was acted upon and not dealt with appropriately by suppression, explanation, or interpretation. The new therapist must establish the reason for the patient's vulnerability at that time and must use this information to prevent further abuse of the patient by him or herself or others, including the new therapist, thereby resolving the impasse and establishing conditions that will help avoid future impasses.

There are other, less dramatic impasses that result from transference mismanagement. Inappropriate dependency gratification is one example. The main factor in inappropriate dependency gratification is not the length of treatment, but the quality of the relationship, the frequency of visits, and the goal of treatment.

Many patients who have major psychiatric disorders benefit from periodic contact with a benevolent parent-substitute. Such a relationship can easily be maintained with a frequency of visits of once a month or less. It can also be maintained without the therapist presenting him or herself as an authority on all of life's problems. The rational part of all patients recognizes the impossibility of the therapist's omniscience, and it is the rational part of the patient that psychotherapists seek to cultivate.

Frequent visits—i.e., twice or more a week—extending over many years with no evident change in the patient's way of thinking is an obvious impasse, but many patients and therapists would not dream of altering their quest for curative insight. It may be difficult for the therapist in this circumstance to see that the goal of insight is merely a vehicle for the patient to stay in contact with the symbolically nurturing aspect of the therapist. By saying that they are striving for insight, the conscience of each is satisfied. If this arrangement prevents a decompensation, it is worthwhile. If it merely continues a stalemate, it should be terminated.

It is in connection with the goal of therapy that we find the next type of transference mismanagement, the cultivation of transference guilt by the therapist. Cultivation of guilt typically occurs when patient and therapist contract for a type of therapy that is beyond the patient's conceptual and emotional means. The contract is made without an adequate assessment of a patient's assets and liabilities and offers fulfillment of the transference wish to be transformed from a limited, caterpillar-like existence to the seemingly unlimited radiant butterfly-like existence of the therapist and all those whom the patient idealizes.

We will examine the alexithymic person as a patient who may stay in insight-oriented treatment modalities because he or she knows he is doing something wrong (otherwise, he or she would have been cured). From the therapist's point of view, the fact that a person sticks with therapy means that he or she is motivated and will begin to change as his or her resistances are worked through. It is an entirely different story from the patient's point of view, as we will see with the alexithymic and later, the "uptight" patient.

The concept of alexithymia is based on the observation that many patients with physical disorders in which a significant emotional component is suspected report very limited fantasy lives and have difficulty putting feelings into words other than those which describe physical discomfort. It is not repression that makes these people unable to tell their feelings and fantasies (Nemiah, 1978), nor is it a partial regression to a preconceptual stage of development (Schur, 1955). Rather, it is a lack of capacity to symbolize emotions, without which there can be no repression of symbols and no regression to a preconceptual state.

Alexithymia manifests as a deficiency disorder in which there is little capacity to symbolize unconscious drives and their conflict with reality, or to elaborate fantasy. As a result, psychic tensions have no symbolic outlet and may discharge directly through the autonomic or neuroendocrine system.

This means that verbal interventions that are aimed at making the unconscious meaning of symptoms conscious are doomed to failure. These patients can learn the therapist's formulas by rote, but never experience them as emotional insights. They can repeat what they are told, but it has no emotional or therapeutic impact.

We can take an entirely different type of patient and treatment approach as our next example: the uptight patient and the approach that encourages the patient to get out of his or her head and to be spontaneous, to follow "gut reactions," and to stop trying to figure everything out. Constrained, uptight people marvel at the openness of those whom they see in encounter sessions and attempt to emulate them only to find that their need for predictability or their need to know others before opening up limits their spontaneity. Because they cannot respond in an unrestrained or unpremeditated fashion, they feel they are hiding something awful that must somehow be purged, and that failure to do so means they are not doing what is best for them. If they drop out without having achieved exquisite openness, they experience shame and guilt for not having become fully human.

Using the alexithymic and the uptight person as examples, we can see the potential for stimulation of transference guilt, based on guilty memories from childhood when, because of failure to follow parents' instructions to the letter, some calamity occurred. The unconscious formula that makes these people continue with an inappropriate therapy is the idea that if authority is followed, all will be well, and that all not being well is prima facie evidence of not conforming adequately. The patient deals with this transference guilt by trying harder to make therapy work. The impasse which results is only compounded by the patient's increased efforts.

Countertransference

Countertransference is exactly equivalent to transference in the patient (Greenson, 1967). It is a reaction to some aspect of the patient as a person or to the patient's transference to the therapist, and must be distinguished from a personality mismatch between therapist and patient and from an appropriate emotional reaction to the patient. A personality mismatch is an incompatibility between the character of the therapist and the character of the patient. It is ordinarily not reversible, and the proper means to deal with it is to help the patient to find a therapist with whom he or she fits better.

Significant countertransference is probably present when the therapist's feelings and behavior toward his or her patient vary considerably from what he or she would expect another therapist to feel and to do with a similar patient under similar circumstances. The therapist can be defensive, angry, indifferent, restless, obtuse, overconcerned, or even bored.

Fenichel (1953) conceptualized the therapist's boredom as a defense against unconscious fantasy stirred up by the patient. The therapist attempts to maintain repression by becoming bored and sleepy. Altshul (1977) adds another dimension to therapist's boredom. He suggests that it can also be a reaction to narcissistic depletion by a patient to whom one gives and gives without emotional returns. By fostering withdrawal from the patient, boredom blocks further narcissistic depletion, and also indicates to the therapist that he or she is being drained actively or is being depleted by being ignored.

When therapists experience intense emotional reactions toward patients, they tend to assume that countertransference is at work, but such is often not the case. In particular, patients with borderline personality organizations stimulate intense, but appropriate feelings in the therapist. Because of their intensity, therapists often make the error of thinking that their reactions are countertransference-based (Nadelson, 1977). When therapists experience an intense feeling toward a patient, it is most useful first to ask themselves what the patient is doing to them and next to ask if their response is out of proportion to the stimulus. Havens (1973) has catalogued some of these noncounter-transference reactions. *Praecox gefuhl* is the eerie feeling conveyed by some schizophrenics. Havens' sign is feeling the small hairs on the back of one's neck rise upon hearing schizophrenics' accounts of *déjà vu*, derealization, or strange bodily sensations.

Hendrick's sign is what young female hysterics convey to the male therapist's penis. The therapist's yawn is a sign of the ruminative obsessive patient. Sullivan's sign is the tightening of the male therapist's anal sphincter in the presence of a male homosexual patient. To this brief list, I add Weiner's sign: the insistent reverie that tells the therapist that he or she has scheduled too many patients that day and has overtaxed his or her ability to concentrate. Finally, I suggest the borderline sign: a mixture of intense, chaotic emotions in the therapist that mirror the emotions of the borderline patient.

All the emotional reactions listed above are important diagnostic clues. In themselves, they do not indicate an impending impasse. The therapist's management of his or her response to his or her own reactions determines whether or not an impasse develops.

Unlike a personality mismatch, countertransference can be dealt with in the treatment relationship as a means to prevent or reverse an impasse. Like the appropriate emotional reactions experienced by the therapist, it can be an important diagnostic clue. It is important not to confuse countertransference with an inappropriate defense by the therapist against feelings such as anger which are entirely appropriate reactions to certain patients (Chrzanowski, 1980). This inappropriate defensiveness may stem from an overzealous self-control, a sense that the therapist owes the patient a calm reaction under all circumstances. Each emotional reaction of the therapist must be dealt with in the context of his or her real relationship with the patient at that moment, as well as in the context of the therapist's unconscious mental life (Weiner, 1978).

Countertransference usually develops over a period of time, but it can develop in the first session with a patient as a reaction to his or her personality, or as a reaction to the presenting complaint.

The first of the two following clinical examples is an impasse based on countertransference and counterhostility. In the second clinical example, an impasse was avoided because the therapist was aware of the impasse (probably countertransference-based) reached with the patient's prior therapist.

Mrs. A.A. was a 34-year-old married Jewish woman who had been raised in upstate New York. She, her husband, and her 8-year-old son had been in Dallas only a few months, and she had been very lonely since her arrival. About a month before her first consultation with the therapist, she was visited by her older sister and the sister's son. Her nephew brought marijuana with him, and the sister, the nephew, the patient, and the patient's 8-year-old son all ate marijuana brownies. Mrs. A.A. had two brownies and was the only apparent casualty. After eating the brownies, she experienced waves of unpleasant feelings, and was calmed down only with great difficulty. She was asymptomatic for two-weeks, after which she experienced an episode of dizziness and a sense of being outside of herself. She was then hospitalized for a general medical workup, which proved negative. While in the hospital, she felt she was having a religious experience and that she was choosing between God and the devil. After her discharge from the hospital, she continued to fear a recurrence of dizziness or of the unpleasant feeling she experienced when she ate the marijuana brownies.

In the month before her visits with this therapist, her internist had prescribed Valium, Triavil, and Dilantin for her. Valium had had no effect. Dilantin had disorganized her, and Triavil had made her muscles stiff. She had been given a prescription for 50 mg. Thorazine tablets, but she was afraid to try them.

Mrs. A.A. was the younger of two children. She felt that her parents and her older sister had been unconcerned about her. She graduated from high school, spent a year in business school, and then worked overseas as a secretary for the U.S. Foreign Service for two years. She had hoped to become the mistress of a rich man, but she did not succeed. When she returned from overseas, she met her future husband and married. She did not want children, but finally acquiesced to her husband. She began to hate her child when he was 20 days old, but felt better about him after a period of therapy with a psychologist. Prior to her visits with the psychologist, she had an unpleasant short period of treatment with a psychiatrist which was precipitated by a panic after the death of a neighbor's husband. She was started on an antidepressant, which helped more than talking to the doctor. She had a similar reaction to her father's death.

The more history the therapist obtained, the more physical and emotional complaints emerged. Before coming to Texas, for example, she suffered from the sensation of a lump in her throat which gave her great discomfort and concern. She finally admitted to having been chronically anxious and chronically concerned with thoughts about death.

During her interview with this therapist, Mrs. A.A. was anxious, and demanded to be reassured about the nature of her symptoms. She did not appear depressed. There was no gross evidence of an organic brain syndrome or a thinking disorder. Her chief defensive mechanisms were denial, rationalization, projection, and somatization.

Mrs. A.A. and her husband had come to Dallas because he had been chosen by his superiors as scapegoat for certain cheating in which he and his former employers had engaged. He was fired when his company was caught and was now in training for a job with a new company.

The therapist explained to Mrs. A.A. that her symptoms were flashbacks that were due to drug use and to her own anxiety. He said that she might experience recurrences, but that they could be controlled with small doses of Thorazine. He did not attempt to deal with her chronic anxiety state because she said that she and her husband would be in town for only a few months. At the end of the session, she was puzzled that the therapist did not suggest another visit. He said that he would be happy to see her again, and set an appointment for ten days later. He made the same suggestions at the end of the second session, and suggested that she return as necessary. The therapist did not hear from her again.

Five months later, at a local psychiatric society meeting, the therapist was asked if he recalled a certain Mrs. A.A. He learned that after seeing him twice, she was very dissatisfied. Afterward, she visited Dr. B., was again dissatisfied, and saw Dr. C. Dr. C. did not treat her. He instead referred her back to Dr. B. with whom she began twice-a-week psychotherapy. Dr. C. felt that she and the first therapist were probably poorly matched, and did not understand his telling her that she did not need treatment. The therapist told Dr. C. that he suspected his recommendations were not based on a reasonable appraisal of her treatment needs.

At a later date, the therapist encountered Dr. B. who reported that he had seen Mrs. A.A. twice a week until she moved. She got over her dizzy spells, had stopped hyperventilating, and had become able to drive on freeways. Dr. B. referred her for continued psychotherapy in her new location.

The problem that I, as the therapist, initially failed to identify was easy to see in retrospect as I examined my conscious reaction to this woman. I had felt angry with her, was critical of her, and wanted as little as possible to do with her, hardly an attitude that would stimulate rapport. She probably was aware of my attitude during our first session, but, not being entirely certain, brought to my attention my failure to suggest a second appointment. I had wanted to dismiss her with an explanation of her symptoms and a suggestion about medication. She was interested in treatment, but I found it impossible to hear that. To me, her voice had been harsh and grating, her attitude demanding, and her interests deplorably selfish.

It was difficult for me to assume a neutral attitude toward her administering an unknown quantity of a toxic substance to her child, even bearing in mind the stress of geographic dislocation, the fact that her child was unwanted, and the fact that he had been the object of angry rejection by her when he had been an infant. I may even have been glad that she was the only casualty of her poor judgment.

Instead of appearing fragile and vulnerable to me, she appeared shallow and crass. My morality was offended by her offhand manner of dealing with her husband's complicity with his former company's activities and with her ease in blaming his superiors.

I had expected her to be calmed by concrete reassurance that she was having flashbacks, especially because I assured her that her symptoms were self-limited. In trying to reassure her, I avoided listening to her say that her difficulties were longstanding, and that she needed more than a few words of reassurance and some pills to get over her most recent crisis.

As I sought further in myself, I realized that she epitomized for me a personality and a lifestyle with which I felt uncomfortable and had usually sought to avoid. I conjectured that at a deeper level I may have envied her easy conscience and her comfort in demanding of others. My responses to her were undoubtedly a mixture of countertransference and counterhostility. My suspicion of countertransference is based on similar reactions to similar people whom I have seen in my practice for short periods of time. The only one of these people with whom I did well required electroshock treatment, which alleviated her depression and probably satisfied enough of my sadistic impulses to enable me to work with her at that time and many years later when she became upset after her husband's death.

The next case demonstrates that a patient who has reached an impasse with one therapist will not necessarily reach an impasse with every therapist. When a patient is self-referred or is referred by another professional because of an impasse reached with another therapist, careful diagnosis of the nature of the impasse can lead to a better outcome of treatment.

> Mrs. A.H., a woman with a borderline personality disorder, was referred for treatment because of continued suicidal urges following hospitalization and treatment at two psychiatric facilities. She was referred by her hospital physician at the second facility. She and her first therapist had been involved in a self-perpetuating, sadomasochistic relationship in which the psychiatrist's efforts to be kind stimulated her aggression toward him and toward herself, and intensified her infantile clinging.
>
> From the outset, the second therapist confronted her with the mutually hostile nature of her interaction with her first therapist, and tied her interaction with him to her feelings toward her father, with whom she had been unable to achieve a satisfying closeness. As she became more involved in her relationship with the second therapist, she began to provoke him in the same way that she had provoked her first therapist. The greater her professed positive feelings for the therapist, the greater her provocation, including late night phone calls while drunk, suicide threats, and failure to pay her bill. The phone calls and suicide threats diminished, but in spite of repeated warnings about the consequences of nonpayment she paid only token amounts. When the therapist drew the line at a specific amount, she wrote a bad check. She forgot her checkbook at the session after he told her that he would not see her unless she paid for each session. She offered to pay for that session and for two sessions in advance at their next meeting. She returned the following time with a check that she asked the therapist to hold until after their next visit. He did, and the check bounced. He then notified her that her treatment was discontinued. She responded by arriving unannounced at the therapist's office at the end of a work day insisting that she had to see him. He responded with overt anger. She was surprised.

> She did not see the connection between her behavior and his response. When he finally began to shout, she understood that he was angry and retreated from his office. Later, she asked a lawyer friend to appeal to the therapist on her behalf. She told him that the therapist really understood her. The therapist spoke to her friend, showed him the record of her payments, and he understood the situation. The therapist also pointed out that in spite of her professed wish to return to his care she had not yet paid her bill. Her friend asked what therapy would be most effective for her, and the therapist replied that his angry rejection would be. She had at last been openly confronted by someone with whom she had dealt unfairly, and she was having to deal with the consequences. Her friends and her first therapist had been accustomed to picking up the pieces and making apologies for her. This therapist had finally been able to expose her capitalizing on the guilt of people who cared about her as a means to turn their anger with her toward themselves.
>
> Ten months later, she sent the therapist a small payment. Several months after that, she expressed a wish through her lawyer friend to continue working with him. He said that he would continue with her if she paid her past due bill and would agree to pay for each session. She paid, and they continued.
>
> After a few sessions, she again failed to pay, and they terminated. Nearly a year later, she asked to continue with the therapist during a period of crisis, and he agreed to see her on a pay-as-you-go basis. She paid four sessions in advance, used them well, and they discontinued again.

I, as the therapist, was not taken off guard by this woman's aggression. My aggressive responses to her were well-timed and appropriate. I had neither ignored nor bludgeoned her.

I cooperated with Mrs. A.A. to help create an impasse. I failed to respond to the cry for help which lay beneath her superficiality. I was aware, before Mrs. A.H. reached my office, that she and her former psychiatrist had reached an impasse, and was consequently more alert to my own reactions. Neither patient triggered a warm personal response in me, but the fact that Mrs. A.A. and I are both Jewish and originally from the same geographical area probable made me more judgmental and more sensitive to her behavior. In short, countertransference factors were the predominant cause of my impasse with Mrs. A.A.

Mrs. A.H. was far more provocative and certainly less cooperative. She frequently refused to talk, was belligerant, often lied about her thoughts, feelings, and activities, and gave me a hard time about my bill, but I did well with her.

Countertransference is difficult to recognize until the therapist has had prolonged experience with many patient types, and has had many types of interaction with patients. In addition to being aware of their personality traits, such as generosity, therapists must also know generous with whom, generous under what circumstances, and generous in what way. Having an awareness of themselves interpersonally and as individuals, therapists can compare their feelings and behavior with similar patients, or can ask themselves with whom else and under what circumstances in the past they have felt, thought, or behaved in the same way. Having made these comparisons, they are able to ask themselves the cardinal question which differentiates countertransference from an appropriate reaction to the patient and from a personality mismatch: do I behave, think, or feel substantially differently with this patient than I do with similar patients under similar circumstances? If the answer is yes, therapists must ask if anything in their relationship has stirred something in their unconscious and if so, must determine its nature. My countertransference response to Mrs. A.A. was so ego syntonic that I never asked myself this question. On the other hand, I easily anticipated the anger that arose with Mrs. A.H., and was therefore able to dose and time its overt manifestations effectively. Even a countertransference-based act toward a patient, however, can be useful in the proper context. It can demonstrate that therapists, too, have unconscious processes to which they are responsive and with which they must deal in their own daily lives. In those situations where the therapist's countertransference thoughts and feelings are transparent, the patient can be asked if others have ever reacted to him or her in the same way. Many patients are aware that they stimulate competitiveness, envy, or rescue fantasies in others. Therapists are not immune to being stirred up by their own repressed urges and conflicts, but they accept the responsibility for them and for their reactions to them. In this way, they tell the patient that everyone has irrational aspects to his or her personality, but that one need not be totally governed by them.

There are many signs of countertransference, such as preoccupation with the patient away from the therapy hour, repetitive dreams about the patient, sexual or hostile fantasies about the patient, seductiveness or quarrelsomeness with the patient, or an increase in the therapist's defensiveness (Langs, 1973). Stereotyped behavior toward the patient may also stem from countertransference, as we will see in the following case report.

> Mr. K. had originally sought treatment because of low self-esteem, depression, mild paranoid ideation, and difficulty maintaining social relationships. He was, for several years, unable to tolerate an empathic smile by the therapist or the therapist's attempts to recapitulate or summarize Mr. K.'s statements. Over a long period of time, Mr. K. was able to say that he experienced these behaviors as sexual penetrations, but he was no better able to tolerate the therapist's behavior, which persisted in spite of his inability to deal with it. It eventually occurred to the therapist that his behavior was partly a countertransference-based sadistic attack on the patient, and he reduced his smiling and began to summarize only when the patient asked for a summary. This greatly increased the patient's comfort with the therapist. The patient began to disengage himself from his sadomasochistic relationship with the therapist and began dating relationships with women.

The therapist's best defense against countertransference interfering with therapy is the adoption of a neutral professional attitude toward his patient. The therapist's real concern for and interest in the patient is best tempered (except in times of crisis) by a period of calm reflection before any action is undertaken toward the patient.

Summary

Mismatch, transference, and countertransference can all be impediments to therapy, but all can be dealt with by appropriate action stemming from the therapist's mature self-awareness.

Mismatches of personality require that the patient be transferred to another therapist in a way that maintains the patient's self-esteem.

Transference may be interpreted, avoided, or explained away. The frequent occurrence of certain kinds of transference toward the same therapist may point to a characteristic behavior or attitude of the therapist.

The manifestations of countertransference should be reduced to a level at which the patient and therapist can deal with them in the context of the therapist relationship after careful determination that the therapist's reactions to the patient are, in fact, inappropriate.

4 Stage of Psychotherapy

An impasse can arise at any time or at any stage of therapy. It can develop in one session, or may evolve over many months or years.

For convenience, we may speak of the psychotherapeutic process as having beginning, middle, and ending stages. In the beginning stage, the therapeutic contract is established. In the middle stage, the contract is carried out and is modified to meet the needs of the patient best. Therapist and patient accept their work as finished and part company in the ending stage. These three stages may take years, or they may occur in the course of a single session.

The bulk of the therapeutic work may occur in any of these three stages. The experience of potency that comes through contract making or the experience of acceptance by the therapist may satisfy the treatment needs of some people. Others require the insights and identifications gained by prolonged participant observation with the therapist. For many patients, learning how to relinquish is the crux of therapy. Early impasses, then, are often contractual issues. Later impasses are more likely to stem from process issues.

Early Impasse

The studies of premature dropouts cited in Chapter 1 show that a fundamental cause of early termination of psychotherapy is a covert contractual disagreement between patient and therapist about the approach to the patient's problems. The patient objects to the therapist's approach by dropping out instead of attempting to negotiate for a type of treatment that he or she experiences as more directly helpful. These studies underscore the need to help patients understand what the therapist has to offer and how it works, as well as enough concrete, immediate assistance to motivate patients to continue.

It may be argued that only the charlatan offers quick, easy answers, and that the legitimate therapist can only offer the hard work of self-examination or of facing reality. This ignores the basic human need for hope and people's reasonable need to see some results of treatment (Puryear, 1979). Asking patients to cooperate for long periods of time without tangible results goes counter to their common sense. If something works, there should be evidence that it works.

Early impasses also involve other contractual matters: reality factors, unclear contract, invalid contract, and inappropriate context for therapy. Process issues have their origins in the early stage of psychotherapy, but often do not manifest as impasse until the middle stage.

Reality Factors

Reality factors are a frequent source of early impasse. These factors include the patient's ability to conform to the therapist's schedule, to pay the bill, to secure transportation, or to enlist appropriate family support. They also include reality factors in the life of the therapist.

Payment

A discussion of payment arrangements is an important part of planning for therapy. If the patient's resources are limited, the patient and the therapist are faced with the alternatives of reducing the therapist's fee, of undertaking a time-limited course of therapy, or of referral to a reduced-fee clinic. Failure to consider the patient's resources adequately may result in premature termination. As the patient becomes unable to manage the bill, he or she may be unwilling to deal with the issue and may terminate therapy instead.

If the therapist finds that a patient is not paying as agreed, it is important to raise the question before it becomes an overwhelming embarrassment to the patient and a great financial loss to the therapist. Therapists often feel that they will be perceived as money hungry if the question of payment is raised before two or three months of unpaid bills elapse. The patient can be reassured that the therapist wants to be certain that the patient is not having financial difficulty in addition to wanting his fee paid.

Not raising questions about the bill implies that one can get something for nothing or that the therapist and the patient have a special relationship. The longer the therapist waits before disillusioning a patient, the more strongly and self-destructively such a patient may behave when the therapist raises the financial issue. Not asking about the bill also suggests that the therapist is an easy mark, and encourages the patient to continue making promises that he or she does not intend to fulfill.

Family Support

Family support is especially important for the person who is dependent on others for maintenance, but mustering family support is difficult for many patients. When a troubled person first seeks help with emotional problems, the family will often denigrate the mental health professions, assure the patient that any difficulties can be handled by will power, and browbeat, coerce, or shame the patient into discontinuing treatment. This is especially true in highly dysfunctional families in which the identified patient is struggling against the role he or she has been assigned by his or her family. An important consideration in treating members of highly dysfunctional families is the increased tension in the family system that may occur when the person who is seeking help changes. In these instances, prospective patients need to be told that by undertaking therapy for themselves, they are risking severe family disruptions which may alter their family relationships in ways that cannot be predicted.

The mobilization of family support is especially needed when the family member who is designated as the patient is symptomatic of other family members' difficulties as well as his or her own. Attempts to treat this person individually will be inadequate until a state of reasonable equilibrium is reached in the family. This was taken into account in the following case and an impasse was avoided.

> An 18-year-old boy was referred for evaluation of difficulties that began after a severe head injury which he had suffered in a motorcycle accident a year previously. The therapist saw him for one session, during which he told of his medically stormy postoperative course involving 14 surgical procedures. He still had a draining sinus in his chest and was unable to coordinate his eyes well. He said that he felt badly about himself because of his parents' chronic criticism and their unfair comparison of him with his older brother. He was not interested in psychotherapy and preferred to work on raising his self-esteem by starting to carry a small academic load at a local junior college.
>
> The therapist saw his parents a few days later. They reported that their son's judgment was poor, that his academic performance was poor, and they that found dealing with him very frustrating. They said they had taken him to a counselor, but that he had not been interested in counseling.
>
> Several important aspects of the family relationship emerged. The identified patient was the younger brother of a highly successful young man who was an all-around scholar and athlete, while the identified patient had a mediocre athletic and scholastic record. The parents said that their younger son now felt he would not be able to compete with his older brother, and that this had crushed his spirit and made him less willing to exert effort. It was also obvious that the parents were having enormous difficulty reconciling themselves to their son's brain damage and his limited emotional and intellectual abilities. The session was focused on enabling the parents to support their son emotionally instead of trying to find ways to get him to come to the office. They discussed means to provide more structure, dealt with their own grief, and dealt with their disappointment in him and their wish that he could be like his older brother. They were assured that because their son had made consistent progress he would probably continue to do so, but that his judgment would continue to recover slowly.

> The parents were greatly relieved as a result of this interview. They told their son that he didn't have to see the therapist, but that should he ever want someone to talk to, the therapist would be available.

Had the therapist tried to deal with this young man as an individual therapy patient, an impasse would have developed. Instead, the therapist supported his parents and left the door open for him. As a result, he sought the therapist out a number of months later to discuss further problems that had arisen, and was attentive to the advice he was given. He felt he required only a single session, and said that he would return if he felt he needed further advice. He said that his parents were having difficulty with his adopting a lifestyle different from his brother's, and that he had to become himself.

Reality Factors for the Therapist

Reality factors in the life of the therapist can be a source of early impasse. The therapist may have insufficient time to evaluate or to meet the treatment needs of the patient adequately, but may try to squeeze the patient in for a host of reasons. The result may be a poor evaluation and an inappropriate treatment plan.

The therapist's office arrangement, such as a large, shared waiting room, may cause difficulty for some patients, who may need to be referred to a therapist in less public surroundings.

The therapist's energy level at the time of day that the patient can be seen may not be adequate for the patient in question.

Finally, the therapist's relationship to the patient, with the patient's employer, or with his or her referral source may preclude objectivity and may require the therapist to re-refer the patient.

Invalid Therapeutic Contract

Invalid therapeutic contract may stem from misdiagnosis, from failure to heed the biological component of an emotional illness, from failure to appreciate the physical component of disorders which are triggered by emotions, and from the therapist overvaluing a certain treatment modality.

Misdiagnosis

An invalid therapeutic contract commonly results from misdiagnosis, usually an overestimation of coping ability or impulse control. A misdiagnosis is less likely to occur if the patient is evaluated in more than one interview, and if he or she is evaluated over a period of time, during which the therapist might carefully note the quality of the interaction while taking a detailed history with emphasis on coping ability and impulse control, as reflected in ability to complete schooling, hold jobs, and maintain stable, positive relationships. If the therapist is in a hurry to fill a vacant hour or performs a hurried evaluation for a reduced fee, he or she may fail to observe that his prospective patient's thinking is quite concrete and is involved with direct alleviation of symptoms. Patients of this sort fare poorly in psychological treatment.

Even when therapists make correct descriptive diagnoses they may incorrectly assess the patient's potential for change, assuming, for example, that because the patient suffers an anxiety neurosis rather than schizophrenia, he or she is better treated by uncovering and resolving unconscious conflict than by use of medication. Unfortunately, many anxiety neurotics have few coping skills, few healthy defenses, and little capacity for developing insight beyond rote recitation of the therapist's psychodynamic hypotheses. By contrast, occasionally a person who has been overtly psychotic can make use of an ego-supportive psychotherapy.

Biologic Aspects of Emotional Illness

Invalid therapeutic contracts frequently stem from failure to heed the biological component of a patient's symptoms adequately. The affective disorders are probably the largest source of this type of error. Genetic studies show that bipolar affective disorders have a strong hereditary component (Klerman, 1978). Hence, the history of a bipolar illness or of significant depression in a first degree relative of the patient must alert the psychotherapist to the possible need for biological intervention in addition to psychotherapy. This is crucial when treating a depressed person because it can reduce the duration and degree of the patient's suffering and his or her family's disruption, and also because of the danger of suicide when a person remains depressed.

Other findings that suggest a strong biological (but not necessarily hereditary) component to a complaint of depression are the presence of vegetative signs: slowing down, early morning awakening, weight loss, and unreactivity. The onset of such symptoms in an older patient with a stable premorbid personality and in the absence of overt life stress points to the need for biological intervention in addition to psychological measures (Klerman, 1978).

Many patients do not desire medication and express this as wishing not to be "drugged." The psychotherapist may see this as a sign of emotional health and as a positive prognostic indicator for psychotherapy. It is not always so, especially if the patient is depressed. It often reflects the patient's unwillingness to see him- or herself as ill, or as having the same biological vulnerability as his or her mother, father, or sibling.

When a strong biological component is suspected, the treatment contract must specify that psychotherapy is undertaken only as a trial, and that medication or other biological intervention will become necessary if the patient's symptoms do not abate or worsen. This principle is illustrated below.

> M. had begun a professional practice in a new city a year before seeking therapy for depression. His practice had developed sluggishly. He and his wife had also experienced a sense of social isolation. He gradually began to feel that he had failed, had difficulty concentrating on his work, experienced weight loss, early morning insomnia, and loss of libido. He had no prior history of depression, and there was no significant tension between him and his wife. His mother had experienced severe episodes of depression for many years, and had finally been stabilized on an antidepressant and lithium carbonate.
>
> M. responded negatively to the suggestion that antidepressant medication might be indicated. He was told that the prognosis for the episode of depression was good; it was merely a question of the most efficacious treatment. He thought that he was failing in business and that his basic problem was inability to accept his failure. After a period of ineffective psychotherapy, he accepted an antidepressant to which he responded well in four weeks. He continued in psychotherapy for three years, and intermittently required antidepressant medication.

Psychotherapy and drug therapy were mutually augmenting. M.'s psychotherapeutic experience broadened his interpersonal skills, helped him to deal more effectively with life changes, and helped to make his depressive symptoms ego-alien. As he became able to see his depressed mood as a symptom, he was enabled to begin antidepressant medication early and to avoid full blown episodes of depression. Had the therapist agreed to treat him with psychotherapy alone and felt bound to that contract, his life might have been ruined.

Psychologically Triggered Physical Disorders

An invalid therapeutic contract may also be established because of the therapist's presumption that, because a physical illness is triggered, worsened, or improved by psychological events, some form of psychological therapy is the treatment of choice.

Virtually all physical illnesses may be triggered, worsened, or improved by changes in emotional state and in psychological environment. Engel (1967) has described a specific psychological complex in which vulnerability to illness is increased. Simonton, Matthews-Simonton, and Sparks (1980) find that enhancement of hope may help to prolong the lives of cancer patients.

The degree to which purely psychological measures can alter a physiologic state depends on the degree to which the physiology has been altered, the amount of structural change that has occurred, and the accessibility of the final physiologic pathway to further influence by psychological events.

It has long been known that peptic ulcer, asthmatic attacks, and diabetic acidosis, among other disorders, can be triggered by psychological events. It has even been possible to predict the onset of peptic ulcer in a susceptible population (H. Weiner et al., 1957). Once the physiologic dysfunction is initiated by psychological events, however, it is usually the end result of a complex chain of neurohormonal events that involve physical processes beyond the reach of psychological influences and requires physical or chemical intervention.

There are physical disorders in which the chain of physiologic events is not so complex as in the above examples, and in which the altered physiology can be directly influenced by conscious will or by a change in feeling state.

This is the case in tension headaches, air swallowing, irritable colon, several disorders of orgastic function, enuresis, and encopresis. These physically minor disorders are not life threatening, do not ordinarily cause permanent structural change in the affected organs, and have all been successfully treated in some patients by purely psychological means (Williams & Gentry, 1977).

The therapist must not lose sight of the fact that the complex interaction of physical and emotional factors may require physical intervention, even in a minor psychosomatic disorder. For example, functional vaginismus, which is a purely psychogenic disorder, often requires dilation of the vaginal canal with a graduated series of dilators before penile penetration can be accomplished (Weiner, 1973). Although no structural narrowing actually exists, the painful involuntary spasm that occurs upon penetration can only be overcome in some cases by gradually increasing the size of the penetrating object.

The following case indicates the interplay of physical and emotional factors in a purely psychogenic physical disorder.

> N., a 14-year-old boy, was referred by his pediatrician for a longstanding problem of soiling. N.'s mother complained that he frequently smelled bad, that his underwear was constantly stained with feces, and that he often hid his stained, smelly underwear to avoid confronting the issue. N. steadfastly denied any problem at all, except for rare occasions on which he found feces in his underwear. He denied awareness of having had bowel movements at these times, but he did say that he ordinarily had bowel movements only once a week.
>
> There was no history of significant medical disorder. His early toilet training was uneventful. His bowel difficulties had begun shortly after the death of an older brother.
>
> In addition to his bowel problems, N. was a procrastinator. He rarely did his homework on time, delayed his reading assignments at school until the very last moment, and completed his schoolwork only under great duress.
>
> The psychological picture was one of all-round retentiveness. With the pediatrician's reassurance that there was no physical abnormality, psychological treatment was attempted but proved ineffective. Consultation with a proctologist revealed the reason. The boy had a huge mass of feces in his rectum which had stretched the rectum until it could not contract and expel its contents. His soiled underwear was due to leakage of semiliquid fecal matter around the hard-packed mass of feces in his rectum. Successful treatment of the soiling problem was accomplished in a two-week hospital stay during which he was given daily enemas to break up the impacted

> fecal mass and was given stool softeners to prevent further impaction. Reduction of the fecal mass relieved the overdistention of the colon, which became able to contract normally and to empty itself.
>
> Needless to say, this physical treatment had no impact on N.'s procrastination, which he later acknowledged as a problem and dealt with psychologically.

The therapist must always be aware that the interaction between mind and body is complex and that the physical aspect of psychologically based physical disorders may require direct treatment.

Overvalued Therapy

An invalid therapeutic contract often results from a therapist trying to impose a highly personally valued therapeutic procedure on an unwilling patient-designate. Because it is coercive, such therapeutic practice violates a prime requisite of a contractual relationship.

In the following case, a therapist reached an impasse because he attempted to impose a treatment contract on a woman who came for help in dealing with a problem that she saw as external to herself.

> Mrs. T. was concerned about her teenage daughter who was in treatment with another therapist. She wanted advice to help her deal with the child. The child's therapist had earlier referred Mrs. T. for casework treatment to help her understand and resolve her conflict with the child. The child's therapist said he would discontinue treatment of the child if the mother did not continue in treatment. She sought this therapist out, and said that she felt no need for personal therapy. She did feel that her daughter's therapist was unaware of the extent of the child's difficulties. Soon after the second therapist saw Mrs. T., her daughter's treatment was terminated by her original therapist. The child saw another therapist who advised hospital treatment. The mother calmed down rapidly after the daughter's hospitalization, and required only a few more visits to reassure her that her panic had been justified and that environmental control for her daughter was a more appropriate immediate measure than dynamic insight into herself. The mother may have had intrapsychic problems for which treatment would have been helpful, but that was not her area of concern. Attempting to treat her only served to alienate her.

A prospective patient may agree to a therapist's treatment approach because of the therapist's credentials or professional reputation, even though the proposed treatment does not make sense to the patient. The therapist, on the other hand, must be certain that the patient wants to be treated by a method, and not by a reputation. This, of course, means that the therapist must describe the proposed treatment to the patient.

Unclear Therapeutic Contract

Unclear therapeutic contract means that the patient and the therapist are not sure if they have agreed to work together, how they have agreed to work together, or on what issues. An unclear therapeutic contract commonly stems from the therapist's carelessness. In the haste to acquire a patient, he or she neglects to determine if the prospective patient has a treatable emotional disorder or sufficient motivation to work in a treatment relationship. This often occurs when the therapist's case load is low, when he or she is impressed by a potential patient's social standing, or when he or she is physically attracted to the person. The therapist attempts to make an emotional tie first and to establish a treatment contract later. This can be like grabbing the proverbial tiger by the tail. Once entrapped, many people scratch and claw at the therapist until he lets go and roar that they have been abandoned, but when asked why they entered therapy, they say that it was all the therapist's idea.

An unclear contract produced an impasse in the following case because of the therapist's reluctance to tell the referring physician and the patient that he felt group therapy was not an appropriate treatment.

> Miss K. was referred for group therapy. She had been hospitalized for a psychotic illness ten years before, but had made a good recovery and was on no medication. At the time of referral, she was mildly depressed, felt isolated, and wanted help to improve her interpersonal relationships, which were few and remote. She sought therapy with her former physician, who referred her for group treatment, feeling that a group experience would be the best way to help her establish and maintain social relationships.

> Miss K. grudgingly agreed to a reassessment before entering group therapy. During the evaluation sessions, it became evident that her bitter, quarrelsome interpersonal style that endangered her job and her social relationships also reflected a very brittle defensive system. In the third session, in spite of poor rapport, the group therapist told her that they were both adequately prepared for her to enter a group. When he then told her the time of day that the session was held, she became livid. She worked across town, and had only 15 minutes to make the 30-minute drive, and could not get off work early. She would not consider coming to the group a few minutes late, nor would she consider referral to another therapist's group. She decided to seek out a self-help group at a junior college and stormed out of the office.

During the evaluation, this woman's characterologic rigidity emerged, an alliance did not develop, and she self-selected out of the group. The therapist was relieved at not having to deal with her in his group. She had little latitude for a change, and virtually no tolerance for another point of view. Failing to tell her the time of the group meeting may have been in part the therapist's acting out of anger toward the referring physician who had referred a number of similarly unsuitable candidates for group therapy. These candidates had consequently been treated individually by the group therapist or referred back for continuation of individual psychotherapy. While it was fortunate for the group that this woman was unable to attend, her difficulty with trust was reinforced.

Working out of an impasse that stems from an unclear therapeutic contract requires that the therapist and patient realize that they do not understand their contract. The next step is for each to state what he or she thought the contract was, and for each to indicate what sort of contract he or she is willing to enter. The lack of clarity in establishing the treatment relationship can also be a useful diagnostic aid.

It may be an extension of the characteristic modus operandi of one or both, and as such may point to character pathology that needs to be resolved or at least examined. It may also point to transference-countertransference issues that have arisen early in the treatment relationship and may suggest that the therapist needs to begin discussing the case with a colleague who has some awareness of the therapist's blind spots.

Inappropriate Context for Therapy

Certain environmental contexts facilitate treatment for some people and block effective treatment for others. Contextual considerations include the time, place, and manner in which the therapeutic techniques are carried out, as well as the interpersonal context in which they occur. Psychotherapy offered by a clergyman may be quite effective for many people, but ineffective for others solely because it is offered by a clergyman. The same can hold true for a psychiatrist or a probation officer.

Psychotherapy offered in the context of a penal institution is frequently ineffective because the basic staff-resident relationship is coercive. Further, the resident group norm is antistaff, and members of the resident group who work cooperatively with staff are seen as traitors to the resident group and thereby jeopardize their group standing and physical safety.

The temptation to see someone in one's own organization or circle of friends can be rationalized in many ways, including convenience, lower cost, and keeping it in the family. I have known an occasional therapist who did this successfully, but this is not within the ability of the average professional therapist, no matter what his professional discipline. It usually enables the person in the role of patient to deal superficially with problems and allows the person in the role of therapist to feel omniscient. It also allows the therapist to get the inside scoop on people about whom he or she would not ordinarily hear gossip, and greatly prejudices work and social relationships.

It is not necessary that the life or personality of the therapist be completely unknown to the patient. It is necessary that they have a professional relationship in which the important information can be shared. Trying to work therapeutically with someone who has significant influence over one's life colors and alters the exchange of information, even in training analyses (Greenson, 1967).

To extricate one's self from an inappropriate context for therapy, one may suggest an appropriate context. If the person seeking help becomes defensive and insists that he or she does not have a serious enough problem to warrant formal consultation, the therapist may say that reasonable advice is not possible without the fuller understanding that a formal consultation would provide. The therapist can express fear that the advice he or she gives will be taken as knowledgeable professional advice, which it cannot be since he is only partially informed. Many non-patients who seek professional advice will go away angry, but none will think the therapist as much a fool as the one who manages to solicit advice based on incomplete information.

If the person seeking help agrees to formal consultation with the therapist, the therapist can make an appropriate referral instead of having to guess at the real nature of the advice-seeker's problem.

Mid-Stage Impasses

Transference resistance and countertransference are the major sources of mid-stage impasses. To have reached mid-therapy, the therapist and patient will ordinarily have made a valid therapeutic contract based on an accurate assessment of the patient's ego strength, adaptive mechanisms, and psychodynamics. In spite of all this, the therapy may stall and the patient may feel or act worse. The therapist is often tempted to apply a new technique or a new method of therapy at this time, but before doing so, he or she should examine the relationship with the patient, and the place to start is with the transference relationship.

Transference Resistances

All patients experience transferences toward their therapists. Transferences that impede therapy are called transference resistances. Transference resistances manifest directly in the therapeutic relationship. The patient's reenactment of some feared or desired aspect of past relationships in the therapy hour may be called acting in. In its most extreme form, the patient is unaware that he or she is behaving irrationally, responding to the therapist as if he or she were an important person from his or her past. Patients with little ego strength lose the "as if" perception of their therapists and begin to see them as their persecutors and as the cause of their troubles. Therapists who work with psychotic patients are aware that they may become included in their patients' delusional systems (Searles, 1965). Healthier patients, although aware of the "as if" quality of their perceptions, may still be overwhelmed by the intensity of their feelings. One woman who required hospital treatment actually cowered in her chair, expecting the therapist to attack her sadistically as her parents had done. Her terror of the therapist blocked her therapy for a significant amount of time.

Transference resistances also manifest outside the therapeutic relationship as acting out. Patients who act out displace their transference feelings away from their relationship with the therapist onto other relationships. For example, sexual transference feelings aroused by the therapist may result in the patient entering an extramarital liaison. Aggressive transference feelings displaced outside of the therapeutic setting may result in quarrels at home or at work.

Transference resistances can best be detected by therapists viewing themselves as the center of their patients' emotional world. They need to view all of a patient's behavior as if it might have some relationship to them, while keeping in mind that there are other significant occurrences and relationships in the patient's life. In this way, the therapist can detect transference and will also be alert to the host of nontransference communications that patients make through their actions and through metaphor. The therapist's alertness to metaphor and other indirect forms of communication enables him or her to help patients face and begin to assume the responsibility for their feelings and to express them directly.

In repressive and ego-supportive therapies, the therapist periodically elicits patients' dreams and fantasies, and tries to keep transference feelings at a minimum by explaining them away as they arise in dreams and daydreams. Patients can be told that people in psychotherapy frequently develop sexual feelings toward their therapists or react to their therapists as though they were like some important loved or feared person from the patient's past with whom the patient has unfinished business. Patients can be told that everyone has unfinished business like this, and that as patients differentiate therapists from the important people of their past, such feelings will subside.

When the therapist suspects acting in or acting out, but cannot identify the nature of the transference, the content and the affective quality of dreams can tell the therapist what is being avoided, and can give a feel for the intensity of the transference feelings. They can also help the therapist decide whether to allow the further development of the transference or to limit or suppress it.

In psychoanalysis, transference resistances are dealt with by interpretation. This is possible in psychoanalysis because the patient is sufficiently psychologically intact and sufficiently psychologically minded to understand the carryover from one relationship to another. When the patient is more in need of support than analysis, other approaches must be used.

The intensity of the transference may be reduced by reducing the frequency of visits so that the patient has less of the therapist to react to and can be more easily focused on external events. It may also be reduced by increasing the frequency of visits so that the transference issues can be more sharply defined and explained. It is difficult to do more in a once-a-week therapy than focus on reactions to life events and behavior outside the therapeutic hour. Dealing directly with transference issues usually requires more than one session per week to maintain the emotional intensity of the relationship without having to ignore the patient's reality situation altogether.

Structuring sessions is another way to reduce the intensity of the transference. Assigning greater priority to the patient's life situation outside the therapeutic hour than to his or her reactions to the therapist can help to keep the transference relationship from becoming the central issue in the therapy if developing transference feelings threaten the ability of the therapist and the patient to work together.

The rapid development of acting in or acting out points to poor ego integration, and suggests poor impulse control and the capacity for severe regression. It requires a shift in the focus of therapy away from the unconscious and past relationships toward the development of coping skills and impulse control if one is to avoid an impasse.

Countertransference

The possibility of countertransference reactions by the therapist is the next consideration after transference difficulties have been explored. Mid-therapy countertransferences may not be accompanied by significant dysphoria for the therapist. In fact, the therapeutic sessions may be relatively comfortable, with the therapist noting a lack of significant conflictual material in the session, and only occasional feelings of boredom. For example, Mrs. A.K.'s transference wish (see Chapter 1) was to care for the therapist by not raising difficult issues during a period of crisis in his life. The therapist's countertransference response was to let her do for him what his superego would not allow him to do for himself: allow a few moments of peace and quiet during his day. Their mutual awareness that therapy was not progressing forced the issue, and they got back to work.

As indicated in Chapter 3, countertransference is easier to spot if one knows one's self and knows one's typical interactions with patients. One becomes aware of those patients who stimulate one's own sadism or seductiveness, and strives to be more neutral with those patients.

Mid-therapy countertransference reactions may be spotted by the patient, who notes that something about the therapist has changed. He or she is less caring. Or more critical. Or less sensitive to the patient. The therapist tends to view these comments by the patient as transference manifestations, but having ruled out transference, he or she should make a presumption of countertransference difficulties and ask him or herself what might be the nature of the countertransference.

A self-examination for countertransference begins with the therapist's conscious attitude toward the patient. What is it, how has it changed, when did it change, and in relation to what? How does the therapist's conscious attitude toward this patient resemble or differ from his or her attitude toward similar patients in the past? If different, why? If similar, were there countertransference problems with those patients?

The therapist's fantasies and dreams about the patient can also give clues to the nature of the countertransference. If the therapist is unaware of fantasies or dreams that might shed light on the subject, he or she can construct a fantasy about the patient. He can imagine himself and the patient together in various settings: at a cocktail party, in bed together, sharing a meal, or engaging in some competitive activity with one another. Fantasies that come easily and that are readily elaborated, or the inability to fantasy a patient in a particular setting give important clues.

When the therapist feels that he or she has spotted the countertransference difficulty, he can take action. If the countertransference problem is in the sexual realm, the therapist examines his or her behavior with the patient to see if he or she has been behaving seductively, or at the opposite extreme, if he or she has been unwilling to acknowledge the patient as a sexual person. If the countertransference problem concerns nurturance, the therapist may be overly accepting of the patient's tendency to come late or of the patient's excuses for failing to keep appointments. On the other hand, the therapist may be sharply critical of the patient for the same behavior.

Having identified the countertransference and the behavior resulting from it, the therapist diminishes his or her countertransference-based behavior by increased attention to the area in which he or she has been slipping or by greater activity in the area in which he had formerly been passive.

If the diagnosis of a countertransference-based impasse is correct, some change in the patient will follow: a change in behavior toward the therapist, a change in mood, or a change in behavior outside the therapy hour. In some cases, there will be an apparent change for the worse as the patient begins to express negative feelings that were formerly withheld. Mrs. A.K., for example, was first upset with herself for having negative feelings toward her therapist, but she worked through her guilt and became more comfortable with her ambivalence.

The patient can help to make the diagnosis of countertransference problems, and can help to straighten them out. The patient can be asked if he has noticed a change in the therapist. He can be asked when he noticed the change, the nature of the change, and the patient's idea of what the therapist may have been reacting to. When the therapist has made the diagnosis of countertransference-based impasse and has instituted corrective action, he can ask the patient about further changes, and ask the patient's reaction to them. Because countertransference problems are usually linked to the patient's transference expectations, they often involve transference gratification. If the patient's wish for transference gratification is totally ego syntonic, one may expect that the patient will feel hurt or angry at the deprivation he or she is now suffering. When the patient is aware that his wish for certain things from the therapist was not entirely in his best interest, he may grudgingly praise the therapist for having taken the best course of action.

End-Stage Impasses

End-stage impasses result from the accumulated errors that go unnoticed until therapist and patient become aware that therapy is dragging on beyond the time that either might reasonably have expected. They also become apparent when either therapist or patient attempts to conclude the therapeutic relationship.

The therapeutic relationship that extends indefinitely without thought of termination by patient or therapist usually involves substantial gratification for both, and frequently involves avoidance of experiences and feelings concerning separation, grief, and loss. Impasses that arise when the therapist attempts to terminate treatment may stem from an inappropriate termination. On the other hand, the threat of termination may be a potent impasse breaker and may be the crucial element in therapy for some patients.

Inappropriate Termination

Some patients require permanent psychological support by a designated therapist to maintain their psychological balance. For these people, contact with the psychotherapist enhances coping, stabilizes mood, and maintains contact with reality. Patients who require permanent psychological support belong to no single diagnostic category. Some have affective disorders, many are schizophrenic, and many have anxiety and personality disorders. The common denominator is a need for an external psychological prop that is not supplied by ordinary means.

Contact with the therapist can be intermittent or can be regular biweekly, bimonthly, or biannual visits. The length of the visit and the content of the interchange are probably less relevant than the patient's sense of stability and continuity in the relationship with the therapist.

One discovers that one's patient requires a permanent ego auxiliary by attempting to terminate therapy or to space out visits. The patient becomes more symptomatic, often without attributing this increased symptomatology to the threat of termination. Ordinarily, the therapist's first assumption is that the patient is experiencing the ordinary separation anxiety that occurs at the end of the treatment relationship. One senses not merely a return of symptoms with the interminable patient, but a certain instability of the ego that suggests that the therapist somehow supplies the framework about which the patient's ego is organized.

Again, the patient usually fails to make the connection. Or, if he does, the connection sounds superficial and like a parroting of the therapist's explanation. The rote quality of the patient's insight suggests that it has not been integrated by the patient and that it has not become the basis of a substantial identification with the therapist. It suggests instead that there has been only a tenuous introjection that requires the real or imminent presence of the therapist for reinforcement.

Difficulty assimilating the psychotherapeutic experience stems at times from lack of basic trust (Erickson, 1950), or from such problems in the transference relationship as fear of being swallowed up or anally penetrated by the therapist. Other difficulties have to do with how patients learn. Many people can best understand an idea which is expressed in a concrete form that is analogous to the idea, something that can be seen or touched. Their absorption of the idea may only be possible through continued exposure to the concrete form. In the case of psychotherapy, the therapist's physical presence or the memory of the therapist may reinforce the ideas and values he or she attempted to inculcate, and without this real or anticipated presence the patient loses what he had gained. Icons and talismans serve the same purpose in religion.

Other patients, of course, ingest insight after insight without ever becoming able to translate them into useful action.

Patients are usually disappointed with themselves when the therapist proposes slowing down or halting the process of termination. The therapist must be careful not to support their idea that if they had really been trying or fully cooperating, they would have finished therapy by now.

A patient's ability to terminate may be demonstrated, on the other hand, by the therapist dragging his feet until the patient literally demands to be more independent. In this instance, the patient mobilizes his or her emotional resources to pull against the therapist. The patient who cannot pull strongly against the therapist may require prolonged or permanent shoring up.

It may be more necessary than has been previously suspected for the therapist to remain as a permanent, symbolic parent-surrogate in virtually all cases. Even the most mature, well-analyzed person can use a symbolic shoulder to cry on now and again.

There are many reasons why therapists terminate patients who need to stay in the treatment relationship. Inability to get someone well may threaten therapists' sense of potency. Indeed, if they have not made significant progress with a patient, they may have good reason to feel impotent.

The patient who clings to the therapeutic relationship may also remind the therapist of unacceptable wishes of his or her own: wishes for fusion or for an external source of support. This may produce a strong countertransference-based insistence that the patient stand on his or her own two feet. Inability to see maintaining the status quo as a valid goal for the treatment of persons who have been severely decompensated can be a problem for ambitious therapists. It may be difficult to face the fact that one is more often a temporary or permanent crutch than a powerful instrument for personality change.

A therapist can also tire of seeing the same old face and of hearing variations of the same old complaints. The lack of excitement in the relationship and the banality of the therapist-patient interaction discourage ardent healers, but chronic patients form a large percentage of psychiatric patients. They tax therapists' patience more than their skill, their tolerance more than their psychological knowledge, and they are the biggest affront to the therapist's narcissism.

A final reason for premature termination of therapy is to begin a social relationship with the patient. The therapist's admiration of certain qualities of a patient may lead him or her to turn the relationship into a friendship before it is in the patient's best interest, if it is ever in the patient's best interest at all. It is difficult to know under what circumstances it is reasonable to establish a social relationship with an ex-patient. It is probably unwise for the therapist to broach the idea. Perhaps the best way to approach the issue is for the therapist to say, in response to the patient's suggestion of an eventual social relationship, that he or she, too, would like a social relationship with the patient (if this is true) and to discuss what therapist and patient would like from the relationship. After that, they might agree to wait after termination for an arbitrary period before contacting each other to give each a better perspective on his or her own needs. At the end of the stated period, patient and therapist might convene in a neutral place, as equals, to discuss their attraction (whether social or sexual) and to decide how or whether to proceed. Most patients have little interest in a continuing social relationship with an ex-therapist after a cooling-off period. Those who do may be colluding with their ex-therapists to avoid dealing with important aspects of each other's psychopathology or interpersonal needs.

If the patient raises the question of a social relationship with a therapist who is not interested, the therapist need not say no. He or she need only explore the patient's motivation and help the patient work through any feelings of abandonment, frustration, and anger if they exist, and to help turn him or her toward people who can be more accepting.

Therapist Unwilling to Terminate

Patients who are able to terminate therapy may be kept in therapy because of the therapist's unwillingness to let go. Chesler (1971) has described therapists whose patients serve as their surrogate families and as important social outlets. For these therapists, to let go of a patient is to suffer a severe personal loss. When the patient suggests the possibility of termination, the therapist reminds him or her how much unfinished business there is, or becomes distressed, allegedly for the patient's sake. He does not realize how much of his own needs he has projected onto the patient and the extent to which they are gratified in the treatment relationship.

The termination of the patient's treatment reminds the therapist that separation and loss are inevitable and recurrently brings to mind the memories of past losses and feelings connected with them. Some patients, of course, have greater emotional significance to the therapist because of the quality of their present relationship or because of the thoughts and feelings they arouse in the therapist that are based on past relationships.

A therapist's unwillingness to terminate a patient's treatment may also be due to unrealistic treatment goals. It is possible to continue making progress after more than ten years of therapy, but there is some doubt that the therapeutic sessions need be more frequent than once a month after such a length of time.

How long should therapy proceed when there is no appreciable gain? When does one call it an impasse? These questions can only be answered if the therapist is willing to raise them with the patient. One may reasonably ask what harm is done if therapist and patient are willing to see each other indefinitely, but again one cannot deal with this question unless the patient is asked how he or she reacts to the prospect of termination. In some instances, the patient is awaiting the therapist's permission to discuss the subject, perhaps out of awareness that the therapist wishes to continue treatment, but without any certainty as to why the therapist wants to continue.

A number of patients will be startled and uncomfortable when the therapist asks how the treatment is going and raises the question of eventual termination. These people feel that the therapist is withdrawing love (if, indeed, there was any). The therapist who is overly attached may react defensively and assure the patient that he or she has only raised these questions out of concern for the patient's well-being, thus tightening his or her hold on the patient and assuring that the patient's negative feelings will be discharged away from the therapist. A patient who has been in treatment for many years and hears these questions for the first time may be justifiably angry if there has been no significant change.

Raising questions about the progress of therapy and about its possible termination can also stimulate reflection by therapist and patient on their individual and mutual goals. These questions can stimulate a significant reexamination of their explicit agreements and their implicit expectations. The therapist must ask himself why he is raising the questions of progress and termination at this time. They may reflect a change in his overall attitude as a therapist, in his attitude toward the patient, or in his own intrapsychic or interpersonal life. As some therapists change during their lives, they become less tolerant of certain types of personalities and eliminate these persons from their practices by raising questions about the therapy that could have been more profitably raised years earlier.

Borderline personalities can make each session a fascinating, spine-tingling adventure for the young professional. For the experienced professional, the prospect of working with yet another borderline personality may stimulate only unpleasant tension. Those therapists who carry borderline patients from early career to mid-career may become worn out and drive the patient away by sheer indifference to his or her escapades and interactions.

Patient Unwilling to Terminate

Patients are unwilling to terminate therapy for many reasons. For example, the patient's agenda may not include termination. He or she may instead wish for permanent support. Patients may fear termination, based on a realistic appraisal of their need for support or on fear of dealing with separation and loss. The therapist may, of course, have become very important to the patient as a real person and as a part of his or her emotional life. These issues need to be separated from the need of the patient for formal therapy and from his or her avoidance of important issues.

Forced Termination by the Therapist

Events in therapists' personal and professional lives may require that they terminate treatment of patients who are not yet ready to discontinue treatment. This occurs most often when a therapist graduates from professional training or takes a new job. This type of termination has the potential for compounding the patient's problem and for creating an impasse with the next therapist.

Problems can arise from failure of the therapist to give the patient adequate notice of termination and adequate opportunity to work it through. Failure to notify the patient and to encourage expression of his or her feelings on the subject is frequently due to the therapist's feelings about leaving the patient and his or her wish to avoid the patient's reaction to his leaving.

Frequently, the therapist wants to avoid his or her own feeling of guilt. As a graduating trainee, he often feels guilty because he has used the patient for his own education without having cured him completely. For the therapist who is terminating a patient because of job change, there may be guilt over leaving a person who is still in need. In both instances, guilt may be compounded if there is no readily available professional to take the therapist's place, and the patient must be left to cope as best he or she can without professional help.

Therapists react to their own guilt in many ways. They rationalize it away by telling themselves that their leaving cannot be avoided, and that the patient is better off having had some treatment than no treatment at all. They may also attempt to assuage their irrational guilt by indulging the patient—giving advice more freely and offering more of themselves as people. In spite of the lessening of the therapist's guilt, there is often an adverse result from the departing therapist's generosity. It blunts the ability of the patient to recognize or to express his or her anger at being left. If the patient begins therapy with a new therapist, the latter usually becomes the target of the anger that has been displaced away from the former therapist. The new therapist is chastized by the patient for being less giving and less open than the departed, now idealized, former therapist. The avoidance of an impasse in an interrupted therapy often depends on the new therapist's ability to point out the real source (and later, if appropriate, the transference source) of the patient's anger without demeaning the former therapist, who has usually been transformed by the patient into a paragon of virtue. In some cases, it is necessary to challenge this idealization vigorously in order to keep the patient from turning an excessive amount of aggression inward toward himself and attempting suicide.

The therapist's attempts to minimize and to avoid the patient's anger often have the same effect as the therapist's avoidance of his or her own guilt. There are times when it is appropriate to help the patient suppress anger, especially when intense affects directed toward an important person in the patient's life have triggered severe ego decompensations. In these instances, it is best if the therapist actively assures the patient that he or she is better off having had some treatment than no treatment at all, and that the therapist is willing to remain available for periodic, brief telephone contact. When a transfer has been arranged, the departing therapist can emphasize that he or she believes that the patient and the new therapist will do well together, and may even arrange for patient and new therapist to meet before he or she actually leaves.

Summary

There is a relationship between types of impasse and stages of therapy. Early impasses stem from contractual issues, including reality factors, unclear contract, invalid contract, and inappropriate context for therapy. Transference resistances and countertransference are the major sources of mid-therapy impasses. End-stage impasses are the culmination of contractual and process errors, and result in prolonged therapy or premature termination. They often stem from inappropriate gratification of therapist and patient. Additionally, they result from avoidance of dealing with separation and loss.

5

The Therapist's Life Cycle

Introduction

The psychological changes in the therapist that come about in response to aging, life events, and a changing culture all influence the therapist-patient interaction. Both the therapist's view of patients and his or her behavior toward them change, and have the potential for influencing the process of psychotherapy for better or for worse. Researchers of the adult life cycle agree that significant personality changes normally occur during adult life. In existential terms, we are all becoming.

There have been many attempts to show that the changes of adult life occur independently of life events at predictable ages or predictable intervals, and that these changes occur serially or depend on the successful completion of an earlier change or stage of life (Levinson, 1978; Gould, 1978). The preponderance of evidence at present suggests only that change occurs, sometimes in reaction to external events, and sometimes not (Neugarten, 1979).

The fact that the psychotherapist is subject to changes in adult life makes self-awareness for the psychotherapist a lifelong process of inquiry. No single period of self-scrutiny can last a lifetime, and in this context Freud's (1912) suggestion of a periodic reanalysis for the analyst makes sense in principle.

This chapter explores the personal and professional development of the psychiatrist. The psychiatrist's life cycle is not proposed as a prototype for all mental health professionals. It is examined because it is the life cycle about which most has been written and with which the author is the most familiar.

Much of the material in this chapter is derived from personal experience. In the 18 years since the completion of my own psychiatric training, I have supervised and taught formal courses for psychiatric trainees. I have observed and interacted with many of these trainees in the years since the completion of their training. Consequently, I believe that I have a good overview of the professional development of the early career and mid-career psychiatrist in my own locale.

Motivation

Before describing the life cycle of the psychiatrist, it will be useful to discuss briefly the motivation of persons who enter psychiatry and who do psychotherapy. Often cited as reasons are love of mankind, the wish to have power over people's lives, financial reward, prestige, fascination with the mind, and the wish to solve one's own problems. Feifel (1965) notes that physicians have greater than average fears of death and illness. He suggests that entering the field of medicine is an attempt to manipulate these realities.

The need to cure can be an extension of one's omnipotent urges, a reaction against feelings of impotence, a reflection of one's wish to be psychologically healed, or of one's wish to cure one's parents (Groesbeck & Taylor, 1977). Attempting to cure by use of words may also be a product of the wish to utter magical incantations. It is important that people who work with other people's problems distinguish clearly between their own need to cure and the patient's need to be cured, what they wish to be cured of themselves, and what the patient wishes or needs to be treated for.

People who enter psychiatry often choose medical school late in their college careers, having flirted with the social sciences and the humanities (Nemetz & Weiner, 1965). Future psychiatrists are frequently uncomfortable in medical school. They are often traumatized by their first year of residency, during which they are responsible for the treatment of severely mentally ill patients. As they recover from the dysphoria of the beginning psychiatry syndrome, they become increasingly comfortable with their choice of profession (Mecklin & Little, 1967).

With this brief background, let us now turn to the new psychiatrist.

The New Psychiatrist

If the average college graduate is 22, and a psychiatrist's education is continuous, he graduates from medical school at 26, and completes residency training at 30. Those who have military experience add an extra two years before completion of residency.

This approximate age range is indicated as a transitional period by Levinson (1978), but the transition for the young psychiatrist is quite different from the transition for the person whose period of professional training is considerably shorter. Levinson's prototype person has reached a time of doubt and reevaluation by age 30. For the budding psychiatrist, it is the beginning of professional autonomy, and is usually greeted enthusiastically (Looney et al., 1980). The psychiatrist's periods of indecision were experienced as a college student, as a medical student, and during the early days of residency training. At age 30, he or she has committed himself and is getting a career underway.

In a sense, the psychiatrist undergoes a maturational delay for the sake of developing as a professional. He or she continues throughout training to be designated as a student, to depend on parent surrogates, to experience pressure for conformity to standards of learning and behavior, and to set aside financial remuneration, society's primary validator of worth.

These institutional blocks to interpersonal and intrapsychic maturation have positive and negative effects. By delaying the crystallization of character, they enable incorporation of the role of psychiatrist as a professional tool, and also as an interpersonal defense.

The typical new psychiatrist can make an accurate descriptive diagnosis and can formulate a reasonable plan of treatment for most psychiatric problems. Beginning psychiatrists generally work with the most difficult cases. These cases come their way because they are readily available and because they more readily accept the difficult cases. Their assets are intellectual curiosity, knowledge of recent developments in the field, enthusiasm, and high energy level. Their liabilities are the expectation that they can apply their expertise to individual patients without significant modification, their tendency to force their frame of reference onto patients, and their tendency to overgeneralize from limited experience.

Some psychiatrists are open to experimentation. Others use only well-worn paths. The former attitude allows the development of new ways of looking at and dealing with patients, but may result in repeating the mistakes of one's elders if one fails to talk over such new ideas with professional colleagues or fails to read the professional literature. On the other hand, following traditional methods may help to avoid some technical errors, but may also promote a stereotyped therapeutic approach.

The typical mistakes of the young psychiatrist are based on inadequate skills and knowledge, lack of self-awareness, overenthusiasm, overly rigid following of rules, hunger, and grandiosity. The last-named is partly due to an identification with presumably omnipotent teachers and partly due to a reaction against the discomfort of leaving the nest. The omnipotent appearance of a teacher and the adoption of his technique based on his or her personal power can be greatly reduced if students have the opportunity to witness ongoing therapy conducted by the teacher. Trainees' anxiety about leaving the nest can be reduced by gradually increasing their extramural contacts and responsibilities and by allowing them to maintain institutional ties through continuing attendance at conferences or by becoming part-time teachers themselves.

Few new graduates of psychiatric residencies are well equipped to deal effectively with the wide range of psychotherapeutic problems they encounter, but it doesn't show at first because of the placebo effect of psychotherapy, and because of patients' response to the therapist's enthusiasm. After the first year in practice, impasses begin to arise because of overestimating ego strength, failure to consider the patient's dynamics in addition to his diagnosis, and failure to spot transference and countertransference problems.

At some time after the first year in practice, new psychiatrists begin to seek supervision or therapy for themselves (many have had earlier experiences with therapy as medical students or residents). A certain number seek gurus or new systems as they encounter treatment blockages and failures, feeling that the traditional system has failed before having adequately mastered it, and instead of examining themselves.

The new psychotherapist's enthusiasm and eagerness can be positive attributes. Tempered enthusiasm and willingness to be personally involved may facilitate the treatment of severely mentally ill persons who have been dehumanized by their families and by the institutions which house them. Their families have told them how they must perceive their world. The staff of the mental hospital tells them how they must behave in it. In this group of patients, it is likely that in the establishment of rapport the human qualities of the therapist are of far greater significance than technical skills or formal knowledge. Unfortunately, studies of specific personality variables in the therapist which significantly influence his or her therapeutic impact have not held up well as more sophisticated outcome studies have been done (Razin, 1977; Mitchell, Bozarth, & Krauft, 1977).

It is easy to understand why young therapists who have had the experience of mobilizing a schizophrenic patient may fancy themselves to have special attributes. After facing and dealing with schizophrenia, the treatment of neurotic outpatients should be a breeze by comparison. What neurosis can withstand the force that has rehabilitated a schizophrenic?

The answer is, most neuroses. Neuroses respond to religious experiences, outright chicanery, or technical expertise. Thus, it is usually a tough neurotic who, by defying professional expertise, common sense, empathy, and enthusiasm, drives the young psychotherapist into supervision or into therapy for him or herself. Those who take Freud's (1912) rule of abstinence too seriously also create difficulties for themselves and their patients. In attempting to be "pure," they become sterile, wooden mockeries of human beings. A bit of friendliness and obvious personal interest go a long way toward making self-investigation by the patient less tedious and less like an inventory of faults. It helps the patient avoid feeling like an insect on a pin.

In their eagerness to earn a living, to attain the lifestyle of their seniors, and to catch up with peers who entered the working world eight to ten years earlier, hungry, socially competitive professionals are therefore more likely to accept an unmotivated exhibitionist or shoplifter for treatment and develop an impasse instead of noting the person's lack of motivation and telling the referring judge that closely supervised probation is more appropriate than going through a charade of therapy.

The Mid-Career Psychiatrist

The psychiatrist who has spent ten to twenty years in the practice of his or her profession is biologically and psychologically different from the young professional.

By the time they have reached their forties, psychiatrists have frequently experienced the loss of a parent, illness in themselves or a family member, marital disharmony, and often divorce and remarriage. Their narcissism is tarnished and their omnipotence dented. They are tired, often from overwork due to their own need to accomplish or accumulate. They may also be tired of sitting in one place and repeatedly asking patients, "Tell me more," "What do you mean by that?" "What does that bring to mind?" and "Can you clarify a little further?" Just staying awake eight (or more) hours a day in the office may have become a chore.

Certain aspects of the psychiatrist's character also create difficulties. An important character trait of the person who undergoes prolonged professional training is the ability to absorb, regurgitate, and apply (in an approved manner) a certain body of specialized information. Personal openness and creativeness are not always assets in this situation and their lack of cultivation begins to show in later years. Studying to achieve the professional goal was often the first priority, and family members were often relegated to secondary positions. As their profession becomes part of their character, psychiatrists' families may continue to be secondary to professional practice, based on the righteous assumption that the welfare of patients comes first. The problem in this case is not the demands of the professional practice but the character of the professional, who has little ability to do other than minister to patients. The assimilation of the role of psychiatrist has become so complete that it cannot be set aside any more than thinking or talking in one's native tongue.

At mid-life, the ability to look unswervingly ahead and the

incorporation of a professional role into one's character, which were assets in training, may become pronounced interpersonal liabilities. The loneliness that this creates pushes the psychiatrist toward making the professional life his or her entire social life (Chessick, 1977).

Isolated psychotherapists become even more compromised when they lose an important source of emotional support or sense their own physical or emotional decline. In Dahlberg's (1970) study of sexual approaches or contact between therapist and patient, the therapist was invariably over 40, the patient was 10 to 25 years younger, and the therapist was either separated or recently divorced. Chesler (1971) found that therapists who were sexually involved with their patients had unsatisfactory sex lives at home and that some created surrogate families with their patients.

In spite of McCartney's (1966) claim that sexual involvement with patients can help them master developmental hurdles and the fact that 5 to 10 percent of physicians report having had sexual intimacy with patients (Kardener, Fuller, & Marsh, 1973), there is little evidence that emotional growth is enhanced by physical intimacy with a psychotherapist.

The lonely, interpersonally isolated therapist is more likely to respond in kind than to frustrate the patient and stimulate the emergence of the unpleasant feelings that are often masked by the expression of positive feelings toward the therapist. He or she is likely to miss the defensive aspect of patients' positive or erotic emotional responses. The following example points out this potential danger.

> Mrs. A.E.'s therapist noticed that her anxiety diminished if she expressed erotic feeling toward him. Instead of responding in kind or accepting her comments as confirming his sexual attractiveness, he asked her to focus on the events in her own mind. This brought a dream to mind. A man who she presumed to have been her mother's lover after her father's death was threatening her with a small penknife. In earlier dreams and in daydreams, she had seen her mother attacking her with a large butcher knife. The message was clear enough in terms of what the therapist had learned about her previously. She felt safer dealing with the sexual aspect of a man than with the phallus she had imagined concealed beneath her mother's thick thatch of pubic hair, which had been abundantly exposed to her as a child while her mother sat in bed, legs akimbo, talking to her man friend.

The lonely, emotionally deprived therapist would be inclined under these circumstances to accept the patient's positive feelings unquestioningly and to stimulate the patient to tell more of her positive feelings instead of helping her to deal with intrapsychic issues, and would thus set the stage for a mutually gratifying impasse.

Bermak (1977) found that isolation was a problem for psychiatrists, including physical aloneness, lack of satisfaction of intimacy needs, and an inability to talk about patients because of confidentiality constraints. Many found that the need to control their emotions was a problem, and that it was heightened by awareness of their own deep emotional issues that resulted in part from dealing with the problems of their patients.

Professional isolation results, I think, from the interaction of the psychiatrist's character with the frustrations of his or her daily life and with the frustrations and gratifications from his practice. It also stems from a need to be seen as personally competent which may cut the psychiatrist off from the peer support that is so important to everyone else in maintaining day-to-day functioning. Psychiatrists may see themselves in all-or-none terms as being competent or as being in need of therapy, instead of seeing themselves in need of ordinary social support.

From other quarters come comments of a different sort—that working as a psychotherapist may be inherently hazardous and that like radiation hazard, prolonged exposure may result in a cumulative toxic effect (Lewis, 1980). Jung (1968) has said that a typical occupational hazard of psychotherapists is to become psychologically infected and poisoned by the projections to which they are exposed.

Being middle-aged may make it more difficult for therapists to deal with certain problems, and easier to deal with others. Eissler (1951), for example, has suggested that the active, assertive, almost omnipotent approach of the youthful therapist seems to be most effective in acute schizophrenia. Watching the course of many schizophrenias may well dull the older psychiatrist's enthusiasm. A study of age-related attitudes (Lionells & Mann, 1978) indicates that the middle years are characterized by movement toward greater interiority and greater individuation. The younger middle-aged person is reported to see himself in relation to others around him. Satisfactions and security are linked to and supplied by others. Older persons who have gone beyond the middle years arrive at a sense of identity independent of others, with less symbiosis and more individuation and separateness. In other words, middle-aged therapists may be more inclined to focus on unique, personal issues than on relationship issues because of their own position in life in which, having established their interpersonal ties, they now look inward to find themselves.

It is quite clear that in spite of having comfortably identified themselves interpersonally and professionally, middle-aged therapists' stability will be further enhanced by maintaining skills and interests outside their daily work that connect them to the important people in their lives and that offer the possibility of continued gratification. Most desirable would be an array of sedentary and physically active pursuits, some intellectually challenging, some physically challenging, and others functioning as simple diversions. In this way, there is a wide range of choices that can be made under different circumstances, such as physical indisposition or emotional fatigue.

A clear defect in the preparation of people for psychiatry is the demand for preparatory education that does not prepare the future professional to live during the hours when he or she is not practicing his or her profession. Having no background in sports, parlor games, literature, or music leaves little for the professional to do but to live through his or her work, making a balanced view of life more difficult and impasses more likely to occur and more likely to cause emotional overreaction when they do occur.

The Late-Career Psychiatrist

I was able to find only one reference on the effect of aging on the therapist. In a brief note, Eissler (1977) states that aging produces an accretion of narcissism. If it concentrates within the superego or the ego-ideal, the analyst becomes more rigid, compulsive, and intolerant. If the narcissistic accretion occurs within the analyst's ego, he or she will expect admiration, awe, and respect from patients. If, however, the narcissistic accretion is evenly distributed over the personality and is aided by the lessening of the conflict produced by diminishing id drives, superego and ego will be more harmonious. The analyst under these circumstances will be more tolerant, have reduced therapeutic ambition, and greater acceptance of his or her patient's humanity. Eissler feels that aging reduces the tendency toward activity and increases the desire for knowledge and insight. He also feels that the increased recall of childhood that accompanies aging stimulates more of the analyst's empathy for the childhood of the patient. The successful integration of death as a part of life by the aging analyst may help him or her deal with the inevitability of the patient's death and help the patient analyze his death wishes and fears. The death of contemporaries, however, may increase the aging analyst's investment in the patient.

Eissler also notes that weakening of the analyst's memory is detrimental to therapy, but he does not elaborate. He suggests that the elderly analyst discuss what the patient should do in the event of his death, and that if the analyst knows his death is imminent, he should arrange a transfer before he dies.

I am not at all certain how one can so closely ascertain one's impending death, and I am not certain what Eissler had in mind by suggesting that a transfer be arranged while the therapist is still alive. I think that a more reasonable position is that a therapist can treat a patient as long as the therapy is productive for the patient and within the physical means of the therapist.

Because of the paucity of literature on the subject of the aging, I undertook an informal, conversational survey of older practicing psychiatrists in the Dallas area. My sample was small. It included five men and one woman who ranged in age from 69 to 77. All but one were in private practice. Their schooling ranged from completion of analytic training to informal on-the-job training in psychiatry. Psychotherapy had been, and continued to be a major portion of five of the six interviewees' practices.

Most of the psychiatrists in private practice no longer worked with children or young adults, even if trained in child psychiatry. They preferred to work with adults in their late twenties or older.

Denial of illness and incapacity were significant factors in the lives of these people. Five of the six claimed robust good health. None found his concentration significantly impaired, but all worked part-time schedules in contrast to the extraordinarily demanding schedules they reported having handled earlier in their lives.

Each of the people interviewed was married. Two were married to second spouses. All valued marriage highly and saw it as a significant stabilizing force in their lives.

Each had also evolved his own style of psychotherapy. One had developed a casual style in which he saw patients only a few times and asked them to try out their own new awareness before returning. Others felt that continued regularly scheduled appointments were important to promoting change. Two of the group (one of whom was trained in psychoanalysis) saw their patients twice a week. The others did psychotherapy on a once-a-week basis. Estimates of the duration of treatment needed to produce significant change ranged from a few sessions to three or four years.

Two psychiatrists in private practice felt that their ways of dealing with patients had changed little over the years. The others reported changes in style, including reducing the frequency of sessions, feeling freer to give advice, and sharing aspects of their personal lives.

In spite of their advanced ages, each gave the impression of handling the aging process well. All were aware that their patients responded to their age, sometimes positively and sometimes adversely. None reported physical difficulties to be a significant distraction. Two had suffered myocardial infarctions, three had back complaints, and two of these three suffered from severe chronic back difficulties. One of these two denied his chronic pain. The other said that his pain enabled him to appreciate his patients' emotional pain better.

Each conceded that he worked better with some persons than with others, but only one person made an active attempt to screen certain personality types from his practice. The others saw patients as they came, and tried to work with them in whatever manner seemed appropriate. There was a general consensus that the consistent application of a rational technique over time was likely to yield positive results.

Only one of the six persons surveyed made active attempts to keep abreast of new developments in the field of psychotherapy. They were generally content with their psychotherapeutic skills and concentrated on applying what they already knew instead of seeking new knowledge in psychotherapy.

In spite of vigorous efforts, I was unable to uncover significant transference difficulties related to these psychiatrists' age or physical health. A benevolent grandfather transference was noted by several; patients saw themselves as less harshly judged by an elderly therapist. There also seemed to be little by way of sexualized transference resistances, which could have been due to a tendency by patients to sexualize the relationship less, or a tendency of the therapist to sexualize it less. (I did not ask people I surveyed about their sexual lives, and only one volunteered such information.)

The professional activities of these psychiatrists were important parts of their lives, but were not so engulfing as they had been earlier in life. It was difficult for me to estimate how broad a range of nonprofessional interests was held by these people, but it was my impression that their lives outside their professions gave considerable satisfaction. Three were widely traveled and all seemed actively interested in life and in living.

Fear of death was not a prominent concern for any of these people, contrary to Roth's (1978) finding of widespread fear of death in the aged. All had made their peace with the idea of death, and all indicated that they had led full, satisfying lives, as the following letter from one of the interviewees indicates:

> I have, through the years, periodically commented that I have had the feeling of living a charmed life. The feeling continues. My father lived a rich and full life until he died suddenly in his 93rd year. My mother was a productive, thinking person until she died at 89½. Their ancestors were long-lived persons. Children tend to outlive their parents. Your note raises for the first time the question of my attitude about aging and death. I think I never thought about it before, but now that I do, death holds no terror. My goal for my old age is to continue practice and to attempt to grow old gracefully and graciously, and charmingly. I have had . . . honors . . . but I haven't taken time to reminisce about them.

None of this group regularly discussed with patients what to do in the event of the therapist's death and, I think, all would disagree in this respect with Eissler.

No significant countertransference difficulties were reported. There was a trend away from seeing younger patients because children and especially adolescents, were seen as too demanding. One therapist preferred to deal with successful, aggressive people; several reported dislike of manipulative people, but none found patient types or diagnostic categories that were more difficult to deal with than they had been earlier in life. I think it fair to say that their reduced energy level probably also contributed to the lack of interest in dealing with manipulative patients. In spite of their generally reduced level of energy, all seemed able to become involved with patients but, as one psychiatrist put it, with a different perspective that allowed continued equanimity in spite of patients' ups and downs. All felt they had a broader view of life and of their patients than they had earlier in life.

This impressionistic study led me to the surprising conclusion that emotionally healthy elderly psychiatrists who are in good health may stimulate fewer impasses than newly trained or mid-career psychiatrists. They have overcome their naivete, are no longer driven by professional ambition, and have come to terms with life.

On the other hand, they tend to be content with what they know and do not actively seek to broaden their psychotherapeutic skills. They seem less inclined to extend themselves for patients or to become entangled in countertransference issues, but their grandfatherly or grandmotherly appearance may sharply limit the transference possibilities of the therapeutic relationship, thereby limiting the patient's ability to explore him or herself.

Areas of potential impasse might be found in the therapist's inability to extend himself at critical moments, difficulties with memory that would cause him or her to fail to connect important events, and difficulty with abstract thinking that might cause him or her to be less alert to the symbolic value of the patients' productions.

Traumatic Events

The therapist's management of information about events in his or her life that directly affect dealings with patients as well as the therapist's management of his or her practice during a time of stress or illness can affect the outcome of therapy.

> On a Saturday night in 1972, the therapist became ill in another city, where he was hospitalized. His secretary was told to cancel his next week's appointments, telling patients only that he was ill. Several days later, when his physician was certain that he had suffered a myocardial infarction and would need to remain in the hospital a total of four weeks, his secretary was instructed to cancel his appointments until further notice, to tell patients that he had suffered a mild heart attack and would return to practice as soon as he was able.

The therapist began seeing patients at his home in the three weeks before he returned to the office, beginning with one a day, and saw patients at his home in the afternoons during the first month of his return to the office.

His illness and seeing some patients at home had adverse effects on several relationships. Two patients did not return after the therapist's illness. One transferred to another therapist while he was gone. The other found it impossible to make an appointment time, even though her old time was offered to her again. The therapist felt that both of these patients had been unable to tolerate his ordinary human frailty, and unfortunately gave no opportunity for him to deal with the issue. Of the 20 or more patients who were asked to see the therapist at his home, one refused and two were markedly uncomfortable. They were relieved to see him in his office again. For one patient, being seen at the therapist's home was a clear technical error. It was a strongly positive experience for her, but rekindled a wish for regressive closeness that they were never able to resolve and eventuated in his transferring her to another therapist. The first therapist had seen her in combined individual and group therapy and began the process of transfer by her working with the other physician (whom she had met during a hospital stay) individually while she continued in his group, and then terminating her group treatment after her relationship with the second therapist was on sufficiently solid ground. After a stormy period with her new therapist and many letters and telephone calls in which she pleaded to return to the first therapist, she settled into the new therapeutic relationship, and eventually did well.

Other patient management problems arose directly from the therapist's illness, usually stemming from patients' altruistic concern for him, fear of damaging him, or fear that he would desert them if they overburdened him. When one woman told the therapist that she feared that she was taking too much from him, he replied that he chose to spend his time with her, and that what she took was given freely.

Over the intervening years, patients who know of his illness occasionally inquire about the therapist's health. Some are concerned about his physical vulnerability. Others are pleased that he takes good care of himself.

Minor stalemates can be compounded into impasses by the therapist's defensiveness, which he or she may rationalize as protecting the patient or as a need to remain a neutral screen for the development of transferences. I have dealt with this subject at great length in another work (Weiner, 1978) and wish only to state here that therapists' refusal to deal openly with patients about crises in their own lives is more related to their wish to present an omnipotent facade than it is a real need to withhold information for the sake of the patient or the treatment. It is not necessary or desirable that therapists bring all of the upheavals in their lives into the therapeutic situation. On the other hand, when patients make discoveries about the therapist's personal life or when there is an obvious alteration in their working relationship (the therapist is gone for a month, fatigues easily, or cannot concentrate well), these issues must be dealt with. In repressive therapies, the patient is given concrete information and reassurance. In evocative therapies, the interpersonal implications are dealt with, the difficulty is acknowledged, and the patient is encouraged to explore the reactions which occur in his or her unconscious mental life.

Dewald (1980) sheds further light on this subject in discussing the impact of his illness on his practice of psychoanalysis. He suggests that in an evocative therapy, giving factual information about a mild illness might unnecessarily alleviate anxiety and the occurrence of transference fantasies, but too much information about a serious illness might unnecessarily frighten the patient. He found that serious countertransference issues arose from the role reversal when he, as a patient, received his patients' wishes for recovery. His patients' expressions of positive regard also complicated his relationship with his wife.

Dewald reported that he had never considered becoming seriously ill or disabled, and that part of his feeling of pressure to resume practice was a fear that he might be professionally displaced or that he might lose his professional skills. He gave the most immediate and detailed information to patients in supportive therapy and early analysis. Patients in mid-analysis were given little factual information, and were encouraged to explore their reactions. Two patients in the terminal phase of analysis continued without needing any factual information.

He points to the potential for impasse in the transference-countertransference reactions which arose. Therapists, for example, may expect patients to appreciate the effort they are making when they return to practice, but patients, on the other hand, may be preoccupied with hostile or depressed feelings about having been abandoned. The therapist's exhibitionism or masochism may be stimulated and the therapist may expect patients to give to him, partly to make up for the pain and suffering the therapist has undergone. The therapist, expecting to be loved on return, may be abused instead, and may react by abusing the patient in turn.

Both Dewald and Little (1967) point out the need to allow patients *not* to discuss the therapist's illness if it does not concern them or if it is too threatening, even though it may frustrate the therapist's need for acknowledgement as a person. The working-through period can be prolonged, and may require many repetitions, especially for those people with significant conflict over aggression who cannot express their anger over desertion and their wish to retaliate.

The therapeutic problem as seen by Dewald is to explore the full gamut of patients' responses, affects, and associations to the illness in the face of countertransference temptations to promote premature closure, to avoid more threatening feelings, or to use the experience for exhibitionistic, masochistic, or other neurotic satisfaction.

The death of significant persons, divorce, illness, and injury all have impact on therapists. All may increase their sense of aloneness and intensify their object needs or may result in decathexis of relationships with patients. All initially lower the amount of energy available to therapists to invest in their patients. Later, they may stimulate therapists to incorporate their patients into their social and emotional life as other pathways seem blocked.

All life events which drain the therapist's emotional energy change the type and degree of the therapist's narcissistic vulnerability. At times, the therapist may have difficulty tolerating patients' aggression, sexuality, dependence, and so forth.

The therapist's narcissistic vulnerability is an important determinant of the outcome of psychotherapy (Saretsky, 1980). Therapists need to be treated in certain ways by their patients in order to treat their patients effectively. Certain patients deny their therapists the gratifications that the therapists need in order to work effectively. The changes that occur within the therapist and in his or her life alter the degree and nature of narcissistic vulnerability to patients. One well-trained therapist turned away adolescent patients for a period of time because of the struggle he was having with his own adolescent children. An elderly psychiatrist discontinued treatment of adolescents because he found them too demanding.

At times, referring sources are aware of a particular therapist's vulnerabilities, whether they are part of his or her character or a product of his current life situation. Basically, however, it is up to the individual therapist to ascertain that his or her personal limitations make it impossible to work with a particular patient and to arrange for referral of the patient to someone with whom the patient can work more productively.

Occasionally, a therapist-patient encounter in which each agrees to modify a significant aspect of him or herself in order to establish a therapeutic relationship heralds a significant change for both, but we must also heed Kernberg's (1975) warning to avoid feeding our own narcissism and the messianic hopes of our patients.

Therapists obviously need some cushion against the negative affects of important life changes and life events. These are to be found in the cultivation of personal relationships and varied recreational pursuits that can serve as ends in themselves or as bridges to other people during times of narcissistic depletion.

Another issue that is largely undiscussed in the scientific literature is the issue of permanent or progressive disability of the therapist. Dewald suggests that a chronic, recurring, or disabling illness makes transference-countertransference problems more difficult to resolve, and their effects in therapy considerably more intense and prolonged. He feels that the tendency of the therapists to deny disability is probably high and would interfere with technical judgment and with the therapist operating in the best interest of his or her patients.

This is in contrast to my findings with the six elderly psychiatrists I interviewed. All were more limited in their activity and all had suffered significant impairments at one time or another, but their denial of disability and this insistence on continued functioning at a high level served them well. I suspect that adequately trained, self-aware psychiatrists usually know when it is time to quit, and if they don't, their referral sources do.

The last important topic is the impaired therapist who lacks sufficient judgment to know that he or she is impaired. This person's welfare and the welfare of his patients depends on his peers, who owe it to the impaired therapist and his patients to intervene through personal contact or through professional organizations.

The greatest leverage can be exercised with impaired therapists who belong to licensed professions. The threat of removal or suspension of licensure is a potent motivating force for the impaired therapist to seek help, and many professional societies have provided nonpejorative pathways through which such help can be given. The Impaired Physician Program of many state medical societies is a good example of this type of humane treatment approach for the impaired professional (Kempthorne, 1970; Talbott et al., 1976).

Summary

Each stage of a professional's life and the events in his or her life color his or her dealings with patients. Each stage has its advantages and liabilities for the therapist and patient. Youth has enthusiasm and naivete. Age has reduced energy and broad perspective. Each event has its damaging and growth-producing potential for therapist and patient. A therapist's illness can block patients' dealing with hostile feelings. It can also open wider vistas of self-acceptance and acceptance of others by patients.

It is clear that socially isolated professionals with a narrow educational and vocational background are at a significant disadvantage in dealing with the changes and events in their lives, placing both themselves and their patients at risk. These observations should help us with the selection of people for training as mental health professionals and should help us in their training and their later career development. The fact that we need to make significant alterations in these areas is attested by the fact that psychiatric patients lose their therapists by suicide at twice the expected rate for other physicians (Rich & Pitts, 1980). The suicide of one's therapist is hardly conducive to a positive outcome of therapy. Professional colleagues, aware of significant professional impairment of their peers, need to accept some responsibility for aiding their fellow therapists.

We must stress the building of appropriate social, professional, and recreational activities to maximize the potential for growth instead of damage by life's predictable crises. Attention to all of these factors may not only decrease the frequency of impasses, but may also reduce the lethality of psychiatry (and perhaps psychotherapy) as a profession.

Repressive Therapy: Dealing with Ego Deficit

6

Introduction

This chapter deals with impasses that develop in the psychotherapy of two patient populations that superficially appear dissimilar: borderline personalities and psychotics (including psychosis-prone persons). Indeed, there are many dissimilarities but one important similarity, inadequate ego function, outweighs all dissimilarities and deserves close scrutiny.

The impasses that develop with these two groups are frequently caused by failure to appreciate the nature and degree of ego impairment that exists. Instead, patients are approached psychologically as if their egos were intact. Therapists then frustrate themselves because of the difficulty communicating with the patient, who cannot make the therapeutic split into observing and participant ego, and who cannot grasp the symbolism of his or her activities. The patient becomes discouraged because he is aware of the therapist's annoyance and impatience, and because he feels scrutinized and criticized instead of helped to obtain symptomatic relief or helped to deal with what he perceives to be overwhelming external pressures. If the therapist probes enthusiastically into the psyche of a patient who appears lucid, he or she may also provoke a severe psychotic retreat (Lambert et al., 1977).

Ego function is not an all-or-nothing phenomenon. There are not only degrees, but levels of ego function, as we will see from a brief review of Vaillant's (1977) concept of hierarchical adaptive mechanisms.

Vaillant's concept is based on longitudinal observation of 95 men (a subsample of a larger sample) who were selected for high all-around functioning as college students, and who were studied at regular intervals by teams of multidisciplinary researchers for more than 30 years. This is a far different sample and a far different method of sampling from those of earlier psychoanalytic observers who drew their conclusions about healthy functioning and about psychopathology from retrospective accounts given by emotionally disturbed people in psychological treatment. Vaillant's information is derived from interview and psychological test data obtained at regular intervals and not given in the context of seeking help.

Vaillant suggests that there are four levels of psychological adaptive mechanisms. At the first level are the psychotic mechanisms, which occur when the ego is greatly impaired. They are: denial of external reality, distortion, and delusional projection. At level two are the mechanisms classed as immature, which are commonly seen in severe depression, in adolescents, and in personality disorders: fantasy (or denial in fantasy), projection, hypochondriasis, passively aggressive behavior, turning against one's self, and the repetitive acting out of impulses that are better dealt with by suppression or repression. At level three are the neurotic mechanisms, which Vaillant finds ubiquitous, and not confined to persons with diagnosable neurotic disorders: intellectualization, isolation, compulsive behavior, undoing, rationalization, repression, reaction formation, displacement (conversion, phobias), and dissociation (neurotic denial). The mature mechanisms of sublimation, altruism, suppression, anticipation, and humor are at level four, and are frequent in healthy adults.

Implementation of most healthy mechanisms requires the three characteristic behaviors of the emotionally healthy person described earlier: constructively attempting to alter one's environment, assuming appropriate responsibility for oneself and others, and assuming different roles toward oneself and others as needed to meet the demands of life. The mechanism of anticipation is a searching for potential difficulties as a means to plan purposeful behavior and constructive alternative behaviors. Suppression is conscious waiting until the best time (if ever) to do something. Sublimation is taking the trouble to learn a skill that will allow the acceptable expression of one's inner drives. Altruism is operating from the viewpoint that one has a responsibility toward others as well as oneself, and humor is the ability to enjoy the uncertainty and fumbling of ordinary life.

These mature mechanisms are not inborn. They require work by the ego, and therefore require a relatively intact nervous system, a psychic apparatus capable of supporting ego maturation, and an environment that will support the development of ego functioning. When ego functioning is compromised, the ego uses mechanisms that require less work and less organization.

It should be noted, however, that a composite profile of the most psychologically healthy men showed that they used level-four mechanisms somewhat less than half of the time (based on evaluation of transcribed interviews), and that the majority of the mechanisms used by these men fell into the level-three, or neurotic range. In short, people do not function at a very mature level very much of the time.

This chapter deals with the underdeveloped or impaired ego and how it causes impasse if undetected or inappropriately treated. It deals with people whose ego functioning is fixated at a suboptimal level, or is regressed to a disorganized and ineffective level. As figure 6.1 indicates, ego impairment is first evident in the loss of the capability for creativeness, for dealing with extraordinary situations or emergencies and for mature play. (Mature play is use of the ego's surplus energy for pleasurable activities while the ego continues to deal effectively with the other demands of life.) As the ego is further depleted, it loses the ability to deal constructively with the ordinary demands of external reality, with the id, and with the superego, and symptoms or symptomatic behavior develop. At this level of impairment, one may seek refuge in play-like activity as a refusal to face life's tasks and as a denial in fantasy.

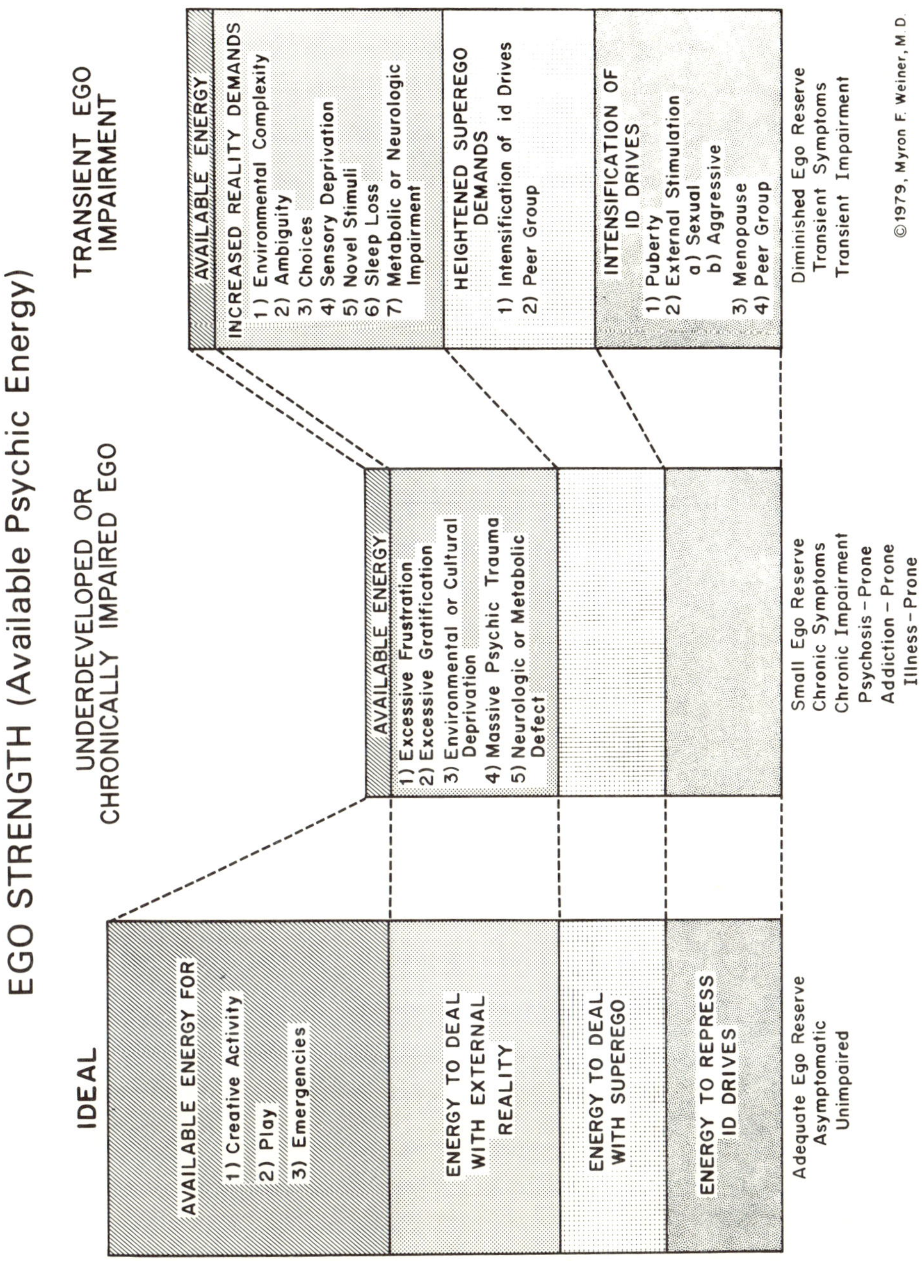
EGO STRENGTH (Available Psychic Energy)
IDEAL
AVAILABLE ENERGY FOR
1) Creative Activity
2) Play
3) Emergencies
ENERGY TO DEAL WITH EXTERNAL REALITY
ENERGY TO DEAL WITH SUPEREGO
ENERGY TO REPRESS ID DRIVES
Adequate Ego Reserve
Asymptomatic
Unimpaired
UNDERDEVELOPED OR CHRONICALLY IMPAIRED EGO
AVAILABLE ENERGY
1) Excessive Frustration
2) Excessive Gratification
3) Environmental or Cultural Deprivation
4) Massive Psychic Trauma
5) Neurologic or Metabolic Defect
Small Ego Reserve
Chronic Symptoms
Chronic Impairment
Psychosis - Prone
Addiction - Prone
Illness - Prone
TRANSIENT EGO IMPAIRMENT
AVAILABLE ENERGY
INCREASED REALITY DEMANDS
1) Environmental Complexity
2) Ambiguity
3) Choices
4) Sensory Deprivation
5) Novel Stimuli
6) Sleep Loss
7) Metabolic or Neurologic Impairment
HEIGHTENED SUPEREGO DEMANDS
1) Intensification of id Drives
2) Peer Group
INTENSIFICATION OF ID DRIVES
1) Puberty
2) External Stimulation
a) Sexual
b) Aggressive
3) Menopause
4) Peer Group
Diminished Ego Reserve
Transient Symptoms
Transient Impairment
©1979, Myron F. Weiner, M.D.

FIGURE 6.1

General Considerations for Psychotherapy

My view of the psychotherapy of the ego-impaired person differs considerably from Kernberg (1980), who feels that an ego-supportive therapy offers more hope for achieving a higher level of function than a repressive therapy. Kernberg bases his position on a study of 42 patients at the Menninger Foundation which found that ego-impaired nonpsychotic patients improved more with ego-supportive therapy than with repressive techniques (Kernberg et al., 1972). Eight of the sixteen cases, however, treated with ego-supportive or combined ego-supportive-repressed techniques required hospitalization, while only two of the eight patients treated by repressive means required hospitalization. The number of cases is too small for these data to be of statistical significance, but they do confirm my own clinical observations. If one probes or confronts the ego-impaired person too much, one produces a psychological decompensation which can be of devastating magnitude. It is too risky for the average therapist who does not have the backup of a tailor-made environment. Furthermore, Kernberg essentially discounts the hospital treatment of these people, which I suspect was more useful in stabilizing them than was their psychotherapy.

The most important general considerations for psychotherapy are the means for dealing with the inadequate ego, for preventing further ego decompensation, and for stimulating the maturation or reintegration of the ego. In my opinion, these goals are accomplished by structuring the psychotherapeutic interview in a repressive manner, by structuring the patient's environment, by capitalizing on the positive transference, and by minimizing the negative transference.

The Structuring of Repressive Psychotherapy

Repressive psychotherapeutic techniques enhance ego development and reintegration and avoid impasse by promoting impulse control, the capacity to tolerate dysphoria, self-observation, the differentiation of internal from external stimuli, secondary process thinking, and accurate perception of external reality. The interventions in repressive therapy develop or restore appropriate suppression and repression and develop adequate coping skills through direct teaching, through stimulation of identification with the therapist, and through other means to help the patient to see and to deal with the world more rationally.

Repressive interviews generally lead the patient away from discussing his or her liabilities, delusions, or inability to control him or herself, which are certain pathways to impasse. Generally, they are not highly confronting unless the patient is in a controlled environment, especially if the patient has impaired social judgment and impaired impulse control. Even in controlled settings, the injudicious use of confrontation can provoke physical violence or can permanently alienate the patient and destroy his or her potential for eventual cooperation. The ego-impaired person is frequently given antipsychotic or antidepressant medication to help him deal with his feelings, with reality, and with confrontation by the therapist.

Setting direct limits on the patient's behavior during the interview is appropriate when there is some danger to the patient, the therapist, or the physical environment. With adolescents, it is appropriate to encourage the family to set certain reasonable limits at home, but it is frequently unwise for the therapist to set limits on the patient's behavior outside of the therapeutic session when dealing with the severely ego-impaired person.

The reason the psychotherapist avoids setting limits on behavior outside the therapeutic hour is that it sets the therapist against the patient, and in the patient's struggle to win the battle for control, he or she may lose sight of the real battle for his or her emotional well-being. Where limits are needed for the severely ego-impaired, they can best be supplied through a controlled environment.

Therapists also gently point out the patient's positive aspects; gently, because they are trying to inform, not to sell. The patient's assets may be mathematical ability, a sense of humor, or an interest in helping other people. Therapists encourage their patients to use the assets that are most readily available to them and ask patients to report on their use of them in daily living.

Therapists also notice their patients as people—what interests them, what they dislike, and what pleases them. Therapists must then communicate their awareness of their patients as people to help reduce the patients' sense of alienation. At times it is useful for therapists to indicate that they and the patient have something in common. It may be only the fact that both are people struggling to cope with reality in their own way.

Carl Rogers (1957) suggested a triad of therapist-offered conditions which appear helpful in the treatment of hospitalized schizophrenic patients; genuineness, accurate empathy, and unconditional positive regard. Later, Truax and Mitchell (1971) concluded that therapists who are accurately empathic, nonpossessively warm, and genuine are effective in their treatment of patients. Rogers', and Truax and Mitchell's conclusions are sensible, but they are statistically unconfirmed (Mitchell et al., 1977). The clinician must still rely on his or her own experience while awaiting confirmation of the specific therapist-offered conditions that are the most useful in dealing with certain patient populations, or in dealing with psychotherapy patients in general.

Meanwhile, it must be warned that certain patients find warmth and positive regard to be threatening, and see these qualities as a potential intrusion into their protective isolation. The wish of certain emotionally isolated people to keep their emotional distance must be respected to avoid a worsening of their condition.

Repressive therapy focuses on the patient's real life in the here and now. The patient is drawn out of fantasy and out of his or her concerns stemming from the past except as they directly impinge on his present life situation. He or she is encouraged to seek practical answers to problems by weighing the objective advantages and disadvantages and giving equal weight to the emotional advantages and disadvantages. The therapist does not negate the patient's intrapsychic life, but does encourage the patient to live in reality.

Because of the emphasis on dealing in a practical way with reality, sessions of this sort appear banal. The therapist shows the patient none of his or her ability to weave slim unconscious threads into a multicolored tapestry of insight. Instead, he plods. He encourages the patient to take one step at a time and to face one issue at a time. This is how the ego is built, from early childhood on. No grand leaps. Just one step at a time.

While the therapist gives the surface appearance of preoccupation with ordinary matters, he or she stays alert for signs of increasing ego strength that may eventually allow moving from a repressive approach to a more reflective, ego-supportive approach. He looks for the use of humor by the patient and notes when the patient becomes less self-preoccupied and more interested in others. He stays alert for normalization of sleeping and eating patterns. He notes the patient's increasing capacity for self-observation and a concomitant diminution of self-criticism. He attempts to quantify the patient's self-control, and, in addition, tries to keep the transference positive without shutting off the patient's verbalization of negative feelings.

There are times when the therapist encourages the patient to undertake a task or an encounter that he or she fears. At other times, the therapist lags behind and allows the patient to develop momentum. Whether or not the therapist takes the lead or waits for the patient depends on the way the patient deals with his or her regressed or immature psychological state. If he or she tends to cling to immature ways, the therapist pushes. If the patient is eager to move forward and to cope, the therapist allows him or herself to be pulled along instead of leading.

Structuring the Environment

The borderline personality, the psychosis-prone person, and the psychotic person require ego-supportive and repressive techniques to help with ego development and reintegration of ego function.

An important aspect of the treatment of severe ego dysfunction is controlling the patient's environment and simplifying its demands. Environmental control includes tailoring the environment to meet the patient's needs for predictability and limits. Simplifying the environment includes reducing conflictual demands and reducing the patient's responsibility for himself and others to a level that he or she can manage.

Generally speaking, it is not easy to structure the environment of an adult. One cannot ordinarily prevail upon his or her boss, spouse, and the people with whom he or she carpools to deal with him or her in a certain way. Therefore, if environmental structuring is necessary to help an adult patient onto his feet, psychiatric inpatient care is frequently suggested. A psychiatric inpatient facility attempts to supply a controlled, simplified environment tailored to individual needs, but at the same time it raises certain issues and creates certain problems.

Involuntary Hospitalization

In principle, entering a hospital for treatment should be a contractual agreement in which a person relinquishes a certain amount of control over his or her life in exchange for a chance to improve his psychological health. In practice, psychiatric inpatient treatment is much more often carried out on a noncontractual basis than is outpatient psychotherapy, and is therefore more potentially subject to impasse.

A greater percentage of hospital patients than outpatients are in treatment against their will. The reason for their involuntary admission is danger to themselves or others, not their own perceived discomfort or malfunction. Whether one person has the right to deprive another of his or her freedom for the sake of altering his or her mental state has been hotly debated. The fact remains that many persons are confined to hospitals by judicial process, and that initially, the treatment contract is between the court and the physician, and not between the patient and the physician. The patient is an unwilling participant in a unilateral arrangement which deprives him or her of freedom until others are satisfied with his or her thinking and behavior. The relationship frequently becomes an adversary relationship in which the patient attempts to discover what is expected of him, hoping that he will sufficiently satisfy his captors that they will free him. This process is well known as institutional insight. The paranoid patient learns to keep his delusions to himself, the alcoholic to feign interest in sobriety. A limited degree of social control is achieved, at least until termination of hospitalization. Even after he has won his freedom, the patient with institutional insight may continue to behave acceptably because of the threat of reinstitutionalization.

Ideally, the involuntarily hospitalized patient comes to agree with his or her captors that they are right and begins to invest his or her energy into combatting the symptoms that his or her peers and doctors find so distressing. Viewed in this way, insight is a form of capitulation by the person whose psychosis has conquered a hostile world, or whose drug use has alleviated his or her physical and emotional pain. It is no wonder, when seen from this perspective, that so many struggle against treatment. What the helpers see as symptoms, the patient delusionally sees as his autonomy, or experiences as a protective shield against overwhelming pain or anxiety. We hope to prove to the delusional patient that the world is not so personally hostile and to the addicted person that physical or emotional discomfort can be tolerated. It is only after a patient makes these discoveries that he or she is capable of entering a contractual relationship. The delusional patient comes to appreciate his real potency in negotiating with others and the addicted patient, his potency in withstanding uncomfortable feelings.

Some patients cannot be convinced of the correctness of their captors' views, and will not enter a therapeutic contract. Perhaps we can be more comfortable as professionals if we view this as the best choice the patient can make, and not as recalcitrance or perversity. Acknowledging the patient's unwillingness to interact on our terms after appropriate efforts to convince him fail may concede him enough power to enable his return at a later date without a sense of giving in or giving up.

Voluntary Hospitalization

Many patients who sign themselves into hospitals are voluntary patients in name only. They are frequently coerced into hospitalization, and the potential helpers again find themselves dealing with adversaries. In some cases, the patient's complaint of coercion is a bluff which can be countered by merely opening the hospital door. In other cases, it is a lifestyle of perceived victimization that can only be cut through by the therapist's persistent asking, "What do *you* want from this hospitalization?"

Many of the contracts made with hospital patients are poorly disguised coercive maneuvers, such as telling the emaciated anorexic patient that she must gain a certain amount of weight before discharge, or telling the school-avoidant adolescent patient that she must attend school in the hospital before she can be released. While coercion may not be directly growth promoting for these persons, it helps to protect them against further regression. One may have to sacrifice growth temporarily to maintain function, because the more function is relinquished, the longer the path to appropriate levels of autonomy.

Because of the coercive set of the administrative physician in the hospital, his or her role must often be separated from that of the psychotherapist. The administrative physician is associated with a struggle for control which may so color his or her relationship with the patient that it is impossible for the patient to reflect objectively on his or her own behavior. The administrative physician deals with the regressed aspect of the patient, and his presence may continually stimulate its emergence. The psychotherapist allies with the self-observing part of the patient and avoids struggling with him or her for control of his thinking or behavior in preparation for the time when the patient will no longer require coercive measures to help him maintain his function, but will still need a therapeutic relationship.

Inpatient facilities dealing with addicted persons have found it useful to contract with patients for one of two types of treatment, temporary withdrawal or rehabilitation. Giving the addicted person a choice at the outset reduces the demoralization of staff and patients produced by an unmotivated addict in a motivated population and vice-versa (Robbins & Cowan, 1976).

Transference Management

The transference must be kept positive if one is to maintain a relationship with the person in outpatient treatment who has an impaired or immature ego. With inpatients, the negative transference can usually be displaced from the therapist onto some aspect of the institution, but even when the transference becomes temporarily negative, the other personnel in the institution are often able to keep the patient's negative feelings from disrupting therapy by assuring him or her that everyone goes through such feelings in therapy.

In psychoanalysis, the transference neurosis enables the patient to reconstruct and to reexperience those residuals from his or her past which hamper his daily living. It develops slowly in people with coping skills and relatively healthy ego defenses. Because of its slow development and because of the alliance of the analyst with the patient's observing ego, the transference neurosis is unlikely to disrupt the patient's life and it can be dealt with by interpretation as its historical origins become clear. The transference neurosis is based on the mechanism of projection, which exists in minor forms in the mental lives of all people (Havens, 1973) as racial or religious prejudice.

When the same projective mechanism occurs in persons whose coping ability is poor, whose ego defenses are inadequate or immature, and whose ego boundaries are impaired, the therapist is faced with sudden, massive transference reactions which shift rapidly in valence depending on whether or not the therapist frustrates or gratifies the patient.

I discussed earlier some of the techniques of minimizing the development of transference, such as the use of brief, highly structured therapeutic interviews in which the therapist maintains a high level of activity and allows the patient to know exactly what to expect. In addition, the therapist can discourage the discussion of fantasy, can avoid free association, and can make use of the counterprojective and counterintrojective techniques below, which have been described by Havens (1976) and are based on the work of Henry Stack Sullivan (Mullahy, 1952).

Counterprojective Techniques

In the counterprojective method, the patient's surmises about the therapist and his or her projections onto the therapist are actively combatted. Havens' approach differs from the psychoanalytic approach in that it acts against the transference instead of dealing with the transference by interpretation. It does not require an alliance with a rational, observing ego and, in fact, takes the position that the distorting process in the ego is present at all times. The patient lives as if he or she were surrounded by his introjected objects and as if the therapist were one of them. The therapist's job with the borderline or psychotic patient is to move the patient's projections off the therapist and into the space between them. He or she does this by the use of displacing remarks combined with negative utterances against the introject which has been projected onto himself. This dramatically separates the therapist and the introject, especially when the therapist's actual behavior closely resembles the actual behavior of the introjected person. Havens suggests that the more openly paranoid the patient is, the more directly hostile the therapist will need to be toward the persecuting figures. He reasons that people project feelings because they cannot take sole responsibility for them. They must be shared, partly because one source of the hostile feelings is from the introjects themselves, which were originally external. Therefore, when therapists express what the patients feel toward the now-projected introjects, they help the patients to bear what they cannot bear alone. The next vignette exemplifies this approach.

> A pleasant, paunchy, 65-year-old woman was referred for treatment because of her suspicion (which she recognized as not totally realistic) that her husband was involved in extramarital affairs. She described many years of subjugation and frequent derision by her husband, which had its parallel in her early development. He had recently become more generous toward her and it was in this context that her paranoid ideation began, although she had had jealous tantrums all of their marital life. She reasoned, "He can't be doing all this for me. He must have another woman with whom he will live after he gets rid of me."
>
> The therapist told her that she didn't sound so crazy to him, and that he had no trouble understanding her suspicion. After he made this statement, she blurted out that she felt she actually knew the identity of the other woman. Because they were at the end of the hour, the therapist suggested that they begin their next session with a description of her rival's attributes.
>
> When they reconvened, she told the therapist about the other woman after a bit of prompting, and he again reassured her that he could understand her suspicion. After this, she shamefacedly acknowledged that when her husband had taken a few extra minutes to leave the garage that morning, she presumed that he had put an explosive under the hood of the car. When he asked if she had checked, she replied that she hadn't. She said she didn't know enough about the engine of a car to be able to recognize a bomb.
>
> Her projection onto the therapist was that he would not understand and that he would think she was crazy. He did the very opposite and avoided an impasse. By agreeing with her that her feelings had some basis in reality, and by encouraging her to treat them as realistic, he separated himself from the projected father and husband who had always failed to understand her point of view. By agreeing with her, he allowed her to state the possibility that one could come to other conclu-

sions from the same data. Encouraging her to talk about her rival and to tell how she'd looked for a bomb helped her to gain perspective. The therapist also later suggested that if she were concerned about her attractiveness, she needed to lose a little weight.

Havens' technique can also be described as a radical empathic stance. One takes the patient's point of view, not to mollify or gratify him, but to enable him to gain some distance from the projected aspects of himself.

Havens feels, and I agree, that the counterprojective technique is superior to interpreting or confronting transference distortions as recommended by Kernberg (1968) and by Adler and Myerson (1973). Interpreting and confronting place the therapist against the patient and secondarily require limit setting, which in turn provokes acting against the therapist and often requires that the patient be hospitalized as part of the treatment. In short, transference-based impasses can be avoided by minimizing the possibilities for the development of transference, and by assuming a counterprojective attitude that actively opposes transferences as they develop.

Counterintrojective Techniques

A counterintrojective technique (Havens, 1980) can be used to avoid impasse with persons who hold their introjected objects close, and identify with them. The counterintrojective technique avoids attacking the patient's introjected objects because it would also attack the patient's ego, of which they are a part. This technique has been used as part of the therapeutic milieu of depressed patients since my own days in psychiatric training, and I do not know its origin.

The counterintrojective technique agrees with the patient that he or she may have reason to feel of little worth at present, having abandoned his or her family and responsibilities to enter the hospital in the hope of feeling better. It recognizes the patient's inability to concentrate on complex tasks and urges him to function at very simple repetitive tasks that he can master, like sandpapering a large block of wood, or scrubbing out the grout between bathroom tiles. The therapist or his surrogate becomes an actual, external persecuting object on whom the patient can project introjected impulses and toward whom he or she can feel justified in being angry. The use of this technique ordinarily requires splitting the treatment between an administrative therapist who assumes the role of persecutor, and a psychotherapist who deals with the patient's feelings as they are experienced in relation to the administrative therapist. Often, however, the patient is left with residual negative feelings toward the administrative therapist that may preclude an ongoing psychotherapeutic relationship.

The Psychotic Patient

The psychosis-prone ego has little surplus energy after exerting the necessary intrapsychic repression and after coping with reality. There is therefore constant danger that an additional demand for ego energy will render it unable to maintain repression of the unconscious and unable to maintain its outer boundary, at which reality testing takes place. As a means to preserve energy for coping, the ego allows repressed material to be discharged. The ego shapes the material from the unconscious just as it gives shape to the material from the unconscious recalled by a dreamer on awakening, but it also pays the price of giving up some of its reality-testing ability. The ego is sometimes so overwhelmed that it fails to be aware of common dangers such as the fact that one can be cut or burned.

The shape given by the ego to the material from the unconscious depends on the person's psychological makeup and his or her biologic predisposition. The immature ego of a child and the compromised ego of the elderly person, when further debilitated by sudden impairment of brain function, experience the same intolerable confusion as the person who becomes functionally psychotic before his explanatory delusions and hallucinations begin. Because the organically impaired ego is even more compromised than the functionally impaired ego, a disorganized state of delirium occurs, in which the ego attempts to organize its perceptions in a comprehensible but frequently incorrect manner.

Because the development of a functional psychosis is usually insidious, the ego can systematize and integrate the stimuli it cannot grasp or must disown. It is also likely that the form of a functional psychosis is partly determined by the specific metabolic abnormalities that characterize a schizophrenia or a bipolar affective disorder.

The goal in treating acute disruptions of the ego is to restore continuity to the ego's internal and external boundaries. To minimize difficulties at the boundary between ego and reality, the therapist simplifies and clarifies the patient's environment, and requires as little decision making as possible. This frees some of the ego's energy for reality testing and for repression. Repression is aided by reducing stimulation of those elements in the unconscious that have emerged. As much as possible, acutely psychotic patients are distracted from their troubling and troublesome sexual and aggressive fantasies and behavior and are encouraged to involve themselves in the routines of daily living.

In a hospital environment, the behavior of the personnel and the structure of the patient's activities can be constituted so as to pose the least possible threat. People who fear their own dependent needs can be helped to preserve a feeling of autonomy. People who feel threatened by homosexual impulses can be kept from close personal contact with others of the same sex until their repression becomes more effective.

Contractual Issues

Psychotic patients are dealt with by attributing their thinking and behavior to illness. This enables patients to put distance between themselves and their symptoms and allows them to accept treatment. Persons experiencing a first or second episode of psychosis rarely perceive themselves as ill, but they frequently feel significant distress. After several bouts of overt mental illness, many patients will seek treatment when they begin to experience dysphoria accompanied by delusions, hallucinations, mania, or depression. Unfortunately, many are so severely impaired that they cannot cooperate with the treatment they seek and must be treated in a controlled environment.

The first level of contract making for the psychotic patient is for control of illness-produced thoughts, feelings, and behavior, and for bringing the patient into better contact with the real world. This is augmented by antipsychotic or mood-altering drugs that are administered and taken in the same spirit in which one takes antibiotics: as a means to help defend against invasion by foreign matter.

When there has been significant remission of psychotic symptoms or change of mood toward a reasonable baseline, therapist and patient can begin to consider whether or not to examine the relationship of life events and intrapsychic events to the onset and shaping of the patient's illness. Ordinarily, people who have suffered a psychosis are interested in learning how to decrease interpersonal stresses and the unreasonable demands that they make on themselves. It is usually unwise to contract for insight based on exploration of the patient's unconscious. Few ex-psychotics are able to tolerate this type of treatment (Lambert et al., 1977). They can gain significant self-awareness from accepting the therapist's explanation of what happened and why. The therapist can teach the patient about the unconscious and can discuss with the patient the life events and probable intrapsychic events that caused the failure of repression, the orgy of self-recrimination, or his elated mood.

Absolute confidentiality cannot be promised by the therapist of a hospitalized patient. Hospital treatment is a team effort, and the other members of the team need certain kinds of information, such as the danger patients may pose to themselves or others. The therapist can reasonably promise that he or she will only disclose information relevant to the patients' immediate management, and that their entire past and present lives will not be disclosed to the other members of the staff.

Process Issues

Because of the patient's greatly compromised ego function, the therapist keeps his or her psychological distance while still maintaining a personal and professional interest. The therapist's nonintrusiveness in the early stage of treatment helps patients to reestablish what is inside and what is outside themselves.

Some withdrawn, autistic patients require active intrusion by the therapist into their psychological world as a means to draw them into the real world. This intrusion needs to be gentle, persistent, and neutral so as to avoid creating a transference storm by the patient's misidentification of the therapist with a psychologically devouring or persecuting parent.

If possible, the therapist moves away from being responsible for the patient to being responsible along with the patient, but as noted earlier, a move away from a benevolent paternal or maternal stance may not be possible or desirable for the person with chronic ego impairment.

The Psychosis-Prone Patient

The psychosis-prone person ordinarily has an underdeveloped ego. The exception is the person who becomes psychotic under truly extraordinary duress, whose psychosis recedes in a few days without treatment. Because of an underdeveloped ego and other specific biologic vulnerability, most people retain this vulnerability to severe decompensation (Bowers, Steidl, & Rabinovitch, 1980). There is no specific character structure associated with proneness to psychosis, but even between episodes of psychosis many of these people use Vaillant's first-level adaptive mechanisms to a significant degree. Few psychosis-prone people seek treatment before their first episode of psychosis. Some of those who do seek treatment with naive or unskilled therapists become psychotic as a result of inappropriate treatment.

The most common technique used with the patient who has chronic ego inadequacy and little resistance to psychosis is the encouragement of authority dependence. It is the assumption of the traditional physician-patient role in which the patient comes to the physician for advice, is told what to do, and stays under the physician's care until he or she is released.

This is a useful technique for dealing with many recompensated psychotics who visit the mental health care professional for follow up as one might visit an internist after hospital treatment for heart failure or an orthopedic surgeon after hospital care of a fractured hip. The therapist helps the patient decide what stresses he or she can and cannot handle. The therapist gives advice for dealing with the patient's spouse and children. He or she is a benevolent authority, who is able to understand and respect the patient's point of view, and who offers objective professional advice.

The patient is encouraged to rely on the therapist. The therapist does not object to patients drawing their own conclusions, but also does not frustrate them when they are unable to come to a conclusion. The focus of the therapy is on daily living, but it also includes a great deal of material about the patient's interests and daily life that is purely conversational. Its aim is to keep the patient in contact with reality.

These people are not treated as if their attitudes toward themselves and toward life cause their difficulties. They are treated as people whose illness is the cause of their difficulties, who come to the therapist for treatment of that illness.

Many patients who have recompensated from severe psychosis can be maintained for years with this technique in addition to their prescribed medications. Without the relationship with the therapist, an impasse will develop. They will fail to take their medication and will relapse. Many patients resent long-term medication. They resent the dry mouth, postural hypotension, and constipation caused by some drugs, and the Parkinson-like side effects of others. They may also fear the long-term toxicity of the medication prescribed, such as the tardive dyskinesias that occasionally result from prolonged use of the more potent antipsychotic drugs. The therapist can see that these patients are kept on the lowest possible dose of medication, but should also tell them that the medication provides them with an important chemical insulation that helps keep them from becoming overly stimulated or overly distressed, and that this insulation is an important means to prevent a relapse of their illness and hospitalization.

Visits with these chronic, recompensated patients need not be frequent. They may be once a month or less, but they need to be regular. The therapist's discontinuance of regular visits may be taken to mean that the patient is well and no longer needs to take medication or to be reasonable in his or her demands on himself. Or, discontinuing appointments can mean to the patient that the therapist no longer cares. Many patients react to this feeling by saying to themselves, "If he doesn't care, I don't care either," and discontinue their medications. This response may be due to the patients' need for an external source of acceptance to counter their negative view of themselves. A positive introject of the therapist is used to displace or to nullify other negative introjects. The same response may also be due to the patients' attempt to hurt the therapist-introject, which unfortunately cannot be separated from hurting themselves.

Contractual Issues

The therapeutic contract is usually quite simple; to stay out of the hospital. Some patients express interest in learning why they became mentally ill. Others want to work on their thinking or their patterns of interpersonal relationships.

At times, a patient's discharge from the hospital is contingent upon agreeing to outpatient follow-up. This patient, if no longer under the legal control of the treating institution, ordinarily makes a token visit and drops out of therapy. He or she usually lacks awareness of his or her illness, and sees him or herself as having been unfairly confined. If there is a significant prospect of relapse and the patient is still under the legal control of the institution, the therapist can use the threat of reinstitutionalization to help the patient stay in treatment, usually with medication.

When the patient sees himself as having been ill and is willing to enter a therapeutic contract, he and the therapist contract for a repressive therapy, as described above. The patient is encouraged to see himself as having a specific vulnerability to dealing with certain types of stress, and is encouraged to find ways to compensate for it and avoid the stresses which tend to trigger the illness. The patient who wishes to be cured of his or her vulnerability to mental illness can be told that much can be done to reduce this vulnerability, but there are circumstances that will cause anyone to break down mentally, and that there is no guarantee that such a circumstance will not occur.

In some cases, the physician who treated the patient in the hospital is the best person to continue care outside the hospital. In other cases, the patient prefers to be separated from the hospital and its personnel, and is more comfortable with a new treatment relationship. The patient reasons that if he or she is treated by the hospital personnel, he or she is still seriously ill. Being treated by others means that he or she is better.

Process Issues

As usual, therapists must pay attention to the patient, and not merely to their diagnosis. In this way they will not become too therapeutically ambitious for the severely ego-compromised person or too restrictive of the person who is capable of further emotional growth. They will also stay alert to changes in the patient's status.

As stated previously, negative transference needs to be kept at a minimum, but there is no harm in the patient being angry with his therapist about a real issue in the here and now. The therapist's attempt, however, to escape the real issue by labeling it as transference may do harm to the patient by recalling relationships that he cannot deal with emotionally and by contradicting his valid perceptions.

The attitude of the therapist toward persons who have been mentally ill plays a significant role in the treatment (Rabkin, 1977). The therapist must be able to deal with the patient optimistically and realistically. He or she must appreciate the patients' psychological assets while not losing sight of their liabilities, and he must not use medication as a way to avoid talking to patients about important issues.

Much of what therapists do with ex-psychotic patients is determined by their comfort with their own unconscious impulses. Therapists who are not entirely certain of their own ability to repress may become very uncomfortable with people whose repressive mechanism has failed. They may seek to protect their patients unnecessarily, or avoid as much contact with them as possible. Most therapists' ability to manage an ex-psychotic will depend on the interplay of their personalities: the more reconstruction to be attempted, the greater need for mutual attraction and compatibility (Berzins, 1977).

Treating the Borderline Personality

Persons with borderline personalities seek treatment for a variety of symptoms, including free-floating anxiety, multiple phobias, obsessive-compulsive symptoms, conversion symptoms, dissociative episodes, hypochondriasis, and sexual deviation. As one looks beyond the presenting symptoms during the evaluation, one sees specific and nonspecific signs of ego weakness. The non-specific signs are lack of anxiety tolerance, defective impulse control, minimal capacity for sublimation, and a tendency to shift toward primary process thinking.

The specific ego weaknesses of the borderline personality are due to the predominance of primitive ego defense mechanisms of splitting (actively keeping apart introjections and identifications of opposite quality), primitive idealization, projection (including projective identification), denial, omnipotence, and devaluation. These primitive mechanisms conserve ego energy and ward off psychosis except under extreme environmental pressure or under the influence of alcohol or other drugs (Kernberg, 1975).

Because of multiple developmental failures, the borderline develops insufficient character for smooth handling of internal or external pressures. His or her developmental defects are failure of self-other differentiation; failure to recognize, tolerate, and master separation; loss, and loss of self-esteem; and failure to develop sufficient self-identity and self-esteem to permit relative autonomy and the capacity to maintain stable interpersonal relationships (Weiner, 1978).

Impasses with borderline patients are common because the therapist fails to make the correct diagnosis or, if he makes the correct diagnosis, fails to employ an appropriate treatment. I disagree strongly with Kernberg's (1975) advocacy of an evocative therapy with borderlines, and agree with Zetzel (1971) that because of his impaired reality testing and limited capacity to tolerate painful feelings, the borderline patient requires direct augmentation of these capacities through repressive and ego-supportive techniques.

The repeated experience of therapists who treat borderline personalities by evocative techniques is that the patient requires hospitalization. Unfortunately, therapists see the hospitalization as the result of the patient's psychopathology and not as a result of their interactions with him or her. A severe regressive stalemate is no more a necessary part of the treatment of the borderline personality than it is in the treatment of any other emotional disorder.

A borderline person who becomes clinically worse during the course of treatment is becoming overwhelmed and needs to reintegrate. The core pathology of the borderline personality cannot be exposed and then reworked by regressive means. It is, instead, adapted to and compensated for by the patient's ego under the guidance and tutelage of the therapist.

The focus of the treatment of the borderline is quite different from the focus of treatment for the psychotic person and for the psychosis-prone person, who are dealt with by attributing their symptoms to illness. The borderline personality, on the contrary, is told that his or her symptoms are his means to avoid facing his internal realities and the realities of the external world. Treatment of the borderline personality calls for the patient to become tolerant of unpleasant feelings, to increase his or her ability to distinguish between fantasy and reality, to develop emotional ties and personal relationships that are reciprocal and not parasitic, and to assume responsibility for himself.

Contractual Issues

Borderline patients frequently live so chaotically that in spite of their charm, they fare poorly financially. Thus, the therapist often needs to make financial concessions to such patients at the outset of therapy. This, of course, helps to set the stage for the development of negative feelings by the therapist, whose concessions are usually unappreciated.

The therapeutic contract offered to the borderline should be to help live life more responsibly rather than to alleviate unpleasant feelings, for the unpleasant feelings are frequently the consequences of the patient's behavior. His loneliness, for example, is due to the fact that people actively avoid him to avoid being victimized. His guilt is the result of real transgression against other people.

The borderline patient is the patient who is most likely to turn the therapeutic relationship into a social relationship, reasoning that any acceptance at all means that total acceptance into the therapist's life is forthcoming. The therapist must actively bar the door and insist on his or her own right to privacy. He or she must also insist that therapy takes place within the appointed hour at the therapist's office, and not after hours over the telephone or at a social gathering.

To be adequate therapists for borderline patients, therapists must have their own narcissistic needs well-satisfied. They certainly will not be satisfied by the patient. They must also be able to tolerate direct aggression, and must be capable of standing firmly on their own beliefs, or else they will be steamrollered by the patient. They must not be fearful of their own aggressive impulses, which will be plentifully aroused, and should be in charge of their sadistic impulses, for which they will be given much room and reason to exercise. As part of the therapeutic contract, therapists may wish to include their right to react as people to the proposed patient. The therapeutic rationale is to provide feedback to the patient about his or her interpersonal behavior and to strengthen the patient's ego boundaries by demonstrating his or her separateness from the therapist (Adler, 1970). It also allows need to make it clear that patients cannot do or say whatever they want during the therapeutic hours. The rights of therapists need to be recognized too.

Process Issues

It is difficult to form a therapeutic alliance with a borderline patient. The patient is very busy attempting to incorporate the therapist into his or her real interpersonal world or is busy attempting to spit him or her out. What the patient agrees upon at one moment, he or she negates the next. The therapist resists being drawn too much into the patient's world, but does not engage in defensive withdrawal. From the beginning, he makes the personal relationship between himself and the patient a part of the therapeutic inquiry, uses their relationship to draw conclusions about the way the patient deals with people in general, and does not hesitate to tell the patient about it.

As noted previously, there can be a shift into an antitherapeutic alliance in which therapists make their observations about the patient's interactions a vehicle to discharge their own sadistic impulses. It is easy to engage borderlines in sadomasochistic relationships because they projectively identify with a persecutor and cannot let go. They can only respond with counteraggression that becomes so destructive that hospitalization is required for limit setting , or treatment must be terminated.

The most important process issues, by far, are transference and countertransference. Borderline patients quickly enter into transferences that are characterized by splitting, projective identification, negativistic merger, and serious acting out (Masterson, 1978; Boyer, 1977). The therapist frequently falls victim to these profound, primitive transferences, and there is often a stalemate (Saretsky, 1977). The therapist becomes anxious, angry, confused, or despairing, and begins to wonder if it is he or she or the patient who has the emotional problem. The patient usually works actively to convince the therapist that the therapist is the one who is really out of step with reality. The stirring up of intense transference and countertransference feelings is now regarded by many as a diagnostic criterion of borderline psychopathology (Gunderson, 1977), and Green (1977) contends that the ultimate criterion for the disorder is the affective quality of the patient's communication and the analyst's response to it.

The positive transference feelings the patient has for the therapist are expressed through enticing the therapist to become a real parent or sexual object. When the therapist refuses, the patient attempts to coerce by suicide threats or by threats of blackmail. Negative transference feelings are handled in the same way. When feeling the threat of desertion, the patient often disrupts treatment or makes a suicide attempt. Reality-based positive and negative feelings are handled in the same way: act first and think later.

The therapist is strongly tempted to hospitalize the borderline patient to exert some control over his or her action. Unfortunately, hospitalizing the patient tends to perpetuate a struggle for control, unless the therapist can maintain separation between himself and the staff responsible for the patient's daily management and unless the patient can be hospitalized for an extended period of time (Johansen, 1979). When the borderline patient becomes suicidal, some reasonable person with whom he or she is involved should be told, but the therapist needs to emphasize that a decision about hospitalization needs to be made by the patient, unless he or she has become psychotic. In this way, the patient is made to face his responsibility for his own life, and is made to face the fact that he is not so ill that he cannot think for himself.

While most of the feelings of the patient toward the therapist are based on misidentifications and projective identification, most of the feelings of the therapist toward the patient are reality-based, not countertransference-based. These patients are annoying, frustrating, unpleasant, and unrewarding to the therapist, and it is helpful if they are told in a constructive way

(Weiner, 1978). A great deal can be gained from therapists telling their reactions if they can avoid a shift in the focus of therapy away from the patient's behavior onto their own inner workings. Borderline patients often claim to be startled by therapists' reactions, and attempt to shame them for the feelings they experience in relation to the patient. If therapists are overly concerned about their own aggression, they may feel apologetic because they have struck out at the patient. There is no need for therapists to apologize for having had an ordinary human response, although the patient will tell them that they ought to be above such things. Therapists remind the patients that they are not above having feelings, and that their job in this instance is to show the patient the impact he or she has on others' feelings.

When therapists become angry with the borderline patient, they should ask the patient what he or she may have done to trigger the therapists' anger. The patient will attempt to discount his own behavior, but he will know! This is quite different from the therapist's management of the situation when he or she becomes overtly angry with a neurotic patient in an evocative therapy. In that instance, the therapist starts off by asking him or herself what has been triggered in his or her own unconscious, and then asks the patient his or her reactions and associations to the therapist's behavior. An apology may also be in order, as it would be if the therapist's response to the borderline patient were unreasonable in degree or manner of expression, or if it originated in the therapist's specific vulnerability instead of the patient's provocative behavior.

Summary

The psychotic person, the psychosis-prone person, and the person with a borderline personality all have structural ego weaknesses and therefore require a repressive therapy to avoid impasse. They require different repressive techniques because of the differences in their ego structures.

The psychotic person's environment must be made understandable and predictable. The psychosis-prone person needs a relationship to tie him or her to reality. The borderline needs to be confronted with the effects of his behavior on himself and others. Hospitalization can help the psychotic person to reintegrate, but may require coercion. It is probably unwise to coerce the borderline patient into a controlled environment because he will turn his attention away from himself and onto the struggle for control with the institution. The therapist's relationship to the psychotic person and the person whose psychosis is in remission is that of professional healer to patient. With the borderline, it is a person-to-person relationship in which the therapist, when necessary, confronts the patient with his or her behavior and the therapist's personal reactions to his or her behavior. To the borderline patient, a neutral response or a lack of response is approval of his or her behavior.

7

Ego-supportive Therapy: Treating Adolescents

Introduction

The treatment of adolescents will be used to illustrate the technique of ego-supportive therapy, which is a useful method for dealing with adolescents and adults whose defense mechanisms are classified as immature in Vaillant's hierarchy. While immaturity is a normal developmental stage for adolescents, it usually signifies a developmental arrest in an adult, and therefore suggests a less optimistic prognosis for the adult patient.

Adolescence is a state of life whose beginning is heralded by the biological event of puberty and whose termination point is difficult to ascertain. The age of 18 is the arbitrary chronologic endpoint of adolescence, but it is neither the social nor the psychological endpoint for most people. It is more reasonable to describe adolescence as a state of mind with neither a discrete beginning nor a discrete end in which a relatively unconsolidated ego struggles with the biological sexual drive, with the maturing nervous and musculoskeletal systems, and with the transference of social, psychological, and biological need fulfillment from parents to one's self and to one's peer group. The fundamental task of the therapist is to increase adolescent patients' coping ability by reinforcing their defenses against unconscious conflict, by helping them to develop predictable responses to life's events, and by increasing their ability to observe and to control themselves. The therapist helps to shape the adolescent's character instead of altering character defenses, as he would in an evocative therapy with an adult (Weiner, 1978). The rare exception to this is the well-functioning adolescent with a mild neurotic problem. The ordinary question of the therapist to the adolescent patient is "How can I help you to achieve your goals?" and not "What in you prevents you from reaching your goals?" which is appropriately asked of candidates for evocative therapy. An ego-supportive therapy deals with rational actions instead of rationalizations.

Principles of Psychotherapy with Adolescents

The ordinary adolescent outpatient does not profit from an evocative therapy that brings unconscious motivation and conflict to consciousness. Breaching the adolescent's defenses soon produces an impasse resulting from the child's heightened defensiveness, an antitherapeutic regression, or a misalliance with superego or id.

Adolescents ordinarily cannot distinguish an interpretation from criticism because of the uneasy peace between a suddenly enlarged superego that has been called in by the ego to deal with the rising sexual and aggressive feelings that accompany puberty. An evaluative statement by an adult is equated with an attack on the child's ego by a harsh, punitive superego, and an impasse soon develops.

If adolescents allow themselves to regress, they see the therapist as trying to take over their minds, and rebel against the therapist or collapse onto him.

Generally speaking, it is better to help the adolescent to learn mature ways of defending his or her ego and coping with the world than to reduce his or her intrapsychic defenses. Repressive and ego-supportive techniques or a combination of both are therefore, the most useful approaches with adolescents.

The repressive approach was discussed extensively in the earlier chapter on ego deficit. What was said with regard to treating the borderline, psychosis-prone, and psychotic adult is also true of the borderline, psychosis-prone, and psychotic adolescent.

An ego-supportive approach is appropriate for the adolescent with mild to moderate neurotic or character problems who lives in an adequate family. A more operational definition of the adolescent candidate for ego-supportive psychotherapy is that he or she employs Vaillant's (1977) immature, neurotic, and mature mechanisms of adaptation. He or she can also modify the environment to some degree, can assume a moderate degree of responsibility toward himself and others, and can assume different roles toward himself and others as his life situation demands. The last three criteria also apply to the family of the adolescent who still lives with his or her family of origin. The more flexible the family members and the family structure, the greater the possibility of change for the identified patient.

The Structuring of Ego-Supportive Psychotherapy

Ego-supportive psychotherapy requires a degree of ego development or integration, as manifested by moderate impulse control, moderate capacity to tolerate dysphoria, to observe one's self, to differentiate internal from external stimuli, to use secondary process thinking, and to perceive aspects of external reality accurately. Ego-supportive techniques can also aid in the further development of these abilities.

Generally, promoting impulse control and developing the capacity to tolerate dysphoria are accomplished less directly in ego-supportive therapies than in repressive therapies. Impulse control is modeled by the therapist instead of being enforced externally by granting or taking away privileges from a hospitalized patient. In ego-supportive therapies, the capacity to tolerate dysphoria is developed by gradually raising the frequency and dosage of confrontations on emotionally charged issues. These issues may arise in the here and now between therapist and patient or with a therapeutic group, and are usually managed without the cushion of an antipsychotic or antidepressant drug. The patient is helped to tolerate interpersonal tensions and to become aware of him or herself as a person interacting in the present.

Differentiation of external stimuli from internal stimuli is accomplished by helping the patient to recognize the extent to which he or she blames others or blames external events for his or her behavior, in contrast to repressive treatment in which the person whose hallucinated voices attempt to control him is urged to pay attention to reality instead. Secondary process thinking is encouraged at an interpersonal level by confronting the patient with the fact that others cannot give him what he wants unless he makes his wants known, instead of presuming that if another person cares about him, that person will intuitively meet his needs. Perception of external reality is fostered by interpersonal feedback in which the patient is confronted with the personal impact of his or her behavior on the therapist or on members of a therapeutic group.

Because candidates for ego-supportive therapy have greater ego strength, they can deal with the here-and-now reality of their relationship with their therapist or their peers instead of being taught appropriate behavior, as is done in a repressive approach that seeks to avoid overstimulation of affects. In repressive therapies, patients are taught about themselves. In an ego-supportive therapy, they experience themselves as they interact.

In my experience, a motivated patient who learns in a repressive therapy through active teaching can learn as well as the patient who learns in an ego-supportive therapy through experiencing, and the changes which can come about are no less permanent. The keys in both techniques are mobilizing the patient's wish to learn and addressing the patient's ego at an appropriate level.

The emphasis in most forms of repressive therapy is teaching people how to cope on a day-to-day basis, but active teaching is a large part of any therapeutic approach. In ego-supportive therapies, patients learn through experiencing themselves interact with others. The chief therapeutic mechanisms, in addition to active teaching, are interpersonal feedback and modeling.

Because candidates for ego-supportive therapy can tolerate unpleasant feelings and can control their impulses, they can be confronted with their behavior in the here and now without producing an impasse. Limit setting is usually not required, except for establishing that the therapeutic session is a time to consider personally significant issues and not a social hour.

Patients are allowed more freedom to make their own mistakes in ego-supportive therapy than in repressive therapy. The therapist must still acknowledge the patient's positive attributes, but he can more heavily emphasize the patient's alienating or self-defeating qualities without the fear that he will so inflame the patient's self-critical tendencies that he or she will become psychotic, depressed, or suicidal. There is less need to empathically convey positive regard for the patient because his self-esteem is more stable, but the patient's need to experience positive regard by the therapist still exists.

Dealing with the Patient's Interpersonal Environment

In repressive therapies, there is often need to structure the patient's environment to meet his or her needs. In ego-supportive therapies, the patient's interpersonal environment frequently needs to be dealt with, but does not require active structuring or control by the therapist. In the case of adolescents, parents must be seen for the sake of gaining information and for mobilizing their appropriate support of the treatment and the child's developmental needs. This may call for suggestions by the therapist to the parents, or merely for the therapist to sensitize the patient's family to certain emotional issues. Should there be need for more active structuring of the family, formal family therapy can be proposed and undertaken.

Contractual Issues

Contract making is important with adolescents. It often introduces a relationship in which the child, for one of the first times in his or her life, is acknowledged as a person with his or her own separate thoughts, feelings, and desires, and in whom independent strivings are not taken as rebellion or negativism. Contract making affirms the child as an individual, and also emphasizes that one can negotiate on one's own behalf without a disastrous outcome. Many teenagers who are chronologic or biologic adolescents are psychologically less mature, and must be dealt with according to their level of maturity instead of their age.

When an adolescent adamantly refuses direct involvement with the therapist, the therapist must ascertain alternate routes of intervention which may be family therapy, counseling the parents, or even removal of the child from the home. In all cases except those in which a severely destructive reaction is anticipated, it is useful to include the child in these discussions. If he or she is not willing to be a voluntary, active participant in treatment, he can at least be involved in planning how his difficulties will be approached, or can have the option of stating his feelings about it.

It is usually possible to establish an evaluation contract with children who are 13 or older. Therapist and patient can ordinarily discuss the reasons for the referral if the patient has been informed. If he hasn't, the therapist needs to find out why he wasn't told and why he didn't ask. The therapist needs to state his or her understanding of the referral and to compare it with the adolescent's understanding. The evaluation contract with adolescents can usually include discussion of the child's thoughts, feelings, and behavior.

Confidentiality is a major issue for many adolescents. All adolescents should be asked their wishes about confidentiality, and should be asked their feelings about the therapist contacting their parents. It is possible with older adolescents to avoid all contact with the parents by seeing the child first and by agreeing that conversations with the parents are off limits, except for a telephone call by the therapist to introduce him or herself to the parents, to explain the need of avoiding contact with them, and to ask if they feel there is important information that he or she ought to have. It has been my repeated experience that adolescents who insist on an exclusive relationship with the therapist are concealing significant aspects of themselves and of their relationship with their parents. If adolescents are relied upon to tell their parents that the therapist will not be in touch with them, the therapist can be sure that some of his or her potential working relationship with the parents will be undermined.

The therapist can ordinarily agree that the content of sessions will not be discussed with parents. The exception is when the child's welfare is in danger, and when a responsible adult must be notified so that he or she can be prepared to act. The teenager who is losing control of his aggressive or suicidal impulses must be told that the therapist reserves the right to breach the confidentiality of the therapeutic relationship if there is impending danger. The child, except in the most extreme emergency, should be told in advance when the therapist intends to contact the parents. He need not be told the entirety of what the therapist will tell his or her parents, but certainly should be told the gist of it.

Warning parents that their child is likely to act impulsively and suggesting that he or she be hospitalized for his or her own protection is not a betrayal of the child's confidence. It is assuming reasonable professional responsibility for a person whose judgment is temporarily impaired. Most suicidal teenagers can be told of the therapist's plan to warn their parents and to advise hospitalization. This more commonly triggers a sigh of relief than an impulsive suicide attempt or a runaway.

The ordinary therapeutic contract with teenagers is not to be friends or to play, but to work together on the patient's problems. It is tempting to offer friendship to teenagers who feel misunderstood by other adults. In spite of their seeming objectivity and possible victimization by persecuting or uncaring adults, teenagers can make better use of neutral professional interest than of advocacy by a friend. More than one mental health worker has been made a lemming by an adolescent who convinced him or her to help act out his psychopathology instead of straightening it out.

The contract with the adolescent should include ascertaining who will be responsible for transportation, and informing the child about fees for missed appointments. Older adolescents should be told the fee and, if they are seen without the therapist having been contacted by the parents, they should be asked who will pay the bill. Again, it is unwise to accept the adolescent's word that the parents will pay. The therapist owes it to himself, his patient, and the parents to obtain direct confirmation. Misunderstandings of this sort have arisen in my practice with adolescents as old as 27.

The evaluation and therapeutic contracts of adolescents directly involve their parents. A parent usually makes the initial contact and, except for older adolescents, usually sees the therapist first. Some therapists do not have direct contact with the parents of the children with whom they work unless the child is present. Their rationale is to demonstrate their alliance with the child. By establishing such a contract, therapists may rob themselves of a useful alliance with the parents and of a source of information about the child. While therapists must accept the child's point of view as legitimate, it is often useful to have another point of view or to have background material that the child cannot provide.

Most parents understand the importance of the confidentiality of the therapist-patient relationship when it is adequately explained. Parents tend to object when they do not receive adequate explanation of the need for confidentiality or when the child's behavior is frightening. An occasional parent is so intrusive that he or she will only allow therapy if given a direct pipeline into the child's therapy session. The therapist must be careful in contracting with the parent who is so intrusive. If the parent cannot tolerate the child's individuation, psychotherapy is not likely to be of great value and may negatively affect a family equilibrium. The therapist may need to hand the problem back to the family until they decide they can afford to let an outsider in, or one of the family out.

The therapist can, on the other hand, welcome input by the family, but can also indicate that he will pass along the information to the patient. This ensures that the family will think twice before calling and that the information provided can be used by the patient for self-understanding or for understanding his or her impact on the family.

Periodic progress reports from the family to the therapist and from the therapist to family are very useful. Their frequency usually depends on the degree of tension generated by the identified patient. These reports need not always be direct. They may be funneled through a colleague to whom the family turns directly for periodic advice or for ongoing therapy. On a few occasions, I have been primary therapist for several members of the same family, but not usually at the same time. A sense of having a special relationship to the therapist is so important in treatment that many patients do not fare well if a close relative is in treatment simultaneously. Some children, if they know a parent has been in treatment with a therapist, will refuse to see him or her on the grounds that they want to tell their own story and be seen as an individual instead of somebody's son or daughter. If simultaneous treatment of relatives is undertaken, the therapist must be prepared to deal with themes of jealousy and competition.

Process Issues

The Alliance

It is difficult to form an adequate alliance with adolescents that is also therapeutic. If therapists become overly concerned with developing a positive relationship, they may allow themselves to reinforce behavior that is not in the child's best interest. The distance between an inadequate alliance and an antitherapeutic alliance is small. There must be a positive relationship to facilitate cooperation, but the therapist must be careful of the means he or she employs to facilitate it, as we can see from the treatment of Miss N.

> Miss N., a 17-year-old high school senior, had sought the therapist's advice, suggestions, and approval of her actions during her first month of treatment. The therapist responded with advice, suggestions, and liberal praise for constructive action, hoping to counter her parents' tendency to disparage her moves toward psychological maturation and toward differentiation from them.
>
> In her sixth month of weekly psychotherapy, she told of her experiences asking her mother to help with her homework. As her mother became involved in helping her, Miss N. became less involved. Her mother eventually did her homework for her, and Miss N. learned nothing of her assignment for that day.
>
> She recognized her cooperation with her mother in staying a helpless child and concluded that, given her tendency to be passive in relation to her mother, she would be better off doing her own homework and not asking her mother for help.
>
> The therapist responded by wondering aloud if Miss N. might also be better off if he were to refrain from giving advice and from approving or disapproving of her thoughts and behavior. She grinned, and said she thought that might be a good idea because of her tendency to think the way she thought others wanted her to. She and the therapist agreed that the only way for her to develop her thinking ability and judgment was to think and to make judgments for herself.
>
> Within minutes, she confided to the therapist certain aspects of her behavior that she had formerly withheld, and against which she had resolved, with the therapist's approval,

a month previously. She had been reluctant to admit breaking her resolution for fear of the therapist's disapproval.

Miss N. and her therapist established that she didn't need him to be a better parent than her own parents. Instead, he needed to help her be a better parent to herself.

Adverse Transference Reactions

Adverse transference reactions are common in adolescents because the therapist is readily substituted for a parent. The therapist's neutral inquiries are perceived as attempts to control the child or to undermine his or her autonomy, in spite of the fact that the child's attempts at achieving self-control and autonomy have not been working very well. The child's efforts to separate from parents and parent surrogates manifests as defensiveness and rebellion when they miscarry. Unfortunately, at this stage of development, most people can say more about what they are not that what they are, and what they do not believe in than what they do believe in. An adolescent needs to eschew certain parental values because they are parental values and not because of their content. Even for the ordinary adolescent, the immature mechanisms described by Vaillant are the norm. The child substitutes his or her wishes for reality and action in fantasy for actual potency in dealing with the world. An adverse transference reaction severely impaired treatment of the next patient.

Miss M. was referred for psychiatric treatment by a nonmedical therapist because she had attempted suicide and was threatening suicide again. She told the psychiatrist after a few interviews that *he* was her problem, and that if she were not allowed to return to treatment with her former therapist, she would kill herself. Her unconscious identification of the therapist was with her father, whom she perceived as controlling and uncaring, and whose primary concerns were that she not bother him and that she be what he wanted her to be. Her former therapist was described as unconditionally accepting, loving, warm, and personally open.

It was not possible to deal with the transference by interpretation because there was insufficient therapeutic alliance. Instead, the psychiatrist said that he could not compete with the loving attitude of her former therapist, but that he could offer professional concern and could try to help alleviate her self-hatred and her feeling that nothing was worthwhile in life.

He met her requests to return to her former therapist by saying that he had no objection to her return once she felt better about herself. Over the ensuing months, the patient's demand dwindled down to "just one visit," her adverse transference reaction subsided, and she agreed that her primary therapeutic relationship should be with the psychiatrist because her former therapist's emotional involvement made the necessary objectivity impossible. In the process of negotiating for her visit to her ex-therapist, the transference wish emerged: to be loved and nurtured like a small child and to avoid the pain and loneliness of establishing relationships outside her primary family.

Countertransference Problems

Countertransference-based errors are frequent in the treatment of adolescents. Therapists commonly overidentify with their adolescent patients and see them as victims of unjustifiable persecution. They deal with the sense of helplessness that they felt during their own adolescence by encouraging their adolescent patients to voice their feelings and to take action. They also overidentify with the patient's sense of helplessness and may treat the child as though he or she were actually helpless. It is easy, for example, to blame the child's parents for not consistently providing transportation, but the majority of teenagers can persuade a friend to bring them at a time when the parent finds it inconvenient.

Therapists often attempt to provide the love and warmth which they enjoyed or failed to experience in their own childhood. When the therapist attempts to make up for what the child has missed, he is generally making a mistake. The tender feelings of the therapist block his awareness and ability to deal with certain aspects of the patient. Because tender feelings and love involve some element of projective identification (Weiner, 1980), the therapist loses a clear view of the patient. If one develops tender feelings for a patient, one also becomes subject to manipulation, for the tender feelings that flow back from the patient now have the potential for becoming an item of barter. In exchange for the therapist closing his or her eyes to certain behaviors, he or she is rewarded with tender feeling by the patient.

Truax and Carkhuff (1965) found that application of their triad of therapist-offered conditions to a group of adolescent delinquents did not have a salutary effect. This is not hard to understand on theoretical grounds. Delinquents' problems are not lack of self-acceptance, but the incompatibility of their value systems and their lack of impulse control with society in general.

Another countertransference pitfall for the therapist is seeing his or her own unrealized potential in the child and attempting to encourage the flowering of, say, a writer or a poet, when the development of adequate social skills would be a more appropriate goal.

Seeing the adolescent patient in a group for part of his or her therapy helps in dealing with countertransference-based issues. In the group, for example, the therapist can readily see that the potential poet is, in fact, avoiding the developmental tasks appropriate to his or her age, and the group members can provide the impetus for dealing with social reality that the therapist cannot. Other group members can provide transportation to social get-togethers, can provide support in looking for a job, and can provide acceptance based on the patient's interaction with the people from whom it is most meaningful in the long run—his or her peers.

Other Technical Considerations

Clarification, confrontation, and interpretation—the tools that are the mainstay of psychoanalytic psychotherapy—must be augmented by other techniques if one is to deal effectively with adolescents. Adolescents need help to identify the therapist clearly as a friendly adult who is neither their parent nor the kind of person they feel their parents to be. This often requires the therapist to take a stand on certain issues, but he or she must always be ready to negotiate, as we can see from the next example.

> Miss M. had stolen a gun from her father (whom the therapist had previously asked to get the guns out of the house). She let her psychiatrist know about it indirectly. When he made it clear that he knew she had a gun and that he needed to tell her father, she pleaded that her secret be kept, saying that there were lots of ways she could kill herself, but that if she decided there was no way she could live, using the gun would be the

> most merciful way to end her suffering. Furthermore, the gun was well hidden and she would not surrender it.
>
> Instead of entering a battle for control over her, the therapist told her gently that he understood her wish to have a readily available escape from life, and that knowing this escape was readily available if life were too painful, she might begin to face some of the issues she had feared to face. Then he said that he would keep her secret.
>
> A few days later, no longer feeling that the therapist was trying to control her, she told a sympathetic teacher that she had a gun in her school locker. The teacher had the gun removed, and her father was told by the school authorities. She did what was ultimately best for her on her own terms, and was able to do so because of the therapist's willingness to negotiate.

The adolescent patient requires an active psychotherapy that diminishes the intensity of the patient's transference, and the counterprojective techniques described in the previous chapter are quite useful. While superficially agreeing with the patient's parataxic distortions or with his or her projections, the therapist indirectly questions the patient's perceptions and suggests that there may be other ways to see the situation, without suggesting that the therapist knows the actual truth of the matter. He leaves it to the patient to revise his or her own perception.

I find this technique particularly helpful in working through paralyzing projective identifications with parents that block therapy. In dealing with a patient's perception of an intrusive parent as all-good, I agree that the parent certainly is concerned about the patient, and overemphasize the behavior of the patient that would justify such intense concern. I then wonder aloud if the parent may also have some emotional need for the patient to be dependent on him or her.

It is usually not difficult to elicit and mobilize the adolescent's negative feelings toward a parent, but one must be careful not to mobilize them so rapidly as to frighten the child or to encourage the child to act upon them inappropriately. It is common for adolescent patients to tell their parents that their therapist says they hate them. In this way, a child disowns his or her feelings and starts a fight between the parents and the therapist that frequently results in the child being withdrawn from therapy.

One must not lose sight of the reasons for eliciting the adolescent's negative feelings toward his or her parents in one's haste to uncover them. One reason is to let the child know that he really has freedom of expression with the therapist. He is also, of course, free to air his negative feelings about the therapist. Another reason is to learn what behaviors of the therapist toward his patient will stimulate negative reactions. A third reason is to help the child overcome his fear of his negative feelings, especially if he is concerned that they might destroy his parents. The expression of negative feelings also begins to allow the teenager to place his parents outside himself and to direct his psychic aggression toward them in reality, instead of toward the parental introjects in his own ego.

It must also be remembered that one of the tasks of adolescence is to gain some measure of control over one's emotions, and that to become angry or cry in the presence of an adult says to the patient that he is still a child because he cannot control himself. The therapist's sensitivity to the adolescent as a person enables him to differentiate the persons for whom the expression of emotions threatens a sense of psychological integrity.

In addition to all of the above, the therapist must also concentrate on building adequate coping mechanisms. Adolescent inpatients participate in group projects and group decision making to enhance their ability to cooperate and to deal with others, and to learn responsibility toward others and acceptance of others' point of view. They are shown that they can influence their environment and are shown the usefulness of altruism and of the assumption of supportive roles toward one another.

It is useful to include a group therapy experience in the treatment of many adolescent outpatients. The therapy group allows them to contrast a milieu in which the norm is trying to understand and to deal with one's difficulties with their peer groups, who generally help them to project and to deny their inner conflicts or their conflicts with their real interpersonal world. Impasses are often justified by adolescents by reminding the therapist that all of their friends are the same way.

Peer confrontation in a therapy group is often more effective than confrontation by an adult therapist in breaking up this type of rationalization because communication from peers is often less distorted by transference or by the child's attitude toward adults in general. This, in the next case, a young man was better able to listen to a group of peers than to his therapists.

> Mr. O., an 18 year-old-high school senior, told the members of his therapy group how he drove his car. He said that he always tried to turn his car around corners as tightly as he could without overturning the car. He had had several wrecks because of this, and had been severely injured on one occasion. The leaders did not react to his story. Instead, they asked the group members to voice their reactions and to speculate on the eventual outcome of Mr. O's driving habits. All agreed, to Mr. O.'s amazement, that he would undoubtedly wreck a car again and suffer a severe injury or be killed. Mr. O. was defensive at first and said, to the contrary, that his driving skills were improving. He could now make turns that he never could have made before. The group members replied that each time he gained more skill, he also took more of a chance. Soon, however, he said that the thrill or "rush" that he felt while cornering his car was the way he could best achieve a sense of aliveness. He found interpersonal relationships too painful to risk committing himself.
>
> Over ensuing sessions, he was encouraged by the group to find more satisfaction in interpersonal relationships and less pleasure in risking his life.

Many adolescents are also able to be more emotionally expressive in a group of peers. With peers, there is less regressive connotation to letting go emotionally.

Summary

The fundamental technical errors in working with adolescents and other people with immature defenses are treating them like small children who need external controls and who cannot assume responsibility for their behavior, or treating them like adults and assuming that there is sufficient ego development to permit reflection and introspection. Adolescents and other immature persons need a flexible therapeutic approach that requires the therapist to shift his or her level of intervention frequently from a repressive to an ego-supportive level.

Transference problems abound because adolescents are still children and the therapists are adults and can therefore easily be perceived and reacted to as parents. Because of this, impasses tend to arise if the transference is allowed to develop fully. Countertransference problems leading to transference gratification instead of therapeutic work are also common and result in the therapist's acceptance of the child's unreasonable behavior.

Many of the transference and countertransference problems that arise with adolescents can be dealt with by providing a group therapy experience at some time during the adolescent patient's treatment. In the peer group, confrontation is more effective because it comes from peers and acceptance is based on the patient's work in the group instead of on the therapist's infatuation with the patient's youth and potential.

8

Group Psychotherapy

In spite of the fact that group psychotherapy is much more difficult to observe and control than individual psychotherapy, there is no evidence that the casualty rate or dropout rate is significantly higher for group psychotherapy than for individual psychotherapy. The most carefully documented study of negative group outcomes is a study of encounter groups which showed a decrease in social functioning or psychological comfort in 7.7 percent of the participants (Lieberman, Yalom, & Miles, 1973). Unfortunately, there are few equally well controlled studies in the individual psychotherapy or group psychotherapy literature, but this compares favorably with Bergin's (1971) estimate of an overall damage rate in psychotherapy of 5 to 10 percent.

Since it is so difficult to measure psychological damage, it may be useful to look at cases in which a positive outcome was expected, but the patient dropped out before significant benefit could be achieved.

Yalom (1966) reported a dropout rate of 10 to 35 percent in the first 12 to 20 meetings of groups led by trainees at Stanford. Lothstein (1978) reported a 29 percent dropout rate in the first

12 sessions of groups conducted by several professional disciplines at different levels of training.

These data compare favorably to a 43 percent dropout from individual psychotherapy before the fifth session in a VA clinic (Garfield & Kurz, 1952), and a 43 percent dropout before the fourth individual session in an urban mental health clinic (Craig & Huffine, 1976).

We do not know how many dropouts are failures of treatment, how many are due to a mismatch of a person to a group or to group therapy, and how many are due to other factors. We do know that fewer dropouts occur after the first dozen sessions of an ongoing group.

Lothstein (1978) sees the dropout phenomenon as part of a normal selection process, and finds that the person who drops out usually does not fit well with the group members or with the group's goals. The studies of group therapy dropouts that have been reported, however, have been done in settings in which prospective group members seldom had an ongoing relationship with the group therapist before entering a group and no continued one-to-one relationship with the therapist during the stage of adjustment to the group. This lack of support during the acculturation phase probably contributed significantly to dropouts. In my own experience with combined group and individual psychotherapy, I have found that many patients were extremely uncomfortable in the first few group sessions, and would have dropped out had they not had the support of continued individual sessions through this period of adaptation to the group.

Reality Factors

Patients should not be assigned to groups they cannot attend regularly. Transient persons should not be placed in ongoing groups, but can be seen in time-limited educational groups (Kadis et al., 1974).

Patients who cannot afford individual therapy may be placed in a group as a less expensive alternative, but the group therapist must be aware that individual sessions may be required, which will raise the problem of altering the fee for the individual session. This in turn may establish the transference expectation of the therapist as an all-giving parent, may place the patient in the position of the exceptional child, and may inappropriately stimulate his or her narcissism or guilt. As a practical matter, it is unwise to accept a patient for group therapy who cannot pay the therapist's fee for individual sessions. It is difficult for the patient to ask for individual sessions and irritates the therapist if many individual sessions are required. While there are no absolute rules on making exceptions for certain patients, every exception made requires some reflection by the therapist and some inquiry into its impact on the patient.

Group Therapy Contracts

Group therapy contracts are made according to the type of group the patient is to enter: repressive, ego supportive, or evocative. In repressive groups, the contract is to learn certain skills together with peers experiencing the same problems. In ego-supportive groups, the contract involves freely reacting to the others in the group, coming to understand the impact of one's behavior on others, and making use of the group's support to modify behaviors that are in need of change. In evocative groups, dreams and fantasies are shared, and each patient associates to the others' productions. Contracts for all three levels of therapy involve active participation by the therapist and patient at levels commensurate with the goal of the therapy.

Leaders of ego-supportive and evocative groups commonly build three provisions into their therapeutic contracts to avoid treatment impasses: that outside contacts between group members be reported in the group; that the material discussed in the group is confidential; and that the individual group member stay with the group for a certain minimum time or that he or she give notice of an intention to leave the group so that such a decision can be dealt with by other members of the group. These contracts are made during the individual sessions before entering group therapy, and are reiterated in the group sessions.

Outside contacts need to be reported to prevent subgrouping. Confidentiality is important for maintaining trust. Contracting for a minimum stay in the group is a means to prevent fleeing in the face of the anxiety of entering a new group. A delay before leaving the group helps to deal with acting out and to emphasize the responsibility of each group member toward the group in exchange for what he or she receives from the group.

Many group therapists attempt to minimize potential attendance problems by charging a flat rate for the entire duration of short-term groups or a monthly flat rate for an open-ended group. Charging a flat rate or a monthly rate emphasizes the group members' responsibility for their own attendance and avoids debates over justifiable absences. Furthermore, the flat or monthly rate eliminates the patient's ability to punish the therapist financially by cancelling visits.

Unclear Therapeutic Contract

Lack of clarity about group rules, such as the need for confidentiality, can result in leakage of information to outsiders, erosion of the trust needed for the group's work, and impasse for certain group members or the group as a whole. Group rules need to be simple and explicitly understood by all group members. The group leader must bear in mind, however, that the purpose of the group rules is twofold. Rules facilitate the function of the group and serve as norms. Norms are violated sooner or later by one or more of the members. Violation of group norms are important subjects for discussion: for example, an agreement made between two group members to avoid sharing certain facts with the rest of the group. This is often a manifestation of a transference reaction to the therapist. Group members who secretly become sexually involved with one another frequently do so to avoid issues with the therapist. The sexual involvement can symbolize oedipal rivalry or the gratification of an incestuous wish, to name only two of the possibilities. Without disclosure to the group, investigation and interpretation are impossible.

The therapist who deals legalistically with violations of group rules will often produce an impasse. If, however, a group member's behavior literally endangers others in the group, a threat of termination is appropriate (Weiner, 1970). Ordinarily, the best approach to violations of the group contract is a neutral exploration of the circumstances surrounding the violation, of the possible motives of the violators, and of the reactions of the group members. Based on this exploration, the violator and the group as a whole can determine if the violation demands sanction against the individual(s) concerned or if group discussion alone is sufficient. In the rare instance of repeated absences, prolonged disruptive behavior in the group, or continual betrayal of the group's confidence, a group member such as Mr. K., described below, may be asked to leave.

> After several years of dealing with Mr. K., a frustratingly ruminative monopolizer who seemed unable to benefit from group discussion, the group as a whole demanded that he be dropped. After adequate discussion with Mr. K. and the group, he transferred to individual therapy where meeting his needs would not obstruct the growth of others. Part of Mr. K.'s behavior in the group was based on a misunderstanding of the therapeutic contract. He felt that the group was to provide him a social outlet and unconditional acceptance. Its failure to do so had only intensified his efforts in that direction. Several years later, he had successful experience in another group because of his increased ability to handle frustration and the group's nonacceptance of the interpersonally alienating aspects of his behavior.

Patients with magical expectations attempt to be acted upon by therapists instead of acting in conjunction with them. These expectations need to be partially worked through before a patient can become productively involved in group therapy. To a certain extent, the group itself can be useful in working through magical expectations, but each beginner who requires initiation seriously slows the progress of the group and jeopardizes its therapeutic climate.

Invalid Therapeutic Contract

Patients who are taken into group therapy because they will not accept more appropriate therapy have established invalid contracts with their therapists. Therapists enter into such compromises because their patients supposedly will not accept hospitalization, medication, or the like. Actually, these situations are products of the patient's wish to remain in control of his or her treatment and the therapist's countertransference of his or her narcissism. The therapist is unwilling to let the patient suffer the consequence of his decision to avoid or postpone adequate treatment because of his unconscious reactions to the patient, or the patient's appeal to his omnipotent fantasies.

The therapist's omnipotent fantasies and therapeutic naivete contribute to inappropriate placements of patients in groups. For example, undertaking treatment of a manic-depressive patient in an outpatient group of neurotics invites disaster for the group. When the patient is manic, the group has to struggle against monopolization that does not respond to interpretation. When the patient is depressed, the group feels responsible for the patient's life.

Recent ahistoric group approaches emphasize the development of one's potential through focusing on the positive aspects of one's personality in the here and now (Mintz, 1971). Doubtless, many people gain little by ruminating over the past. On the other hand, much is lost by failure to obtain an adequate history, which may include severe mental illness, outbursts of violence, and serious suicidal danger.

A negative placement frequently invalidates the therapeutic contract. Negative placement is dealing with negative feelings toward a patient by referring him or her to a group (Kadis et al., 1974). Its aim is to avoid awareness of uncharitable feelings toward the patient that might arise if the therapist were more direct. Patients who antagonize or frustrate their therapists are therefore frequently told that they need a group experience. The group experience, however, may devastate patient and group alike. The patient's anger with a former therapist, whether transference-based or a reaction to his or her real behavior, is acted out in the new group, and if caught at a vulnerable moment, group and therapist may react with destructive counter-hostility.

Therapists can avoid making negative placements through mature self-awareness and by asking themselves, when contemplating referral of a patient to a group, "What am I avoiding by making this referral?" Group therapists can avoid experiencing a negative placement by adequately evaluating patients who are referred for group therapy, even if referred by a trusted colleague. The example of Mrs. A.H. is a case in point.

> Mrs. A.H. had been referred for group psychotherapy on the rationale that a group experience would help her achieve insight into her destructive interpersonal behavior. During the evaluation interviews, she told of her extensive sadomasochistic involvements with men, her recent hospitalizations for suicide attempts, and her unresolved attachment to her outpatient therapist. It seemed probable to the therapist that the

reason for her referral was to avoid dealing with her on a one-to-one basis.

Because of her chaotic interpersonal relationships and strongly ambivalent residuals from her last treatment relationship, the group therapist saw her individually. Over the months she was seen, the hypothesis that her referral had been a negative placement was confirmed. Her behavior became more and more infuriating. Her outpatient therapist had been unaware of their mutual provocation: hers active and his passive. Placement in a benevolent permissive group atmosphere would have tied up the energies of the entire group. She was instead treated in a highly structured individual therapy in which she was regularly confronted by the therapist when she repeatedly attempted to abuse him (Weiner, 1980).

Inappropriate Group

Group therapy may be the treatment of choice for a particular person, but he or she may be referred to an inappropriate group. Sometimes this occurs because a therapist only has an opening in a particular group, or an institution is in need of a new member for a certain group. Obviously, the treatment needs of the patient should be placed above the needs of the therapist or the institution.

All patients must be evaluated individually for their fit with the group therapist and the group currently available. Regardless of descriptive diagnosis, the patient must be evaluated in terms of his or her interaction with the therapist and probable interaction with the group, an evaluation that cannot be performed by the referring person or agency.

Group placement may not only be inappropriate for the type of group (repressive, ego-supportive, evocative), but for the life of the group. Patients who enter at a time of group crisis are likely to be traumatized or to be stalemated for long periods of time. Groups should be allowed to work through periods of crisis (loss of important member or other highly charged group interactions) before adding a new person who may become the victim of anger displaced away from other group members or from the leader.

The composition of an otherwise appropriate group may make it temporarily inappropriate. An overabundance of single people may push an evocative group in the direction of a social club. An excess of impulse-ridden teenagers can turn an adolescent group into a gang.

One can, of course, flow with the direction taken by the group instead of insisting that the group conform to the therapist's intended level of function. Thus, an evocative group in which the majority of the members have marital difficulties can shift from its original goal of intrapsychic exploration to examining marital interactions. If the therapist sees a focus on marital difficulties as an important resistance by the group, he or she can deal with it by interpretation or by suggesting more fruitful avenues of exploration, such as the interaction between group members.

The personality structure, culture, or intelligence of a potential group member may be a factor in placement. Groups can tolerate a certain degree of deviance from their norms, but if a person does not conform moderately to the group's norms for behavior during sessions, or does not have some personality attributes or problems with which others can identify or empathize, he or she usually will not be able to function in the group (Yalom, 1975).

Inadequate Alliance

Without an adequate alliance with the group therapist, the patient feels abandoned when transferred from evaluation or individual treatment to that therapist's group. The length of time required to establish a therapeutic alliance is highly variable. It depends partly on the rapidity with which the healthy portion of the patient's ego can establish contact with the mature aspect of the therapist. A positive individual therapy experience realistically heightens the patient's positive expectations of the group therapist, and enhances cooperation in the transition period.

Group treatment is contraindicated until a positive relationship can be established between patient and the prospective group therapist. Otherwise, the patient's negative feelings will be acted upon in the group, but will be uninterpretable because interpretation depends for its effectiveness on the therapeutic alliance. Without the therapeutic alliance, the therapist's comments are seen as hostile, critical, and demeaning. They reinforce the patient's negative feelings, and make change impossible. The group also reacts to the negative relationship between the therapist and patient by deflecting anger from the therapist onto the patient: a scapegoating that can be unconsciously fostered by the therapist who is frustrated by his or her inability to reach the patient in a positive way.

Antitherapeutic Alliance

The following antitherapeutic alliance was based on an error in the assessment of the patient's dynamics that led to a prolonged impasse.

> Mr. J. was a 24-year-old single college graduate, living at home, whose treatment had come to a standstill. He was depressed and felt unable to look for a job. His therapist had told him that, in spite of some homosexual activity, the patient was not basically homosexual. The patient was involved in group therapy, individual therapy, and family therapy. This therapist saw him in consultation for three sessions. They were comfortable together (he and his other therapist were not), and a transfer was arranged. The new therapist decided not to encourage Mr. J. to resist his homosexual feelings. He did oppose further attempts to resolve issues with his parents, feeling that it would perpetuate his regression. The therapist suggested that Mr. J. drop family and group therapy, and worked with him individually for several years, during which time he moved away from home (at first to the home of a domineering homosexual friend) and secured a job.

The therapist had to ally with the patient's homosexual orientation to resolve the impasse and break the patient's regressive tie to his family.

An antitherapeutic alliance develops readily with adolescents. It is tempting to allow adolescent groups to digress into social conversation when tension builds. In allowing digressions, the therapist perpetuates disruptiveness, negativism, and avoidance of age-appropriate responsibility. Conversely, the therapist must take care not to reinforce overly punitive superego precepts and not to become a moralizing parent-surrogate.

Adverse Transference Reactions

Most of the adverse transference reactions I have encountered in group therapy stem from inadequate appraisal of the patient's ego strength, or a failure to appreciate his or her dynamics, coping mechanisms, and defense mechanisms. It is also important to be aware that an individual psychotherapy patient who requests group therapy may be acting upon transference wishes or fears, as the following vignette demonstrates.

> Mrs. A.D., a borderline patient in individual treatment, requested group therapy as a means of dealing with her growing dependent and romantic attachment to her therapist. She reasoned that in the group, their relationship would be diluted, her feelings would diminish and that she would be better able to verbalize because she would have less concern about pleasing the therapist and winning his favor. It seemed to the therapist that there was little alternative. She had not been able to bear the anger she had projected onto her previous therapist, and was unable to bear the intensity of her own positive feelings toward him.
>
> Mrs. A.D. was the youngest child of a large family. Entering the group as a new member recapitulated her position in her family. In the group, she at times withdrew, trying to be a good girl, and at other times occupied the center of the group by staging tantrums, becoming the bad child that she had been in her own family. She was unable to tolerate the warm feelings between the therapist and an older woman in the group, and eventually withdrew from group treatment.

The lesson of Mrs. A.D. is clear. Placement of a patient in his or her own group is not a useful means to deal with an overwhelming transference reaction to the therapist. Another therapist's group would have been more helpful because it would have split the transference.

An overwhelming transference reaction may be an indication for using a group to split the transference, as was done with Mrs. Q.

> Mrs. Q. was hospitalized for treatment of depression. She had been briefly hospitalized once before by another physician. She responded to milieu therapy and psychotherapy, and was

> discharged to outpatient care in four months. Psychological testing during her hospitalization revealed only neurotic elements, but psychotherapeutic sessions, almost from the start, had been excruciatingly painful. She had run from the room in tears on a number of occasions, and had spent the larger part of many sessions cowering in fear that she might say something wrong and that the therapist would do something to hurt her.
>
> She required rehospitalization 16 months later. At that time, the hospital staff felt she was suffering a severe transference regression. Her wish to be emotionally close to her therapist and to have his approval had blocked expression of her negative feelings toward him, and had turned them toward herself.
>
> She received electroshock treatment for her depression, followed by group therapy. In spite of the hospital staff's suggestion that she discontinue with her therapist because of the profound regression she had undergone with him, she returned as an outpatient when she was discharged from the hospital four months later. She continued group therapy at the hospital. He saw her weekly for the next 15 months. She became able to tolerate confrontation by him and also became able to deal with her negative feelings toward him.

Mrs. Q. had formerly seen her therapist as a punitive parent and as her sole source of emotional support. Each effort she had made to be close to him was accompanied by a fantasy of sadistic retribution. She became able to express negative transference feelings toward him only after her depression was relieved and her major source of support was transferred to the hospital staff and her therapy group. As a result of providing additional emotional support, there was sufficient splitting of the transference that she could be angry with him without the fear of total abandonment (Weiner, 1974a).

Although this woman's ego deficit was not evident on psychological testing, her defective coping ability and greatly impaired reality testing in the transference point to a primitive personality organization. This woman could not have been dealt with by means of psychotherapy alone. It was only after she had obtained relief of her depression and support from the hospital milieu that she began to untangle her transference problems and work her way out of the impasse that she and her therapist had reached.

Countertransference

In many instances, it is difficult for the therapist to distinguish between countertransference and appropriate emotional reactions to patients. Congruence between the emotional reaction of the therapist and the emotional reaction of the group suggests that the therapist's emotional reaction is appropriate, but the therapist must ask himself if he is encouraging the group to act out his feelings toward certain patients. In the following case, the reactions of the therapist and group were congruent, but there may have been large countertransference elements to each.

> Mrs. Z., an intensely narcissistic divorced woman, spent several years in group therapy attempting to enable herself to catch a man. To her, marriage was the ultimate solution to her problems. She was unwilling to see men as individuals. Each was only a prospective spouse. All other qualities were ignored or wished away. Over the years, the group and the therapist became angry over their inability to communicate this message and her inability to see them as more than a source of advice on man catching or as people with whom to lament the loss of her most recent man. Eventually, all acknowledged that she was getting nowhere in group therapy, which she terminated in favor of individual treatment, in which she fared no better.

It is difficult, in this situation, to say that the therapist's or the group's anger caused the impasse in treatment. Had the angry input helped her become aware that she was not the pleasant, accommodating person she thought herself, it would have been useful. To the extent that she experienced the therapist's and the group's anger as alienating and demeaning, it was destructive. In this instance, the anger of the therapist and the group was largely based on real frustration. The countertransference aspect was a reaction to the damage to the therapist's and group members' omnipotent strivings.

Countertransference factors were strongly operative in the next case.

> Mr. A. had been in treatment with his therapist intermittently for over four years. He had started in private sessions, but the therapist had encouraged him to enter group therapy because he produced little material during their sessions, and the ther-

apist felt he would do better in a more stimulating therapeutic medium. He had done well in the group, had dropped out because of a heart attack, and returned several months later. As he continued in the group, strong negative feelings toward the therapist took the place of his previously positive attitude. He began to experience a vehement dislike for the therapist, expressed great doubt of his therapeutic abilities, and treatment ground to a halt. The therapist suggested consultation to help alleviate their impasse. Mr. A. agreed, and saw a colleague who reported that Mr. A. was angry because his heart attack had stimulated more regressive needs, and the therapist was intensifying his frustration by refusing to see him in private sessions.

As the therapist reflected, the situation was not hard to understand. He was a large man and had been a bully as a youngster. The therapist was afraid of him. On understanding that the patient was angry because he wished an individual relationship with him, and not because he wanted to hurt him, they agreed that the patient would drop out of the group and see the therapist individually. They brought treatment to a successful conclusion a number of months later. In this instance, the countertransference fear of attack produced an impasse until the therapist could see that Mr. A. wished to be close to him and not to harm him.

Transference Gratification

Transference gratification is probably more common in group psychotherapy than in comparable types of individual psychotherapy, and probably relates more to the personality differences between therapists than to their theoretical orientation. In my experience, therapists who prefer to work with groups more readily blur the distinction between therapist and patient than do therapists who work in one-to-one relationships.

Patients frequently prefer group treatment to individual psychotherapy because of the transference gratification and also because they feel group therapy to be a warmer, more human therapeutic medium in which they feel more like people than like insects on a pin. Patients subjected to the Tavistock model of group psychotherapy, however, in which the therapist responds to the group as a whole instead of to individual patients (much as an analyst might respond only to the patient's verbalizations instead of to the patient as a person), find it an unpleasant, dehumanizing experience from which the few who profit have had earlier successful individual psychotherapy (Malan, et al., 1976).

The principal transference gratifications in group therapy are getting to know the therapist and other group members as people, and having real, personal relationships with them. There are many transference gratifications in having real relationships with the therapist and the other group members, including the wish to incorporate others, to belong to a family, to compete with siblings, and so forth.

The other prominent form of transference gratification in group therapy is physical contact between group members and between group members and the leader, but I have rarely seen patients in groups become greatly involved in physical contact with one another without the leader's demonstration that physical contact is permissible and desirable.

I doubt that the real relationships between group members or physical contact between group members lead to acting out with any greater frequency than occurs in individual psychotherapy, except in weekend groups that are thinly disguised get-togethers for sexually or socially frustrated people. On the rare occasions when sexual intimacy occurs between members of ongoing groups, it is almost invariably discussed and dealt with in the group.

Technical Error

Patients in a well-trained group may be less vulnerable to technical errors than patients in individual therapy who do not have the scrutiny of other concerned, knowledgeable persons, as well as their support. One must be careful, however, to see that the treatment needs of certain members of the group are not compromised by the treatment of others in the group.

Technical errors that are detected by the therapist but undetected by the group need only be dealt with by instituting more suitable interventions. Interventions (or failures to intervene) that have harmed a patient or the group as a whole need to be openly acknowledged by the therapist, as do errors detected by group members. Neither profuse apologies nor lengthy explanations are called for (Weiner, 1978). Patients know that therapists make mistakes. They can deal better with an acknowledged mistake than with a defensive therapist.

When Mrs. L. (p. 69) left therapy as the result of a transference/countertransference impasse with the therapist, the therapist and her therapy group dealt with the fact that Mrs. L. had been special to the therapist in a way that several of the group members envied. Those who had wished for a similar special relationship now expressed gratitude and relief that the therapist had maintained his neutrality with them and had thereby maintained his ability to treat them.

An appropriate discussion of a technical error by the therapist encourages group members to talk about the error as they see it, and facilitates expression of the group members' thoughts and feelings in response to the error. The group is entitled to acknowledgment of the error by the therapist, but is not entitled to a detailed explanation of the therapist's motivation, not because he or she is not accountable, but because an exploration of the therapist's motives changes the focus of discussion from the proper goal of the group: the members' understanding of themselves. The therapist, in addition to acknowledging his or her error, also assumes responsibility for avoiding a repetition of the error.

It is often difficult for group members to deal openly with their feelings about their therapist's error. They fear that their collective rage will annihilate the leader or cause him to desert the group. These fears are based on the group members' fears of their own aggression and of desertion. They project their fears onto the therapist, identify with him as the victim, and avoid putting him in the position that they fear to be in. Raising issues of the group's projective identification with the therapist and their fear of annihilating or being deserted by the therapist can facilitate their expression and the acceptance of negative feelings. Facing the group squarely and nondefensively also lets the group know that the therapist does not fear annihilation, does not intend to desert the group, and also does not expect the group to avoid the therapeutic process. By incorporating and identifying with the therapist's willingness to be responsible for his or her actions and their consequences, group members become more willing to risk new behaviors and to accept the responsibility for them.

If a therapist and a group are deadlocked for reasons unknown to all, the therapist can have a consultant join them as an observer or a coleader for a period of time, or can videotape their sessions for his or her own review, for the group's review, or for review with a consultant.

Coleadership

Coleadership is an intimate professional relationship that can greatly enhance therapy or create impasses. Coleaders must deal with difficulties that arise with patients and with the difficulties that arise form coleadership. Coleaders come to know each other as professionals and as people. Each confronts and supports the other, and works toward resolving their conflicts in the group or in their private meetings, depending on the relationship between the coleaders' difficulties and the group, and on the needs of the group members.

Coleadership Contract

The coleadership contract is as important in preventing impasses in therapy as the patient-therapist contract. It should be established by the prospective coleaders in a series of meetings before they actually begin the group. They must first establish why they want a coleader, and what they expect of coleadership. Beginning therapists often want a mentor. Experienced therapists often want company. They must also discuss their reactions to each other's professional style and, when pertinent, their reactions to each other's personality. These issues arise over and over again during the conduct of the group, and a foundation for this type of interchange must be established early if the coleaders are to function effectively.

Prospective coleaders must also discuss the size and composition of the projected group, their aims for the group, and the type of therapy they will employ. They need to determine how they will obtain new members for the group. If the group is to be composed of the coleaders' individual therapy patients or is to blend two existing groups, both prospective group leaders need to deal with their feelings about sharing their patients.

Each therapist may wish to keep the fees generated by patients he or she has referred to the group, but it is generally wiser to split the fees of all patients in the group in a proportion that the group leaders consider fair. The reason for splitting all fees is that one therapist will generally have greater access to new patients than the other, and the therapist who brings in fewer patients will soon resent working the same amount of time and assuming the same amount of responsibility as his or her coleader, but for fewer wages.

They also need to agree on group rules, the admission of new members, the length and frequency of sessions, the time of day at which sessions will be held, and a time to discuss the group.

The division of leader-patient and leader-leader responsibilities is also important. A more senior coleader may be designated as the principal therapist and as mentor for his or her coleader. A medical coleader bears the responsibility for the type and dosage of medication used to augment the group members' psychotherapy.

Selection of a Coleader

The mutual selection of coleaders for an ongoing psychotherapy group requires much care because these groups have the greatest potential to stimulate untoward reactions between the therapists and therefore require a coleadership relationship that can withstand the confrontations needed to resolve conflict (McGee & Schuman, 1970). Coleaders are most effective if they have common professional backgrounds and similar therapeutic orientations. On the other hand, their effectiveness is enchanced if they have differences in personality that allow them to work in a complementary fashion (Davis & Lohr, 1971).

The matching of coleaders is of less importance in the brief, highly structured treatment of couples and families (Yalom, 1975). Masters and Johnson (1970), however, recommend male-female cotherapy teams for the treatment of marital sexual problems with each therapist serving as an advocate for the same-sexed patient. A male-female coleadership may be useful in other group techniques because a same-sexed therapist may facilitate appropriate identification for some people. Seeing the therapists interchange roles during the course of the group may also be a useful way to cut through sexual stereotypes, such as female nurturing or male authoritarianism.

The Coleaders' Relationship

The relationship between cotherapists calls for more self-disclosure than the ordinary therapist-patient relationship. Knowing each others' reputation or knowing one another socially is not enough. Close friendship may be detrimental, as the honest reactions of one therapist to the other may be suppressed for the sake of maintaining needed emotional supplies from the other.

The coleaders review their reactions to the group members and to each other in their pregroup and postgroup sessions. In this way, the irrational elements of the cotherapy relationship can be brought to the fore and not acted out in the group, as the following example indicates.

> A male coleader felt it imperative that he protect his female coleader from the anger of an adolescent group. In joint supervision, it became clear that his perception of his coleader's fragility was incorrect and served to protect and augment his sense of potency. The consequence for the group, had the problem not been aired and resolved, would have been the establishment of a group norm of masculine potency and feminine helplessness.

It is not necessary that coleaders know about each other's early life, but they must understand each other's major values in life and the reality problems that impinge upon their working relationship. They must be able to compliment and to criticize each other. As in the therapeutic relationship, there must be some gratification of ordinary object needs to make the relationship worth continuing. An absence of emotional reaction to one another suggests that important elements in the relationship are being glossed over and that crucial elements in the group itself are not being faced. On the other hand, the development of intense emotions, whether loving or angry, suggests the operation of factors outside the real relationship between the cotherapists and calls for an appraisal of the unconscious forces in operation. Transferences may be in operation, as well as displacements from each other's daily life. If unable to identify and work through the obvious areas of irrationality in their relationship, they can make use of several means to clarify matters. Group members can be asked to comment on their perception of the cotherapist relationship, audio or videotapes can be reviewed after sessions, or outside consultation may be sought.

Cotherapists reveal more of themselves to group members than do individual leaders of a group. They reveal not only their style of relating to different personalities and problems within the group, but also their style of relating to peers and emotionally important persons. Because cotherapists tend to relax their defenses more than solo therapists, they may be more subject to manipulation, which can lead to impasses.

Group members can develop feelings about the therapists' special relationship with one another that cannot be obtained by themselves. This can restimulate acting upon strivings from all levels of psychosexual development. Feelings of envy and rivalry with the coleaders are even more intensely stimulated by obvious affection of the coleaders for one another. Married cotherapists frequently work with couples in the treatment of marital sexual dysfunction. There have been no reports of the same transference difficulties in working with couples that occur in ongoing, unstructured groups. The highly structured format and the relative briefness of the treatment may account for the diminished transference-based resistances to treatment.

Patients can become confused by differing therapeutic styles. If one cotherapist is more open, patients may assume that the other does not trust the group members or that he or she has something to hide. On the other hand, the more disclosing therapist may be seen as more vulnerable and in need of protection by the group.

Even when group leaders' styles are compatible, there may be problems in their interpersonal relationship that directly or indirectly damage group members. Direct damage comes about when group leaders get so caught up in their own relationship that group members' needs are ignored. Indirect damage results from group members' awareness of hypocrisy and deceit in the relationship between the leaders. Coleaders who are obviously having an extramarital affair with each other certainly raise a question in the group members' minds about dealing openly with interpersonal issues.

As suggested above, the intimacy of the cotherapy relationship may be a hazard for the emotionally frustrated or deprived therapist. The cotherapy relationship can be a burden in other ways that make it function antitherapeutically. Cotherapists who are unwilling to spend the necessary time discussing the content and direction of their sessions and who do not agree on a common pathway may lead the group in divergent directions. Undercutting one's cotherapist may be subtle or overt. Disrespect for one's coleader can be conveyed by a glance, a shake of the head, or an outright contradiction on an important point.

There is room for overt disagreement between cotherapists. More important than whether they agree or disagree is how they manage their disagreements. If disagreements are aired with respect for each other's point of view and are resolved by negotiation based on the validity of each point of view, they may serve as useful models for patients.

Disadvantages for the Therapist

There are significant drawbacks to cotherapy. A cotherapist is one more person with whom to contend. The coleaders must provide adequate time to confer after each group session. They must discuss the entry of new group members and agree on the treatment approach and timing of every new person's entry into the group. This expenditure of time and energy may be experienced as a drain, especially for those therapists who have difficulty with peer relationships. Each may stimulate the immature aspects of the other with resultant competition for the favor of group members or expression of hostile feelings of one group leader toward the other, or may use the protective presence of his or her cotherapist to act out infantile urges.

The cotherapists' relationship can be a model for appropriate dependency, conflict resolution, and cooperation that can be applied by group members to their own interpersonal relations. Cotherapists must also be careful, however, that they do not burden the group with their disagreements at a time when the group is already overwhelmed by dealing with its members' conflicts. For this reason, it is wise if the coleaders sacrifice a bit of spontaneity and discuss in their extragroup session whether or not to disagree openly in the regular group session. Modeling conflict resolution is less important at one stage of group's development than at another, and cotherapists can draw the attention of the group members away from their own inner turmoil into that created by the group leaders.

Disadvantages for the Patients

If the cotherapists have widely divergent techniques or points of view, it is very easy for patients to be caught up in a defensive struggle over who is right instead of examining themselves in the light of the two divergent views or techniques. Unresolved problems in communication and cooperation between the coleaders can significantly undermine group members' hopes of resolving their own interpersonal tensions. The experience of being used by one leader to express negative feelings toward the other may recapitulate patients' earlier experiences in a way that stifles growth and reaffirms the conviction that interpersonal relationships must be managed by covert manipulation rather than direct confrontation or cooperation.

Splitting of the transference may reduce its intensity so much that it cannot be dealt with. While this is an advantage in some repressive therapies, it is a distinct disadvantage in an evocative group psychotherapy.

On the other hand, seeing more of the therapists as real people than one would with a single therapist may be a disadvantage for the patients whose treatment requires an idealized therapist.

Summary

The comparability of the dropout rate from group psychotherapy to individual psychotherapy is surprising, in view of group therapy's greater complexity. This similarity in dropout rate may be partly attributable to attrition in the preparatory individual sessions prior to the group, and to therapists making greater efforts to prepare patients for group therapy than for individual therapy.

Reports comparing the casualty rate for group therapy with individual therapy are difficult to assess because they are largely based on encounter groups, not psychotherapy groups.

The possibility of greater harm in group psychotherapy is offset by its advantages, primarily the provision of a neutral, supportive interpersonal arena for developing interpersonal awareness and trying out new ways of being one's self.

Group therapies require a more explicit contract than individual psychotherapy because the group norms cannot be altered for each newly entering member. The codified therapeutic contract, or group rules, makes dealing with contractual violations a more important part of group therapy than individual therapy. Contract violations are, however, used as points of departure for discussion and not as reasons to punish group members.

Coleadership adds a positive dimension to group therapy by extending the leaders' awareness and their capacity to react, but also adds a complicating relationship that must be dealt with by establishing a coleadership contract and by dealing with the issues that arise between the coleaders.

Couple and Family Therapy

9

Couple and family therapies are repressive methods that focus on current interactions in existing interpersonal relationships. The goals of couple and family therapy are usually stated in behavioral terms: fostering communication of thoughts and feelings, shifting unhealthy or inflexible roles and coalitions, increasing interpersonal options, and puncturing family myths (Glick & Kessler, 1980). As pathological interactions or communications develop in the presence of the therapist, he or she clarifies, confronts, intercedes, or acts as a go between (Zuk, 1966). The couple or family therapist treats the couple or family as a unit, thereby avoiding the tendency to scapegoat individuals that goes with identifying one person as ill or in need of treatment. Couple and family therapists often teach and model healthy behavior, but in spite of their active focus on conscious behavior, they do not ignore intrapsychic dynamics and unconscious mental processes (Framo, 1970).

The chief difficulty in dealing directly with a couple or a family is that one is dealing with well-established patterns of relationship (Bloch, 1976), whereas the individual therapy relationship develops over time, enabling the therapist to point to the difference in the quality of the relationship as transference develops. Particularly in family therapy, one deals with the primary relationships that are the basis for transference relationships. Those primary relationships are mutually reinforcing, where transference relationships to the alert individual therapist are not reinforced if they are to the patient's psychological detriment.

Gurman and Kniskern (1978) found a 5.4 percent deterioration rate in 15 studies of nonbehavioral marital and family therapy. Glick and Kessler (1980) estimate a negative outcome rate of 5 to 10 percent, and present an outline of negative outcomes following the model of Hadley and Strupp (1976): the worsening of present problems, the development of new symptoms, the use of therapy by one member against another, interminable treatment, attempting to reach beyond the couple or family's grasp, and loss of hope. Glick and Kessler also point out that separation or divorce is not a useful measure of negative outcomes, because they may be in the best interest of the couple and their children.

Couple Therapy

Certain resistances are specific to couple and family therapy (Solomon, 1969). They can be categorized as resistances to interaction and family-specific resistances.

The resistances to interaction are: refusing to bring up new or meaningful information while encouraging others to do so; asking questions of other family members to avoid one's own engagement; disrupting conversation on important subjects; refusing to talk in front of other family members; using a second language to exclude family members; and talking about a member only when he or she is absent.

The family-specific resistances are: avoiding dealing with marital conflict; scapegoating; denying the possibility of change; denying change that has occurred in a family member; denying a family member's expressed affect; protecting a family member so that he or she does not change; family secrets, injunctions against family disloyalty; threatening to leave the family if change occurs; or threatening to abandon a family member if he or she leaves.

There are many ways to work with a couple (here defined as two people with a strong emotional tie, whether or not legally married). Each can be seen individually by the same therapist. Each can be seen individually by different therapists. They can be seen jointly by the same therapist, or can work together as a couple in a group, to name a few of the possibilities. The emphasis in this section will be on working with the couple as an individual couple but, before doing so, it will be useful to consider the indications for various types of therapeutic approaches to a couple.

Joint treatment of a couple is usually indicated when the partners see their problems as interpersonal and when they wish to remain together out of mutual respect and affection, not out of fear of financial compromise or fear of loneliness. They cannot be treated jointly, however, when one has insufficient ego strength for coping, when there is intense rivalry between the spouses, when one of the couple is not interested in change, and when the structure of their relationship is such that one partner's gain is always at the other's expense (Weiner, 1975).

Individual therapy of a member of a couple is indicated when that person sees his or her problem as intrapsychic, when there is an obvious treatable emotional disorder such as a depression, when there is a strong need or wish for an individual therapeutic relationship, and when there is need to reveal material that might jeopardize the relationship with the partner. The therapist should avoid making a contract for individual therapy with one member of a couple if it is part of that person's attempt to escape a realistic confrontation with his or her partner, or if it is an attempt to enlist the therapist in blaming the other partner.

Grunebaum et al. (1969) have worked out an overall schema for dealing with troubled couples based on three parameters: (1) whether the couple's problems are in their relationship and, if so, the extent to which the couple is committed and able to work on them; (2) whether the perceived problems are confined to their relationship or are more general; and (3) the extent to which the problems are acute and ego-alien (as opposed to chronic and ego syntonic) in both partners. If problems in the couple's relationship are not a significant issue, or if the couple is uncommitted or unable to work on them, but there are indentifiable personal difficulties, individual treatment for one or both members of the couple is indicated. If the couple's symptoms are experienced largely within the relationship, the couple should be seen together when problems are acute and ego-alien. When chronic, ego syntonic problems occur, couples group therapy is indicated.

Contractual Issues

The evaluation contract for a couple, in addition to requiring historical information that the therapist derives from direct contact with each person, also provides for the therapist to sample the couple's interactions. The therapist uses part of the evaluation time to allow the couple to interact in his or her presence. Some therapists find it useful to see how the partners deal with each other in performing a task that requires cooperation. The task may be to plan a vacation or to play a game together (Ravich, 1969).

The treatment contract offered to a couple incorporates the three elements of emotionally healthy behavior described earlier. The same contract is offered to each member of the couple, but each will often attempt to negotiate a special contract for him or herself. Although the content of the treatment contract is generally the same for both members, it may involve different behaviors for each, depending on the couple's power structure.

One of the four general types of power distribution will usually be seen (Martin, 1976): power may be equally divided; one may be dominant; neither may allow the other power in the relationship; or there may be total avoidance of individual power issues through the couple's insistence on avoiding conflict for the sake of maintaining a stable relationship. Therapists ordinarily attempt to foster an equal power relationship. Characteristically, the dominant partner in the dominant-submissive relationship tries to help the therapist label his or her partner as sick or uncooperative and, therefore, undeserving of equal power. The submissive partner tries to obtain special exemptions based on inequity or on his or her persecuted position, and may actively encourage an alliance between the therapist and the dominant partner to reinforce his or her submissive position. The therapist negotiates for control of sessions with partners who habitually undercut each other and tries to come between partners whose pseudomutuality blocks their individual development. The therapist must be sensitive to the need of each couple for its type of power relationship and to push for a shift only when each person can obtain support in some other way.

Most therapists take a neutral stance about preserving the couple's relationship and emphasize what is best for the partners as individuals. The therapist is entitled to feel that preservation of a marital relationship is primary, but he or she should make this bias explicit.

If the therapist feels it is inappropriate to work with the couple toward a primary goal of preserving the relationship, he or she should say so. This may spare the couple long hours of fruitless discussion, or may force them to reappraise the situation (Weiner, 1975).

If the couple wants to work toward maintaining their relationship against the advice of the therapist, they can be referred to a professional who is willing to work with them on their terms. The first therapist's feeling that the marital relationship cannot be helped can foster a better alliance of the couple with each other and the new therapist.

The vignette below illustrates the rapid assessment of a marital relationship and the tailoring of a therapeutic contract to the needs of each person.

> A couple was referred for last-ditch counseling by their lawyer. They had been seriously talking divorce for five years. The notion of divorce had been entertained strongly by the wife early in their 15-year marriage but she had decided against it because she was pregnant. They were seen together for the initial interview. The wife was in her forties. Her businessman-husband was in his late fifties. It was her first marriage, his second. The wife launched into bitter, tearful reproaches about her husband's involvement with his mother, his son by his first marriage, and his business. She said her husband had ignored her stepson's fondling of their daughter, and voiced resentment of her role, which she regarded as legalized prostitution. While his wife tearfully and angrily voiced her complaints, frequently giving him a killing stare, the husband sat silent and slowly shook his head from side to side as if to say, "She's really crazy." He then stated quietly and simply that he liked living the way he did. He had risen from poverty, and now was suc-

> cessful, and intended to keep himself successful. His job was the number one priority. His children were second. All other considerations came afterward.
>
> The wife appeared strongly motivated for help. Initially, she hoped to change her husband. The therapist told her that her husband had no wish to change. When asked why she wished to remain married to him, she replied that she didn't want to hurt their teenage children (his child by his first marriage was grown). The therapist said that the children would be more damaged in the present situation than if the couple separated. She then said that divorced life would be difficult and that she would need help adjusting.
>
> It was suggested that they work toward a divorce because the husband was unmotivated to change. There would be no further need to see him. The wife wanted therapy through the adjustment period. Any problems the children might develop would be dealt with by appropriate referral at the time they appeared. The next appointment was made with the wife. The interview was concluded, but the husband stayed on briefly with his wife's permission to reassure the therapist that he had no animosity (and also no love) for his wife, but that he would help in any way he could.

The wife's initial motivation was to be seen as maligned and helpless; the husband's was to be seen as benevolent and helpful. Each was looking for a way out that would be acceptable to his or her own conscience and tailored to his or her own assets and liabilities. Beyond encouraging divorce, dealing in a constructive way with one in the presence of the other seemed impossible. The therapist elected to operate with them at a concrete "do this" level, because he felt that pointing out defense mechanisms would serve only to intensify them. He felt it more appropriate to defer discussion of the wife's projection and her difficulty dealing with her own feelings until he could spend enough time with her to establish himself as a helper.

The validity of the therapeutic contract for a couple depends in large measure on the honesty of each member of the couple. Many people who express willingness to work as a couple are biding time until their married paramour's divorce decree becomes final or stay because of the financial advantage of remaining in the realtionship. Carrying on sham therapy can be avoided if the therapist sees each spouse individually and assures each one that he will respect his or her confidence. Under these circumstances, most people admit their conscious hidden agendas and can be induced to give up their pretense at therapy or to become genuinely involved.

Another invalid contract is made by the person who wants to change the behavior of a partner who is not interested in change. The therapist must help the complaining person to face the issue squarely and to live with the partner as he or she is or to get out. If, however, there is clear evidence that the offending partner's behavior is strongly stimulated by one seeking to change him or her, individual therapy is indicated for the partner who voiced the original complaint.

Ordinarily, an impasse will result if one contracts to work with a couple jointly when one of the two is psychologically decompensating. There are exceptions to this general rule, as the following case indicates.

> A woman whose history suggested a transient psychotic episode shortly before her marriage had begun to feel suspicious of her husband. Because they had intercourse infrequently, she suspected an extramarital liaison.
>
> Her husband, a passive man who was doing poorly at his job, was feeling generally overwhelmed. In joint sessions, the therapist pointed out to him that his wife's suspicion was reasonable, based on his behavior with her. During the one individual session the therapist had with him (he felt that more than one might make her suspect a collusion between husband and therapist), he suggested that his wife needed him to be more sexually aggressive instead of waiting for her to invite him. The husband discovered that when he was more sexually aggressive, she was less irritable and suspicious.

Under most circumstances, it is probably better to treat a mental illness directly lest a severe decompensation should occur as a result of a therapist's intervention. Occasionally, a shift in the family structure resulting from the therapist's intervention as described above will turn the tide.

Process Issues

An important part of the process of couple therapy is making explicit the expectations each member of the couple has of each other. Sager (1976) refers to this process as exploring the marriage contract, which he defines as the expressed and unexpressed, conscious and unconscious concepts of obligation within the marital relationship and the expected benefits to be derived. He points out that while each spouse may be aware of his or her own needs and wishes to varying degrees, he or she does not usually realize that his or her attempts to fulfill the partner's needs are based on the covert assumption that his or her own needs will thereby be fulfilled. When significant aspects of the contract are inevitably unfulfilled, and especially those which lie out of awareness, the disappointed partner may react with rage and depression and provoke marital discord as though a formal agreement had been broken. This is especially true when one spouse feels that he or she has fulfilled his or her obligation, but that the other spouse has not.

Sager does not use the word contract as it is employed in this work, but his concept is valuable. Marital relationships are sometimes contractual, but are more commonly based on implicit, unilateral expectations engrafted on romantic love (Weiner, 1980). The common bilateral assumption underlying marital relationships is that with love as the binding force, all tensions are capable of resolution; with love as the primary motivation, each person will want to do what is best for the other. Healthy couples soon learn that explicit agreement is necessary to avoid endless frustration. Poorly integrated persons cling to their view of reality without willingness to accept their failure to meet the real needs of their partners or the destructiveness of retaliating against partners who have failed to live up to their unstated expectations (Lewis et al., 1976), as the following case illustrates.

> A newly married man sought help with a potency problem. He had been unable to penetrate his wife because of erectile difficulty. He felt a failure. She felt angry and frustrated. Taken at face value, this was a case for an educational approach to sexual relations. An exploration of their marriage contract, however, clearly suggested another approach.
>
> He had proposed marriage because he felt romantic love for her, and was strongly attracted to her sexually. She had little romantic interest in him, and no sexual interest. She contended, however, that if he were a real man he would penetrate her and satisfy her sexually. She had a number of complaints about him that made it difficult for her to allow him

near her. He was too heavy, too short, had dandruff, did not speak clearly, and was not sufficiently aggressive on his job.

Further exploration revealed that much of the husband's push to marry came from a conscious decision to be married before he was 30. Much of her decision was an attempt to break from her family without having to be on her own.

Neither could fulfill the other's wishes under the circumstances. He was not the tall, dark, handsome man she wished for, and she was not the loving wife he wanted.

Their marital impasse became an impasse in therapy. Although the husband succeeded in penetrating his wife after a few joint sessions, she withdrew sexually, claiming that she was still not satisfied, and that she would not be frustrated any further. At that point, the therapist resolved the impasse by insisting that each partner be completely open about what he or she wanted from the relationship. When each faced the fact that they could not live up to each other's expectations, the wife moved out, and the couple divorced shortly afterward. Separation of the two parties was the best solution to their contractual dilemma. The husband stayed in therapy briefly to explore and work on some of the problems which had led him into this difficult situation.

As therapy with a couple progresses, it may become clear that formation of an adequate therapeutic alliance is not possible if both spouses are seen together, or by the same therapist, as occurred with the couple described below.

A couple sought treatment because of severe conflict throughout their years of marriage. The wife said she felt too insecure to leave her husband, for whom she felt no great love. He said that he loved her and would do anything to save the marriage. She felt she was the crazy, maladjusted one, and gave a lifelong history of self-dissatisfaction and overreaction to frustration. She complained of frigidity, and found her husband physically unattractive.

Both were strongly motivated for help, she for herself and he for the marriage. The therapist felt that there was sufficient potential for cooperation between them, and that the best place to start was with the marital relationship, reasoning that when their interpersonal turmoil died down, she would begin work on her intrapsychic problems.

There was an initial period of improvement which seemed related to their awareness of mutual provocation. Through the three-month period of joint treatment, it became increasingly

> apparent that the wife wanted an individual therapeutic relationship and that she felt desperately in need of change within herself. Because the therapist felt there would be a disastrous repetition of her unsuccessful rivalry with her siblings if he saw each of them individually, they elected for the husband to work with another therapist while the wife continued with the present therapist. Several months later, the wife was able to climax during intercourse for the first time. Her relationship with her husband temporarily improved as she began to separate him from her idealized image of her father, but even so she found that she still did not love him. They eventually separated and divorced.

In this instance, the wife's growth needs were such that continued joint therapy was impossible. The therapist avoided the antitherapeutic alliance of the husband and the therapist against the wife that would have formed if they had continued in joint therapy.

Transference and countertransference are less of a problem in couple therapy than in individual psychotherapy because the relationship between the therapist and patient is less intense and because the focus is on the interaction between partners, and not between either one of them and the therapist.

The therapist's attitudes toward sharing of responsibility, marital fidelity, and child-rearing practices will, of course, affect his or her attitude toward one or both members of the couple, and the therapist must, therefore, be aware of his or her prejudices and stereotypes of ideal marriage and child rearing.

Family Therapy

Family therapy is a special type of repressive therapy in which direct involvement with the family in action provides grist for the therapeutic mill. The therapist is more than a participant observer. He is an active go-between who also takes the responsibility for restructuring aspects of family communication (Zuk, 1972).

Glick and Kessler (1980) suggest a number of indications for couples or family therapy. The first indication is when the identified patient's symptoms reflect difficulties within the family as a whole, as often occurs with the school phobic child. A family approach may also be useful when other members of the family develop symptoms as the result of the therapy of one member. It may also be useful when a person's primary concerns are family relationships, when a person seems better able to use an interactive rather than an interpretive mode of therapy, when one family member is psychiatrically hospitalized, and when the family has difficulty coping with the loss of a member.

Although family therapy has been described as a powerful treatment technique, I am more impressed with the information that can be derived from a family diagnostic interview than with family therapy as a potent form of intervention. Family therapy is often not possible because of the varying levels of motivation of each family member and their varying perceptions of therapy. For some family members, family sessions are further entrapment in a situation from which they wish to escape. For others, it is a step away from age-appropriate autonomy.

Contractual Issues

Members of families occasionally present with a request for family therapy. More often, the mother or both parents seek help in dealing with one or more of the children. A series of family diagnostic interviews will ordinarily allow the therapist to judge if a family approach is appropriate. Just as in the joint therapy of couples, the family must be able to conceive of its problems as interactional if family therapy is to be useful. The family diagnostic sessions enable the therapist to determine if the family can operate in this way.

The same caveats that apply to couples therapy apply in family therapy. Family therapy should not be undertaken when it helps a family member to blame others and to avoid looking at him or herself or when the most powerful family member cannot be enlisted in a common effort.

The contract in family therapy must be made with all of the participating members of the family at each one's level of understanding and ability to negotiate for him or herself. The parents' level of understanding will often differ from the children's, but it is difficult to say in which direction. Some parents have less apparent understanding of the therapeutic contract than the children for whom they seek help. Negotiating a therapeutic contract allows the therapist to demonstrate his or her roles as clarifier, go-between, and structure provider. Negotiating the contract also helps diagnose the family's level of function.

The family therapist strives for a contract to clarify what is communicated by whom, to whom, and with what intent. Haley (1972) secures agreement among family members to work toward open negotiation without collusion, each person representing and being entitled to his or her own point of view. Family members agree to the contract but soon begin to violate it as they return to their usual means of dealing with their interpersonal environment during family therapy sessions.

The family therapist does not emphasize understanding the present in terms of the historical past. He does not open old wounds. They are usually opened by family members themselves as a means to punish or to control others. The therapist moves the family toward a healthy interaction in the here and now. He contracts with no single family member, but with the family as a unit, thus emphasizing the need of the family to work together, if in no other way than in dealing with the therapist. In many instances, clarifying why the family is seeing a therapist and attempting to make a contract sufficiently mobilizes the family's resources for its members to deal more effectively with one another.

Just as it is wise to interview family members separately to allow them to speak freely, it is often wise to make separate contracts with the children and the adults. It is important to emphasize to the children that the therapist will offer a measure of protection from their parents so that they can speak freely during the therapeutic hour. The parents are asked to listen until the children are finished speaking.

An important part of the first formal therapy session with a family is contracting to deal with a specific issue first. The therapist asks the family to agree on the problem they wish to deal with first. This prevents the therapist from pushing his or her values on the family and allows the family to begin working at a level at which it can function. It is important that all family members agree. For example, it is not useful for the mother and the children to agree that the father's drinking be stopped unless the father agrees as well.

There are many families in which not all members are able to participate in the therapeutic sessions, or in which the therapy sessions would be obstructed by the presence of certain members, such as an active preverbal child. The agreement that certain family members will be included and that certain others will be excluded should be part of the family therapy contract.

The following example shows an impasse in dealing with a family as a whole and resolution of the impasse by developing a treatment relationship with the family member who was most motivated for help.

> Mrs. A.L. sought family therapy to help her deal with her sons who were 11, 13, and 15. She had deserted her alcoholic husband and her children four years previously because, in her words, "They were driving me crazy." She had moved to another city, had divorced her husband, had remarried, and had lived happily in that city until the sudden death of her new spouse. Shortly after his death, she decided to return to her native city and care for her younger two children. They had been placed in an orphanage by their father, who had severe lung disease in addition to his alcoholism, and so was no longer able to manage them. Mrs. A.L.'s conscious motivation for returning to her children was to atone for having deserted them. She was determined to raise them to adulthood on her own.
>
> The therapist agreed to see Mrs. A.L. and her two younger sons (the oldest still lived with his father). The two boys reluctantly joined their mother in the therapist's office, participated to a limited extent, but spent the bulk of their time provoking, blaming, and threatening each other and their mother. Eventually, Mrs. A.L. and the therapist were forced to recognize that including the children was of little value because of their unwillingness to assume responsibility for their own behavior and their inability to view their own behavior in a neutral way, although each had no difficulty pointing out the other's provocations. She and the therapist agreed that she was the one with the ability and the motivation to deal with the problem and that she was the logical one to counsel.
>
> Mrs. A.L. wanted to control her children and to stay calm. The therapist told her that she could not control her children if she wanted to maintain her peace of mind, and that if she wanted to live with them, the best she could do was to seek ways to help her stay calm while attempting to deal with them.

After a time, she saw that she could not control both children at the same time. She found that the most effective means to deal with them was to separate their living quarters and to deal with them individually. In addition, it was also useful to threaten them individually with what they feared most, abandonment by their mother. When things really got out of hand, she took each one aside and conducted a rational discussion about the places he could choose to live as an alternative to living with her. Both children settled down substantially after each of these discussions.

About nine months after her return, her ex-husband died and her oldest child returned to her. The younger children were frightened by the return of their older brother, who they feared would kill them. Their fear was probably based on awareness of their own provocativeness, because he was the most level headed of the three children.

Because of this woman's determination to make the situation work and her refusal to be driven away by the tantrums of her younger children, they developed respect for her and for each other, and after nearly three years, entered a mutually cooperative relationship.

In this family, the only one who could perceive the therapist as a family helper was the mother. The children were only able to see the therapist as someone against whom to rebel and with whom to demonstrate their potency and their willingness to risk almost any consequence to avoid the feelings of helplessness they had experienced in the orphanage. Using their fear of returning to the orphanage proved to be the best way to bring about change in the family relationship.

Process Issues

A significant process issue in family therapy is overidentification with one family member or one group of family members. Overidentification results in alliance with the family's tactic of blaming instead of cooperating.

Another potential source of impasse stems from insisting that the family continue to function as an integrated unit when one or more members is ready to graduate and move on. Both of these antitherapeutic alliances can stem from the therapist's value system, from countertransference, and from the therapist's wish to avoid dealing with his or her feelings about his role in his own family or his feelings about members of his family growing up and moving away.

Inadequate therapeutic alliances occur when the therapist is too eager to begin work with the family as a whole and neglects the need to form an individual relationship with as many of the family members as possible.

Adverse transference reactions are not a great problem in family therapy because the focus is kept away from the therapist and on the interactions between family members. Transference gratification does not become a great issue. The more common issue in family therapy is one of appropriate or inappropriate gratification of the needs and wishes of various family members.

The chief technical errors in family therapy are overemphasis on understanding family interactions or on forcing the family to interact without thinking about what is going on. Therapists trained in one-to-one psychoanalytic psychotherapy tend to overemphasize understanding. Therapists schooled in the interactional approaches tend to err in the direction of too much action. Action and understanding are both necessary, but the degree of each must be tailored to each family's needs (Chasin & Grunebaum, 1980).

Paradoxical Intervention

Paradoxical intervention is a last-ditch technique for resolving impasses in couples and family psychotherapy. It has also been named therapeutic paradox, paradoxical intention, and going with the resistance (Goldberg, 1980), and is probably the essence of Milton Erickson's (1980) hypnotic work with patients.

Paradoxical interventions engage otherwise resistant couples and families in a power struggle. The therapist deliberately imposes a task or a point of view that makes no sense to the patients, or is seen by the patients as counter to their best interest (Whitaker, 1978). Or he merely capitalizes on their oppositionalism. The people in treatment, in struggling against the therapist's (sometimes unreasonable) attitude or task, inadvertently act in a reasonable manner which is in their own best interest. The therapist's suggestion is usually a logical extension of the couple's or family's complaint about one another, like suggesting that a marital partner have an affair to improve his or her relationship with the spouse, that parents send a child to boarding school instead of trying to deal with him or her (Whitaker, 1975), or that a father not involve himself in family meetings with the therapist (Puryear, 1979).

Paradoxical interventions directly or indirectly promote patients' assuming responsibility for dealing with what they fear and for doing what they had formerly felt helpless to do, thereby countering the tendency of people who assign responsibility to others and to external events to place the responsibility for therapeutic change on the therapist. They are a last-ditch technique because they set the therapist against the patient and require sufficient cohesiveness in the couple or family so that it can unite against the therapist. If there is insufficient cohesiveness, the paradoxical intervention serves only to reinforce a feeling of futility in attempting to solve problems or in turning to mental health professionals. The hoped-for result of a paradoxical intervention is that the couple or family will unite, and that they will communicate clearly and act in concert in at least one area of their life together.

There are at least two mechanisms in paradoxical interventions. They extend the patients' well-rationalized irrational behavior or thinking to the point that its irrationality is more readily seen. In other words, the therapist talks more irrationally than his or her patients so that they can see their own irrationality. Even when the couple or family fails to see the therapist's irrationality as the logical extension of their thinking and behavior, they can still unite against the therapist instead of blaming and fearing each other. In the latter case, there is no change in the family's psychological mechanisms, only a change in the direction in which they are employed.

Because this type of intervention pits the therapist against the patient, it is less useful in individual psychotherapy than in a therapy in which the patients have someone in the same situation to turn to. When employed with couples or families, paradoxical interventions also take advantage of the tendency of groups to unite when faced with a threat from without. The art in using paradox is in timing and in the ability of the therapist to convey real concern in spite of the ridiculousness of his or her suggestions (Whitaker, 1975).

A paradoxical intervention will end therapy if it is employed before the therapist has established a positive therapeutic alliance. The therapist must also demonstrate that he or she is capable of rational thought before making an irrational suggestion. The patient's awareness that the therapist probably has a rational basis for his or her irrational stand enables the family to take the suggestion seriously. In addition, the couple or family must know the therapist well enough to be aware that he or she is not making an irrational suggestion to mock them, humiliate them, or get rid of them, and that he is attempting in his own way to break up an impasse.

Whitaker (1975) takes an irrational statement made by a family member, such as "I can't stand my husband," and builds on it by suggesting a logical next step. He suggests that the woman leave her husband. As she balks and brings up reasons why she should not leave her husband, he continues to make suggestions based on the premise that she can't stand her husband until she acknowledges that her tie to her husband is stronger than her wish to leave. He also actively competes for control of couples and families and forces them to establish a workable inner structure, if for no other reason than to deal with the threat of being ordered about by a crazy person outside of the family structure.

Paradoxical interventions differ from counterprojective techniques in that they pit the therapist against the patient. Counterprojective techniques make it clear that the therapist is an ally, not an enemy, and increase the distance between the therapist and transference figures with whom he or she might be identified. Paradoxical interventions ignore transference and make the therapist into a caricature of an unhealthy parent. He or she is arbitrary, intrusive, concrete, and will not negotiate. The patients' reaction is to become better parents to themselves.

Paradoxical interventions share with the counterintrojective technique the therapist's adoption of the role of persecutor. The counterintrojective method, however, is used with the transference in mind. The therapist identifies him or herself with the introjected persecuting objects in the patient's ego and with the critical aspect of the patient's superego in the hope of directing his anger away from his ego. It also involves splitting the therapeutic relationship between a nurturing therapist and a persecuting therapist so that the patient still has someone with whom he or she can ally.

The chief drawback of the paradoxical intervention is that the couple or family may reject the therapist as totally irrational and may discontinue therapy. In many cases, this is a desirable outcome because long-term involvement with some highly dysfunctional families could pose ever-increasing dilemmas for the therapist that could not be dealt with by the continued use of paradoxical techniques. The continued use of paradox in treatment would result in the family or coúple not knowing when to take the therapist seriously.

Another drawback to the use of paradox is that it provides a ready vehicle for the therapist to act out countertransference feelings without adequate awareness of what he or she is acting out. Paradox is probably best employed by a mature, self-aware professional. The younger professional can most safely use paradox after consulting with a more experienced colleague, making certain that all other avenues have been exhausted, and carefully deciding on the dosage and timing of the paradoxical interventions to be used.

Summary

Couples and family therapy are repressive techniques that are best used when members of a couple or family experience their difficulties as relationship problems with their cohabitors, spouses, or families.

Couples and family therapies founder when they become involved with intrapsychic dynamics and when they fail to focus on here-and-now relationships, and when the therapist does not actively intervene in family communication and activities. The therapist actively challenges pathological power structures, sides with family members who require protection, and supplies information about healthy family interaction. Therapists also serve as models of healthy communication and interaction.

The important difference between couples and family therapy and other therapies is that therapists enter an already established social system that they must try partially to disrupt. The therapist's attempts to disrupt pathological communication and behavior within couples and families are frequently met with massive resistances that may require the therapist to struggle actively with the family to assume charge during treatment sessions.

Couples and family therapies are useful means to prevent designating a family member as ill and using him or her as a scapegoat, but they carry the risk of failing to identify a person who requires individual attention for a treatable emotional disorder. There are, however, many reports of severe psychiatric disorders that have become less symptomatic and less damaging to the family when the family as a whole is dealt with (Glick & Kessler, 1980).

Paradoxical intervention, in which the therapist takes an irrational stand to highlight the family's irrationality or to provoke the family to unite, has been recommended for dealing with highly resistive families, but because it sets the therapist against the family, it has very limited usefulness except as a final desperate effort to deal with a couple or a family or as a short-term crisis intervention technique.

10

Summary

From a contractual standpoint, an impasse results from the therapist's failure to depict psychotherapy to prospective patients in such a way that they feel hopeful of securing their goals for themselves, or from failure to structure the therapeutic experience so that patients can be taught constructive coping mechanisms or can learn about themselves through the development and resolution of nodal points in therapy.

From the process standpoint, an impasse results from the therapist's failure to teach the patients useful skills or his or her failure to develop and capitalize on nodal points in therapy.

Impasses also result from allowing certain aspects of therapy to get out of hand, such as the therapist's expectations of the patient. Overexpectation may tax patients' egos to the point of decompensation or stimulate their guilt to the point that they cannot escape their own self-criticism. Underexpectation may relegate a patient to living a constricted, unrewarding life that could have been ameliorated had the therapist been better able to see the patient's assets. Overenthusiastic cultivation of transference feelings, or too vigorous attempts to deal with the patient's liabilities, may result in prolonged defensive regression or the unnecessary intensification of suffering.

We need not be defensive about making mistakes, or having mistakes accumulate and become impasses if we have secured adequate professional training, performed an adequate evaluation of the patient, obtained the patient's consent and enlisted his or her cooperation, and are capable of carrying out the treatment we propose. Mistakes and impasses can be diagnostic and therapeutic tools if the therapist can assess the situation and determine the sources of the difficulties that have arisen. This is hard to do when there is a comfortable stalemate with a patient who pays the bills on time and does not trouble the therapist very much. The overwhelming boredom of this type of relationship should be a red flag to the therapist who is interested in the patient's growth more than the steadiness of his or her own income or the predictability of his or her appointment calendar. It is a sign that something in the patient or the therapist is being avoided (Wangh, 1979).

Therapists can rationalize their patients' decompensation into psychosis. Instead of asking if they contributed to a patient's psychotic regression, therapists may tell themselves that the patient was referred as he or she was moving toward psychosis, and the therapist just happened to be there when the patient went over the edge.

Psychotherapists share with other professional healers the tendency to blame the patient when the treatment they administer is ineffective or if it turns out badly. Surgeons express this by saying, "The operation was a success, but the patient died." Obviously, had the patient's body cooperated, all would have gone well.

Internists speak of "poor protoplasm." The correct medications were prescribed, but the patient's organs and tissues did not respond properly. So it is with psychotherapists, and with relatively similar disclaimers: "The patient used therapy to act out conflicts instead of facing them and working them through"; or, "The patient's characterologic defenses made interpretation impossible." In the first instance, the patient "used" therapy to run amok. In the second, the therapist knew what to do but the patient wouldn't let him do it.

To employ a different psychotherapeutic idiom, "The patient's suicide was a miscarried attempt to force the therapist from an adult-adult relationship to a parent-child relationship." This statement makes it clear that it was entirely the patient's responsibility to keep himself alive and that he would not have suicided had he less strongly valued coercion of his therapist.

The patient's lack of cooperation is a frequent reason given for impasse, but some problems of cooperation are absolutely inherent in the treatment prescribed. For example, a patient can readily see the benefits of hernia surgery. The bulge disappears. The patient with heart failure who is short of breath, has swollen ankles, and cannot lie flat in bed experiences dramatic relief from digitalis. By contrast, patients in psychotherapy are told that they must invest substantial time and money and undergo substantial emotional discomfort in the hope of becoming able to face life and themselves better, with fewer symptoms.

At an intellectual level, cooperation with treatments involving significant inconvenience for little immediate tangible gain depends largely on the patient's ability to understand that significant long-term gains can be achieved at the cost of temporary inconvenience and discomfort. At an emotional level, the story is quite different. One is asked to abandon the easily verified pleasure principle of avoiding discomfort and seeking what is pleasurable and to adopt the hard-to-validate reality principle. For the numerous immature people who live by the pleasure principle, treatments that do not produce immediate change are prima facie ineffective. To suspend their judgment and await long-term results is a regression for many of these people. It is like reverting to a state in which others make judgments for them, and stimulates angry, impulsive attempts to change themselves or reality. Many of these people who have worked themselves and their families into a state of crisis can be helped to cooperate with long-term therapy by first addressing the painful situation in which they are presently caught, and by suggesting concrete common-sense measures to avoid provoking a parent or a spouse's anger, or to give support to that parent or spouse. An adult with marital problems or an adolescent can be told that friction will be reduced if he will keep his word when he makes an agreement, such as agreeing to be home at a certain time. Adults and children can be taught the simple tactic of asking or working for what one wants in life instead of impatiently waiting for it to be delivered by someone else. The relief of pressure that comes from using these simple devices leaves the patient more energy for self-examination and establishes the potency of the psychotherapist.

Many aspects of psychotherapy insult patients' common sense. Insisting that the patient's emotional state is solely a product of his current family relationships is as procrustean as ignoring his current reality and focusing entirely on his history or his unconscious mental processes. Insistence on dealing with presumed causes instead of directly treating certain symptoms does disservice to patients in psychotherapy. For example, allowing patients to continue experiencing crippling anxiety, depression, or functional physical symptoms is demoralizing and can significantly undermine important sources of emotional support because of the interpersonal tensions produced by anxiety, depression, or functional symptoms. Therapists, however, deny medications to their patients on the rationale that symptoms are best treated by dealing with the underlying psychological causes. In many instances, the psychological "cause" is merely a precipitant of the patient's symptoms, which are often based on biological vulnerability. One can, for example, point to the crippling mother-child relationship of an asthmatic patient and to his use of wheezing to avoid stress, but one cannot avoid the fact that he has an altered tissue response which must also be dealt with.

A study of the factors leading to breakdown of the therapeutic relationship presumes a positive outcome if cooperation is achieved and presumes that we have means to measure success or failure.

How do we measure the effectiveness of our treatment techniques so that we know if we are getting someplace, or if we are failing?

How can the psychotherapist quantify the emotional difficulties which patients bring to treatment? Surely this question must be answered before we can begin to measure treatment effectiveness. We are not yet able to quantify feelings of depression, self-hatred, or boredom. Where patients' feelings do not result in overt behavior, we can only rely on indirect measures, including the patient's subjective account, the therapist's appraisal of his or her mental state, and psychological testing by means of questionnaires or projective techniques. Psychological questionnaires such as the Beck Depression Inventory, the Minnesota Multiphasic Personality Inventory, and projective techniques such as the Rorschach Test and the Thematic Apperception Test have been standardized on large populations and are quantifiable. The patient's account and the therapist's appraisal are not.

When feelings or thought processes alter behavior, we are better able to objectify and quantify psychological phenomena. We can measure, for example, the number of dates per month made by a socially inhibited boy before and after his treatment, or, we can measure the frequency with which a sexually inhibited person becomes able to have sexual relations before and after treatment.

How can psychotherapists measure their contribution to the treatment process? How can psychotherapists measure the amount of encouragement they offer? How can they measure the degree to which they interpret unconscious conflict? Or offer themselves as models? These questions are truly unanswerable, even with the use of sophisticated audiovisual equipment. Psychotherapists who use a conversational technique can only measure general trends and attitudes in themselves. Even behavior therapists using standardized instructions and reinforcers must take into account the context and the manner in which they give their instructions and reinforcement.

Measuring progress in psychotherapy is, however, less difficult than one might think. Although a patient's complaints are intangible and frequently unmeasurable, one's current mental state can be compared with one's state at the initiation of treatment through the use of a diary. During the early part of treatment, the patient may be asked to do homework, keeping track of those aspects of his or her life or thinking that disturb him, and to record them as faithfully as possible, as Beck et al. (1979) suggest. He can put aside his diary and at a mutually agreed-upon interval rerecord the thoughts and activities that trouble him. Then, he and his therapist can compare earlier entries with his more recent entries, and an impending impasse can be detected.

Therapists can do the same. They can take an adequate history and obtain a fairly complete picture of the patient's current thinking and functioning through direct interaction with the patient, through interviewing key members of the patient's family, and through interviews in which the patient is seen jointly with the significant other people in his or her life. They can supplement these by psychological tests. Then, at a stated interval, they can reassess in equal depth. Periodic videotaped interviews can serve the same function.

Distortion is obviously possible, no matter how we strive toward objectivity. Many patients who have gained significantly from psychotherapy decry therapy and insist that their lives are no better in spite of the fact that they obviously function at a higher level. For the most part, however, the patient who says that he or she is no better is correct. Therapists are inclined to be defensive at these times, and to point out areas of gain that the patient has overlooked. It is harder for the therapist to be objective about a real impasse than about pessimistic patients' tendency to assess themselves negatively in the face of measurable gain. Obviously, in a real impasse, therapists have much at stake. They have pitted their expertise, effort, narcissism, and omnipotent strivings against the patient's maladaptive psychological state. Therapists have more than a rational, mature involvement in helping patients to change for the better; they also have an irrational involvement tied to their self-esteem and personal needs.

Saretsky (1980) points out the challenges by patients such as the borderline and the narcissistic personality to therapists' basic assumptions that they are engaged in a meaningful encounter, that they have an impact, that they can be helpful, and that there is hope of change. Many of these patients fear being understood because it symbolizes an invasion, a violation of their psychological integrity. They often deny and minimize the importance of the therapist and try to reject his or her influence. They frequently deny that anything worthwhile or productive is going on, and often resent the need to take responsibility for themselves and for the course of their treatment.

The irrational involvement of both patient and therapist in the psychotherapy process mitigates against objectivity in evaluation of psychotherapy, and makes it difficult to diagnose an impasse, to ascertain how it may have developed, or how it may be resolved. Because irrational factors on both sides weigh so heavily, it is important that therapists use the tools now available to determine the presence of an impasse, its nature, and the possibilities for its resolution.

These tools are:

1. An adequate assessment of the patient's environmental assets and liabilities based on knowledge of the supports available to him, the conditions under which they operate, and his relationship to potential sources of support.
2. An adequate assessment of the patient's interactional style, coping skills, defense mechanisms, and biologic vulnerability to mental illness.
3. An adequate assessment of the patient's physical health to ride out physical disorders which might contribute to his or her present symptoms.
4. An adequate assessment of the patient's ability to cooperate with the treatment planned by the therapist.
5. An adequate assessment of the therapist's willingness and ability to deal with this patient at this point in time under the present circumstances in the patient's and his or her own life.
6. The establishment of an appropriate contract with the appropriate person, who often is not the identified patient, and with whom the work may have to be done instead of with the identified patient.
7. Periodic reassessment of the therapist-patient relationship and the patient's progress in relation to the difficulties for which he or she and the therapist have agreed to be the focus of treatment.
8. Willingness and ability to redefine the problem or the therapeutic relationship when there is clear evidence that the problem initially focused upon is not the most relevant or treatable at present, or when another course of action needs to be taken to treat the presenting problem.
9. Obtaining adequate consultation, supervision, and support for the therapist and his or her therapeutic efforts. For the psychiatrist, this may involve psychological testing of the patient or home visits by a visiting nurse or a social worker, or referral to an internist or neurologist. For the nonmedical therapist, consultation with a psychiatrist and referral of the patient to the psychiatrist for consultation may be indicated.

When an impasse develops, the therapist together with the patient, consultants, or concerned others deals with the impasse in a systematic series of steps.

The first step is to *suspect* an impasse. Without a high index of suspicion, many resolvable impasses will become unresolvable because of the secondary effects of the patient's continued or worsening difficulties, such as withdrawal of family support or loss of employment. The second step is to *detect* the impasse by using all means available to appraise the patient's progress or lack of progress. Third, one must *define* the impasse by reevaluating the diagnosis, the appropriateness of the treatment undertaken, and the therapeutic contract. The contract is reexamined to see if the responsibilities agreed upon by each party are actually being carried out and, if not, why not. The elements of the psychotherapeutic process, including transference and countertransference, should be examined. After defining the impasse—whether it is due to inappropriate treatment or a countertransference block to understanding the patient's communications—the fourth step is to *formulate a provisional plan for resolution* of the impasse. After formulating the plan (often with the involvement and agreement of the patient), the therapist begins to implement the plan, noting the positive and negative effects of the various aspects of the new treatment approach. If not entirely satisfactory, the next step is to *modify the provisional plan*, as appropriate.

If the efforts of the therapist and patient to modify the treatment adequately to make it effective do not work, more steps can be taken. They require *consultation* with other professionals and often with family members by therapist and patient together, or by the patient. Mintz (1972) has suggested group consultation by therapists having difficulties with patients, and has used role playing, group associations, and group fantasies to help therapists get unstuck and as a means to circumvent the teacher-pupil dichotomy that blocks the supervisor from making the best possible use of supervision (Saretsky, 1981). Consultation may result in the decision to attempt another modification of treatment or to continue treatment as it is. The outcome of consultation may also be a decision to transfer the patient to another therapist or type of treatment, or to terminate therapy because it cannot be successfully undertaken at this time owing to unavailability of appropriate treatment, or factors in the patient or in his or her situation that make treatment impossible at present. The patient and his or her family can then be told what type of treatment is likely to be effective (if any) and under what circumstances.

References

ADAMS, S., & ORGEL, M. *Through the mental health maze: A consumer's guide to finding a psychiatrist, including a sample consumer/therapist contract.* Washington, D.C.: Public Citizen's Research Group, 1975.

ADLER, G. The myth of the alliance with borderline patients. *Am. J. Psychiatry,* 1979, **136**, 642–645.

———, & MYERSON, P. (Eds.) *Confrontation in psychotherapy.* New York: Aronson, 1973.

ALEXANDER, F., & FRENCH, T.M. *Psychoanalytic therapy: Principles and application.* New York: Ronald Press, 1946.

ALGER, I. Television image confrontation in group therapy. In Sager, C.J., & Kaplan, H.S. (Eds.), *Progress in group and family therapy.* New York: Brunner/Mazel, 1972.

ALTSHUL, V.A. The so-called boring patient. *Am. J. Psychotherapy,* 1977, **31**, 533–545.

AMERICAN PSYCHIATRIC ASSOCIATION. *Diagnostic and Statistical Manual of Mental Disorders.* (3rd ed.) Washington, D.C.: American Psychiatric Association, 1980.

Asch, S.E. Effects of group pressure upon the modification and distortion of judgments. In Swanson, G.E., Newcomb, T.M. & Hartley, E.L. (Eds.), *Readings in social psychology.* New York: Holt, Rinehart, & Winston, 1952.

______. Opinions and social pressure. *Scientific American,* 1955, **193**, 31-35.

Ayllon, T. Behavior modification in institutionalized settings. *Arizona Law Rev.*, 1975, **17**, 3-19.

______, & Skirban, W. Accountability in psychotherapy: A test case. *J. Behav. Ther. & Exp. Psychiatry,* 1973, **4**, 19-29.

Bandura, A. *Social learning theory.* Englewood Cliffs, NJ: Prentice-Hall, 1977.

______, & McDonald, F.J. The influence of social reinforcement and the behavior of models in shaping children's moral judgments. *J. Abnorm. Soc. Psychol.*, 1963, **67**, 274-281.

Barnhouse, R.T. Sex between patient and therapist. *J. Am. Acad. Psychoanal.*, 1978, **6**, 533-546.

Beavers, W.R. *Psychotherapy and Growth.* New York: Brunner/Mazel, 1977.

______; Lewis, J.M.; Gossett, J.T.; & Phillips, V.A. Crucial variables in healthy family systems. *Dallas Med. J.*, 1975, **61**, 313-316.

Beck, A.T. *Cognitive therapy of emotional disorders.* New York: International Universities Press, 1976.

______; Rush, A.J.; Shaw, B.F.; & Emery, G. *Cognitive therapy of depression.* New York: Guilford Press, 1979.

Berger, M.M. (Ed.) *Videotape techniques in psychiatric training and treatment.* New York: Brunner/Mazel, 1970.

Bergin, A.E. The effects of psychotherapy: Negative results revisited. *J. Counseling. Psychol.*, 1963, **10**, 244-250.

______. Some implications of psychotherapy for therapeutic practice. *J. Abnorm. Psychol.*, 1966, **71**, 235-246.

______. The evaluation of therapeutic outcomes. In Bergin, A.E., & Garfield, S.C. (Eds.), *The handbook of psychotherapy and behavior change.* New York: Wiley, 1971.

Bermak, G.E. Do psychiatrists have special emotional problems. *Am. J. Psychoanal.*, 1977, **37**, 141-146.

Berne, E. *Games people play.* New York: Grove Press, 1964.

______. *What do you say after you say hello?.* New York: Grove Press, 1972.

Berzins, J.I. Therapist-patient matching. In Gurman, A.S., & Razin,

A.M. (Eds.), *Effective psychotherapy: A handbook of research.* New York: Pergamon, 1977.

Birk, L. Behavior therapy and behavioral psychotherapy. In Nicholi, A.M. (Ed.), *The Harvard guide to modern psychiatry.* Cambridge: Belknap Press, 1978.

Bloch, D.A. Family therapy, group therapy. *Int. J. Group. Psychother.*, 1976, **26**, 289–300.

Borriello, J. Letter to the editor. Newsletter of the American Group Psychotherapy Association, December, 1977.

Bowers, M.B., Jr., Steidl, J., Rabinovitch, D., et al. Psychotic illness in mid-life. In Norman, W.H., & Scaramella, T.J. (Eds.), *Mid-life: Developmental and clinical issues.* New York: Brunner/Mazel, 1980.

Boyer, L. The treatment of a borderline patient. *Psychoanal. Quart.*, 1977, **46**, 386–424.

Breuer, J., & Freud, S. *Studies on hysteria.* New York: Basic Books, 1957. (Originally published: 1895.)

Chasin, R., & Grunebaum, H. A brief synopsis of current concepts and practices in family therapy. In Pearce, J.K., & Friedman, L.J. (Eds.), *Family therapy: Combining psychodynamics and family systems approaches.* New York: Grune & Stratton, 1980.

Chesler, P. *Women and madness.* New York: Doubleday, 1971.

Chessick, R.D. *Why psychotherapists fail.* New York: Science House, 1971.

______. Intensive psychotherapy for the psychiatrist's family. *Am. J. Psychother.*, 1977, **31**, 516–524.

Chrzanowski, G. Problem patients or troublemakers? Dynamic and therapeutic considerations. *Am. J. Psychother.*, 1980, **34**, 26–28.

Coulson, W.R. From empathy to involvement: A short history of client-centered thinking and beyond. Presented to the North Texas Psychiatric Society, Dallas, Tx., September, 1968.

Craig, T., & Huffine, C. Correlates of patient attendance in an inner-city mental health clinic. *Am. J. Psychiatry*, 1976, **133**, 61–64.

Dahlberg, C.C. Sexual contact between patient and therapist. *J. Contemp. Psychoanal.*, 1970, **6**, 107–124.

Davis, F.B., & Lohr, N.E. Special problems with the use of cotherapists in group psychotherapy. *Int. J. Group Psychother.*, 1971, **21**, 143–149.

Dewald, P.A. Serious illness in the analyst: Countertransference and reality response. Presented at the American Psychoanalytic Association, New York, December, 1980.

EISSLER, K. Remarks on psychoanalysis of schizophrenics. *Int. J. Psychoanal.*, 1951, **32**, 139-156.

______. On the possible effects of aging on the practice of psychoanalysis. *Psychoanal. Quart.*, 1977, **46**, 182-183.

ENGEL, G.L. A psychological setting of somatic disease: The "giving up-given up" complex. *Proc. Roy. Soc. Med.*, 1967, **60**, 553-555.

EPSTEIN, L. The therapeutic function of hate in the counter-transference. *Contemp. Psychoanal.*, 1977, **13**, 442-461.

ERICKSON, E.H. *Childhood and society.* New York: W. W. Norton, 1950.

______. *The collected papers of Milton H. Erickson on hypnosis.* New York: Irvington, 1980. 4 vols.

EYSENCK, H.J. The effects of psychotherapy: an evaluation. *J. Consult. Psychol.*, 1952, **16**, 319-324.

FEIFEL, H. Functions of attitudes toward death. In Group for the Advancement of Psychiatry, *Death and dying: Attitudes of patients and doctors.* New York: Mental Health Materials Center, 1965.

FENICHEL, O. *The psychoanalytic theory of neurosis.* New York: W.W. Norton, 1945.

______. *The collected papers of Otto Fenichel.* New York: W.W. Norton, 1953.

FERENCZI, S. Introjection and transference. *Sex in psychoanalysis.* New York: Basic Books, 1950. (Originally published: 1909).

FIESTER, A.R., & RUDESTAM, K.E.A. A multivariate analysis of the early dropout process. *J. Consult. Clin. Psychol.*, 1975, **43**, 528-535.

FRAMO, J.L. Symptoms from a family transactional viewpoint. *Int. Psychiatry Clinics,* 1970, **7**, 125-171.

FRANK, J.D. *Persuasion and healing.* (2nd ed.) Baltimore: Johns Hopkins Press, 1973.

FREUD, A. *The ego and the mechanisms of defense.* New York: International Universities Press, 1946.

FREUD, S. The psychical mechanism of forgetfulness. *Standard edition of the complete psychological works of Sigmund Freud,* Vol. III. London: Hogarth, 1957. (Originally published: 1898.)

______. The future prospects of psychoanalytic therapy. *Standard edition of the complete psychological works of Sigmund Freud,* Vol. XI. London: Hogarth, 1957. (Originally published: 1910.)

______. Recommendations to physicians practicing psychoanalysis. *Standard edition of the complete psychological works of Sigmund Freud,* Vol. XII. London: Hogarth, 1957. (Originally published: 1912.)

______. Analysis terminable and interminable. *Standard edition of the complete psychological works of Sigmund Freud,* Vol. XXIII. London: Hogarth, 1957. (Originally published: 1937.)

______. An outline of psychoanalysis. *Standard edition of the complete psychological works of Sigmund Freud,* Vol. XXIII. London: Hogarth, 1957. (Originally published: 1940.)

GARFIELD, S.L. *Psychotherapy: An eclectic approach.* New York: Wiley, 1980.

______, & KURZ, M. Evaluation of treatment and related procedures in 1216 cases referred to a mental hygiene clinic. *Psychiatric Quart.,* 1952, **26**, 414-424.

______, & WOLPIN, M. Espectations regarding psychotherapy. *J. Nerv. Ment. Dis.,* 1963, **137**, 353-362.

GLICK, S.D., & KESSLER, D.R. *Marital and family therapy.* New York: Grune & Stratton, 1980.

GOLDBERG, C. The utilization and limitations of paradoxical intervention in group psychotherapy. *Int. J. Group Psychother.,* 1980, **30**, 287-297.

GORNEY, J.E., & WEINSTOCK, S.J. Borderline object relations, therapeutic impasse, and the Rorschach. In Kwawer, J.S., et al. (Eds.), *Borderline phenomena and the Rorschach test.* New York: International Universities Press, 1980.

GOULD, R.L. *Transformations.* New York: Simon & Schuster, 1978.

GOULDING, R.L., & GOULDING, M.M. *The power is in the patient: A TA/Gestalt approach to psychotherapy.* San Francisco: TA Press, 1978.

GREEN, A. The borderline concept. In Hartocollis, P. (Ed.), *Borderline personality disorders: The concept, the syndrome, the patient.* New York: International Universities Press, 1977.

GREENBURG, D. *How to be a Jewish mother.* Los Angeles: Price/Stern/Sloan, 1965.

GREENSON, R.R. The struggle against identification. *J. Am. Psychoanal. Assn.,* 1954, **2**, 200-217.

______. *The technique and practice of psychoanalysis.* New York: International Universities Press, 1967.

______. Beyond transference and interpretation. *Int. J. Psychoanal.,* 1972, **53**, 213-217.

GROESBECK, C.J., & TAYLOR, B. The psychiatrist as wounded physician. *Am. J. Psychoanal.,* 1977, **37**, 131-139.

GRUNEBAUM, H.; CHRIST, J.; & NEIBERG, N. Diagnosis and treatment planning for couples. *Int. J. Group Psychother.,* 1969, **19**, 185-202.

GUNDERSON, J. Characteristics of borderlines. In Hartocollis, P. (Ed.), *Borderline personality disorders: The concept, the syndrome, the patient.* New York: International Universities Press, 1977.

GURMAN, A.S., & KNISKERN, D.P. Research in marital and family therapy: progress, perspectives, and prospect. In Garfield, S.L., & Bergin, A.E. (Eds.), *Handbook of psychotherapy and behavior change.* (2nd. ed.) New York: Wiley, 1978.

HADLEY, S.W., & STRUPP, H.H. Contemporary views of negative effects in psychotherapy. *Arch. Gen. Psychiatry,* 1976, **33**, 1291-1302.

HALEY, J. Family therapy. In Sager, C.J., & Kaplan, H.S. (Eds.), *Progress in group and family therapy.* New York: Brunner/Mazel, 1972.

HARTLEY, D.; ROBACK, H.B.; & ABRAMOWITZ, S.I. Deterioration effects in encounter groups. *Am. Psychologist,* 1976, **31**, 247-255.

HAVENS, L.L. *Approaches to the mind.* Boston: Little, Brown, 1973.

———. The existential use of self. *Am. J. Psychiatry,* 1974, **131**, 1-10.

———. *Participant observation.* New York: Jason Aronson, 1976.

———. Explorations in the uses of language in psychotherapy: Counterprojective statements. *Contemp. Psychoanal.,* 1980, **16**, 53-67.

HEINE, R.W. (Ed.) *The student physician as psychotherapist.* Chicago: University of Chicago Press, 1962.

———, & TROSMAN, H. Initial expectations of the doctor-patient interaction as a factor in continuance of psychotherapy. *Psychiatry,* 1960, **23**, 275-278.

HENRY, J. *Pathways to madness.* New York: Random House, 1965.

JOHANSEN, K.H. A theoretical basis for the management of the hospitalized borderline patient. *Curr. Concepts in Psychiatry,* 1974, **5**, 8-16.

JOURARD, S.M. *Self-disclosure: An experimental analysis of the transparent self.* New York: Wiley-Interscience, 1971.

JUNG, C.G. *Analytical psychology, Its theory and practice.* New York: Vintage, 1968.

KADIS, A.L.; KRASNER, J.; WEINER, M.F.; & WINICK, C. *Practicum of group psychotherapy.* New York: Harper & Row, 1974.

———, & MARKOWITZ, M. Countertransferences between therapists in a couples psychotherapy group. In Wolberg, L.R., & Schwartz, E.K. (Eds.), *Group therapy: 1973.* New York: Intercontinental Medical Book Corporation, 1973.

Kardener, S.H.; Fuller, M.; & Marsh, I.N. A survey of physicians' attitudes and practices regarding erotic and nonerotic contact with patients. *Am. J. Psychiatry,* 1973, **130**, 1077-1081.

Kardiner, A. Traumatic neuroses of war. In Arieti, S. (Ed.), *American handbook of psychiatry.* New York: Basic Books, 1959.

Kempthorne, G.C. The impaired physician-role of the state medical society. *Wisconsin Med. J.,* 1979, **78**, 24-25.

Kepecs, J.G. Tracking errors in psychotherapy. *Am. J. Psychother.,* 1979, **33**, 365-377.

Kernberg, O. The treatment of patients with borderline personality organization. *Int. J. Psychoanal.,* 1968, **49**, 600-619.

______. *Borderline conditions and pathological narcissism.* New York: Jason Aronson, 1975.

______. *Internal world and external reality.* New York: Jason Aronson, 1980.

______; Burstein, E.D.; Coyne, L.; Applebaum, A.; Horwitz, L.; & Voth, H. Psychotherapy and psychoanalysis. *Bull. Menninger Clinic,* 1972, **36**, 1-275.

Klerman, G. Affective disorders. In Nicholi, A.M. (Ed.), *The Harvard guide to modern psychiatry.* Cambridge: Belknap Press, 1978.

Lambert, M.J.; Bergin, A.E.; & Collins, J.L. Therapist-induced deterioration in psychotherapy. In Gurman, A.S., & Razin, A.M. (Eds.), *Effective psychotherapy: A handbook of research.* New York: Pergamon, 1977.

Langs, R.J. *The technique of psychoanalytic psychotherapy.* Vol. I. New York: Jason Aronson, 1973.

______. *The technique of psychoanalytic psychotherapy.* Vol. II. New York: Jason Aronson, 1974.

Levinson, D.J. *The seasons of a man's life.* New York: Alfred A. Knopf, 1978.

Lewis, J.M. The doctor and his marriage. *Texas Med.,* 1965, **61**, 615-619.

______. The dangers of being a therapist. Presented at the Annual Meeting of the Texas District Branch, American Psychiatric Association, Dallas, Texas, 1980.

______; Beavers, W.R.; Gossett, J.T.; & Phillips, V.A. *No single thread: Psychological health in family systems.* New York: Brunner/Mazel, 1976.

Lieberman, M.A.; Yalom, I.D.; & Miles, M.D. *Encounter groups: First facts.* New York: Basic Books, 1973.

LIFF, Z. Impasse: Interpersonal, intergroup, and international. *Group Process,* 1970, **3**, 7-30.

LIONELLS, M., & MANN, C.H. Patterns of mid-life in transition. In Goldman, D.G., & Milman, D.S. (Eds.), *Man and woman in transition.* Dubuque, Iowa: Kendall-Hunt, 1978.

LITTLE, R.E. Transference, countertransference, and survival reactions following an analyst's heart attack. *Psychoanal. Forum,* 1967, **2**, 107-126.

LOMBILLO, J.R.; KIRESCIK, T.J.; & SHERMAN, R.E. Evaluating a community mental health program: contract fulfillment analysis. *Hosp. and Community Psychiatry,* 1973, **24**, 760-763.

LOONEY, J.G.; HARDING, R.K.; BLOTCKY, M.J.; & BARNHART, F.D. Psychiatrists: Transition from training to career: Stress and mastery. *Am. J. Psychiatry,* 1980, **137**, 32-36.

LOTHSTEIN, L.M. The group psychotherapy dropout phenomenon revisited. *Am. J. Psychiatry,* 1975, **135**, 1492-1495.

MALAN, D.H.; BALFOUR, H.F.G.; HOOD, V.G.; & SHOOTER, A.M.N. Group psychotherapy, A long term followup. *Arch. Gen. Psychiatry,* 1976, **33**, 1303-1315.

MANN, C.H. Mid-life and the family: Strains, challenges, and options of the middle years. In Norman, W.H., & Scaramella, T.J. (Eds.), *Mid-life: Developmental and clinical issues.* New York: Brunner/Mazel, 1980.

MARMOR, J. Psychoanalytic therapy and theories of learning. In Marmor, J., & Woods, S.M. (Eds.), *The interface between the psychodynamic and behavioral therapies.* New York: Plenum, 1980.

MARTIN, P.A. *A marital therapy manual.* New York: Brunner/Mazel, 1976.

MASTERS, W.H., & JOHNSON, V. *Human sexual inadequacy.* Boston: Little, Brown, 1970.

MASTERSON, J. *Psychotherapy of the borderline adult.* New York: Brunner/Mazel, 1978.

MCCARTNEY, J.L. Overt transference. *J. Sexual Res.,* 1966, **2**, 227-237.

MCGEE, T.F., & SCHUMAN, B.N. The nature of the cotherapy relationship. *Int. J. Group Psychother.,* 1970, **20**, 25-36.

MECKLIN, L., JR., & LITTLE, R.R. Beginning psychiatry training syndrome. *Am. J. Psychiatry,* 1967, **124**, 193-198.

MEYER, V., & CHESSER, E.S. *Behavior therapy in clinical psychiatry.* New York: Science House, 1970.

MINTZ, E.E. *Marathon groups: Reality and symbol.* New York: Appleton-Century-Crofts, 1971.

______. Group supervision: Experimental approach. *Int. J. Group Psychother.*, 1972, **28**, 467-479.

MITCHELL, K.M.; BOZARTH, J.D.; & KRAUFT, C.C. A reappraisal of the therapeutic effectiveness of accurate empathy, nonpossessive warmth, and genuineness. In Gurman, A.S., & Razin, A.M. (Eds.), *Effective psychotherapy: A handbook of research.* New York: Pergamon, 1977.

MULLAHY, P. (Ed.) *Contributions of Harry Stack Sullivan.* New York: Hermitage House, 1952.

MYINT, S., & WEINER, M.F. Management of a borderline patient in a surgical setting. *Psychosomatics,* 1980, **22**, 71-72.

NADELSON, T. Borderline rage and the therapist's response. *Am. J. Psychiatry,* 1977, **134**, 748-751.

NATIONAL CENTER FOR HEALTH STATISTICS. Characteristics of patients of selected types of medical specialists and practitioners: United States July 1963-June 1964. Washington, D.C.: Public Health Service Publication No. 1000, Series 10, No. 28, 1966.

NEMETZ, P., & WEINER, H. Some factors in the choice of psychiatry as a career. *Arch. Gen. Psychiatry,* 1965, **13**, 299-303.

NEMIAH, J. Alexithymia and psychosomatic illness. *J. Cont. Ed. Psychiatry,* October, 1978, pp. 25-37.

NEUGARTEN, B.L. Time, age, and the life cycle. *Am. J. Psychiatry,* 1979, **136**, 887-894.

OVERALL, B., & ARONSON, H. Expectations of psychotherapy in lower socioeconomic class patients. *Am. J. Orthopsychiatry,* 1962, **33**, 271-272.

PAUL, G.L. Strategy of outcome research in psychotherapy. *J. Consult. Psychology,* 1967, **31**, 109-118.

POPE, K.S.; SIMPSON, N.H.; & WEINER, M.F. Malpractice in outpatient psychotherapy. *Am. J. Psychother.*, 1978, **32**, 593-602.

PURYEAR, D.A. *Helping people in crisis.* San Francisco: Jossey-Bass, 1979.

RABKIN, J.G. Therapists' attitudes toward mental illness and health. In Gurman, A.S., & Razin, A.M. (Eds.), *Effective psychotherapy: A handbook of research.* New York: Pergamon, 1977.

RAVICH, R.A. The use of an interpersonal game-test in joint marital psychotherapy. *Am. J. Psychiatry,* 1969, **23**, 217-229.

RAZIN, A.M. The A-B variables: Still promising after twenty years? In Gurman, A.S., & Razin, A.M. (Eds.), *Effective psychotherapy: A handbook of research.* New York: Pergamon, 1977.

RICH, C.L., & PITTS, F.N. Suicide by psychiatrists: A study of medical specialists among 18,730 consecutive physician deaths during a five year period, 1967-72. *J. Clin. Psychiatry,* 1980, **41**, 261-263.

ROBBINS, M., & COWAN, R.B. Phased inpatient treatment of polydrug abusers. Dept. of Psychiatry, Denver General Hospital, Denver, Colo. Unpublished manuscript, 1976.

ROBERTIELLO, R.C. Iatiogenic psychiatric illness. *J. Contemp. Psychother.,* 1975, **7**, 3-8.

ROGERS, C.R. The necessary and sufficient conditions of therapeutic personality change. *J. Consult. Psychology,* 1957, **21**, 95-103.

______; GENDLIN, E.T.; KIESLER, D.; & TRAUX, C.B. *The therapeutic relationship and its impact: A study of psychotherapy with schizophrenics.* Madison: University of Wisconsin Press, 1967.

ROSENZWEIG, S.P., & FOLMAN, R. Patient and therapist variables affecting premature termination in group psychotherapy. *Psychotherapy: Theory, Research, and Practice,* 1974, **11**, 76-79.

ROTH, N. Fear of death in the aging. *Am. J. Psychother.,* 1978, **32**, 552-560.

ROY v. HARTOGS, 366 N.Y.S. 2d 297 (Civ. Ct. N.Y. County, 1975).

RUTHERFORD, R.B., JR. Establishing behavioral contracts with delinquent adolescents. *Fed. Probation,* 1975, **39**, 29-32.

SAGER, C.J. *Marriage contracts and couple therapy.* New York: Brunner/Mazel, 1976.

SARETSKY, T. The resolution of impasses in borderline states. *Contemp. Psychoanal.,* 1977, **13**, 519-532.

______. The analyst's narcissistic vulnerability. *Contemp. Psychoanal.,* 1980, **16**, 82-89.

______. Innovative approaches to supervision with advanced therapists. In Saretsky, T. (Ed.), *Resolving treatment impasses.* New York: Human Science Press, 1981.

SCHECTMAN, F.; DELATORRE, J.; & GARZA, A.C. Diagnosis separate from psychotherapy: Pros and cons. *Am. J. Psychother.,* 1979, **23**, 291-302.

SCHUR, M. Comments on the metapsychology of somatization. *Psychoanalytic Study of the Child,* 1955, **10**, 110-164.

SCHWITZGEBEL, R.K. *Legal aspects of the enforced treatment of offenders.* Rockville, MD: U.S. Dept. of Health, Education, and Welfare, 1979.

SEARLES, H.F. *Collected papers on schizophrenia and related subjects.* New York: International Universities Press, 1965.

SHAPIRO, R.J. Therapist attitudes and premature termination in family and individual therapy. *J. Nerv. Ment. Dis.*, 1974, **159**, 101-107.

SHARAF, M.R., & LEVINSON, D.J. Quest for omnipotency in professional training. *Psychiatry,* 1964, **27**, 135-150.

SIMONS, R.D.; MORRIS, J.L.; FRANK, H.A.; GREEN, L.C.; & MALIN, R.M. Pain medication contracts in problem patients. *Psychosomatics,* 1979, **20**, 118-127.

SIMONTON, O.C.; MATTHEWS-SIMONTON, S.; & SPARKS, T.F. Cancer treatment: Psychological intervention. *Psychosomatics,* 1980, **21**, 226-233.

SINGER, B.A., & LUBORSKY, L.B. Countertransference: The status of clinical versus quantitative research. In Gurman, A.S., & Razin, A.M. (Eds.), *Effective psychotherapy: A handbook of research.* New York: Pergamon, 1977.

SOLOMON, M. Family therapy dropouts: Resistance to change. *Canadian Psychiatric Assn. J.*, 1969, **14**, 21-29.

STERNBACH, R.A. *Pain patients: Traits and treatment.* New York: Academic Press, 1974.

STONE, L. *The psychoanalytic situation.* New York: International Universities Press, 1961.

STRUPP, H.H. A reformulation of the dynamics of the therapist's contribution. In Gurman, A.S., & Razin, A.M. (Eds.), *Effective psychotherapy: A handbook of research.* New York: Pergamon, 1977.

______. Success and failure in time-limited psychotherapy. *Arch. Gen. Psychiatry,* 1980, **37**, 595-603.

TALBOTT, C.D.; HOLDERFIELD, H.; SHOEMAKER, K.E.; & ALKINS, E.C. The disabled doctors plan for Georgia. *J. Med. Assn. Georgia,* 1976, **65**, 71-76.

TRUAX, C.B. Effective ingredients in psychotherapy. *J. Counsel. Psychology,* 1963, **10**, 256-263.

______, & CARKHUFF, R.R. Client and therapist transparency in the psychotherapeutic encounter. *J. Counsel. Psychology,* 1965, **12**, 3-9.

______, & CARKHUFF, R.R. *Toward effective counseling and psychotherapy: Training and practice.* Chicago: Aldine, 1967.

______, & MITCHELL, K.M. Research in certain therapist skills in relation to process and outcomes. In Bergin, A.E., & Garfield, S.L. (Eds.), *Handbook of psychotherapy and behavior change.* New York: Wiley, 1971.

ULANOV, A.B. Followup treatment in cases of patient/therapist sex. *J. Am. Acad. Psychoanal.*, 1979, **7**, 101-110.

Vaillant, G.E. *Adaptation to life.* Boston: Little, Brown, 1977.

Wangh, M. Some psychoanalytic observations on boredom. *Int. J. Psychoanal.,* 1979, **60**, 515-527.

Weiner, H.; Thaler, M.; Reiser, M.F.; & Mirsky, I.A. Etiology of duodenal ulcer. *Psychosom. Med.,* 1957, **19**, 1-10.

Weiner, M.F. Levels of intervention in group psychotherapy. *Group Process,* 1970, **3**, 67-81.

______. Wives who refuse their husbands. *Psychosomatics,* 1973, **14**, 277-282.

______. The psychotherapeutic impasse. *Dis. Nerv. System,* 1974, **35**, 259-261. (a)

______. Self-disclosure by the therapist. *Am. J. Psychiatry,* 1974, **131**, 930. (b)

______. Reply to Roemer. *Am. J. Psychiatry,* 1974, **132**, 85-86. (c)

______. Individual versus conjoint therapy. *Dis. Nerv. System,* 1975, **10**, 546-549.

______. *Therapist disclosure.* Boston: Butterworths, 1978.

______. Personal openness with patients, help or hindrance? *Texas Med.,* 1980, **76**, 60-65. (a)

______. Healthy and pathological love—psychodynamic views. In Pope, K.S. (Ed.), *On love and loving.* San Francisco: Jossey-Bass, 1980. (b)

______. Contracts in psychotherapy. *J. Psychiatric Treat. and Eval.,* 1981, **3**, 127-131.

______, & King, J.S. Self-disclosure by the therapist to the adolescent patient. In Giovacchini, P., & Feinstein, S. (Eds.), *Adolescent psychiatry.* Vol. 5. New York: Jason Aronson, 1977.

Whitaker, C.A. Psychotherapy of the absurd: With a special emphasis on the psychotherapy of aggression. *Family Process,* 1975, **14**, 1-16.

______. Struggling with impatient impasse: Absurdity and acting-in. *J. Marriage and Fam. Counsel.,* 1978, **4**, 69-77.

Whitehorn, J.C., & Betz, B.A. A study of psychotherapeutic relationships between physicians and schizophrenic patients. *Am. J. Psychiatry,* 1954, **111**, 321-331.

Will, O.A. Values and the psychotherapist. Presented at the American Psychiatric Association, San Francisco, 1980.

Williams, R.B., Jr., & Gentry, W.D. (Eds.) *Behavioral approaches to medical treatment.* Cambridge, MA: Ballinger, 1977.

Yalom, I.D. A study of group therapy dropouts. *Arch. Gen. Psychiatry,* 1966, **14**, 393-414.

______. *The theory and practice of group psychotherapy.* (2nd ed.) New York: Basic Books, 1975.

ZETZEL, E. A developmental approach to the borderline patient. *Am. J. Psychiatry,* 1971, **127**, 867-871.

ZIPKIN v. FREEMAN, 436 S.W. 2d (Mo. 1968).

ZUK, G. The go-between process in family therapy. *Family Process,* 1966, **5**, 162-178.

______. The side-taking function in family therapy. In Sager, C.J., & Kaplan, H.S. (Eds.), *Progress in group and family therapy.* New York: Brunner/Mazel, 1972.

Index

Abstinence, rule of, 114
Acting in, 97-99
Acting out, 11, 26, 98-99
Adams, S., 42, 44, 60
Adler, G., 141, 151
Adolescence, 155-56
Adolescents
  adverse transference reactions with, 164-65
  alliance with, 163
  character of normal, 156
  confidentiality with, 160
  confrontation of, 168
  contractual issues with, 159-63
  countertransference to, 165-66
  group therapy with, 168
  negative feelings of, 168
  overidentification with, 165
  parents of, 161
  process issues with, 163-66
  transference reactions of, 165
  treatment of, 155-69
  warning parents of, 161
Aging, impact on the therapist, 118-22
Alexander, F., 5
Alexithymia, 72-73
Alger, I., 23
Alliance
  antitherapeutic, 18
  inadequate, 18
Altshul, V.A., 74
Anger, nontransference, 67
Anorexia nervosa, 57
Aronson, H., 9
Ayllon, T., 42, 60

Barnhouse, R.T., 71
Beavers, W.R., ix, 3
Beck, A.T., 48, 66, 216
Beck Depression Inventory, 216
Behavior therapy, 66
Being and staying, 33
Berger, M.M., 23
Bergin, A.E., 2-4, 6, 34, 171
Bermak, G.E., 117

Berne, E., 24, 66
Berzins, J.I., 148
Biological intervention, 89
Bipolar illness, 89
Bloch, D.A., 194
Borderline patient, 38, 74-75, 106-107, 139, 217
  antitherapeutic alliance, 151
  contractual issues of, 150-51
  countertransference to, 151
  hospitalization of, 149, 152
  process issues with, 151-53
  suicidal, 152
  therapeutic alliance with, 151
  transference with, 151
  treatment of, 148-53
Bowers, M.B., Jr., 145
Boyer, L., 152
Bozarth, J.D., 2, 114
Breuer, J., 11

Carkhuff, R.R., 2
Case vignettes
  Mr. A., 182
  Mr. A.A., 76-78
  Mrs. A.B., 180
  Mrs. A.E., 116
  Mrs. A.H., 79-80, 176-77
  Mrs. A.K., 13, 39-40, 100-101
  Mrs. A.L., 205-206
  Mrs. A.M., 57-58
  Mrs. A.P., 16-17
  Mr. J., 179
  Miss K., 94
  Mr. K., 82, 175
  Mrs. L., 33, 69, 185
  M., 90
  Miss M., 67-68, 164-67
  N., 92
  Miss N., 14, 163
  Miss O., 19
  Mr. O., 169
  Mrs. Q., 180-81
  Mrs. T., 93
  Mrs. Z., 182
Chasin, R., 207
Chesler, P., 71, 105
Chesser, E.S., 66
Chessick, R.D., 10, 116
Chrzanowski, G., 75
Clarification, 166
Cognitive therapy, 66
Coleadership, 186-91
  contract, 186-87
  disadvantages of, 190
  disclosure in, 189
  intimacy of, 189
  as modeling, 190
  splitting of transference by, 191
Collins, J.L., 2
Communication, pathological, 3
Compliance, *see* Noncompliance
Concerned relatives, 55-57
Confidentiality, 144
Confrontation, 133, 141, 158, 166
Consultant, use of, 25, 28-30, 219
Consultation, peers, 23
Context, inappropriate, 18, 96-97
Contract, definition of, 43
Contracts
  and ego strength, 51
  evaluation, 45-47
  imposing, 46
  invalid, 18, 88
  level of therapy and, 50
  making, 42-43
  marital, 199-200
  negotiating, 55, 57-58
  with psychosis-prone patients, 147
  with psychotic patients, 143
  with spouse or relative, 55-57
  therapeutic, 21, 47-50
  unclear, 18, 94-95
  written, 60
Corrective emotional experience, 5
Counterintrojective technique, 141-42, 209-210
Counterprojective technique, 139-41, 167, 209
Countertransference, 12, 38, 74-82, 99-102, 121, 124
  definition of, 74
  diagnosis of, 100-101
  resolution of, 101
  signs of, 81-82
Couple and family therapy, negative outcome rate of, 194
  impasse in, 199

contraindications to, 195
contracts in, 196-99
countertransference in, 202
indications for, 195-96
negative outcome of, 194
process issues in, 199-202
resistances in, 194-95
transference in, 202
power distribution in, 196
Cowan, R.B., 138
Craig, T., 9, 172
Creative partnership, 40

Dahlberg, C.C., 71
Davis, F.B., 187
De La Torre, J., 45
Depression, 89-90
Deterioration effect, 6; *see also* Therapy, harm by
Dewald, P.A., 124-26
Diary, use of, 216
Dropouts, *see* Termination, premature
Drug therapy, 90, 146

Ego
boundaries, 37, 51, 143, 151
defenses, 12
deficit, dealing with, 128-54
function, 129-30
immature, 142
impairment, 128, 130, 145, 149, 153
integration, 99
observing, 128, 139
organically impaired, 142
participant, 128
regression, 54
reintegration, 132
strength, signs of, 135
strength, illustration of, 131*t*
Eissler, K., 117-19, 121
Electroshock treatment, 181
Emery, G., 48
Encounter groups, 2
Engel, G.L., 91
Erickson, E.H., 103, 207
Evaluation contract, consultative, 29
Eysenck, H.J., 2, 5

Families
dysfunctional, 3, 86
healthy, 3
Family support, mobilizing, 86-88
Family therapy, 202-210
adverse transference reactions in, 207
antitherapeutic alliances in, 206
contractual issues in, 203-206
contraindications to, 203
indications for, 202-203
negative outcome of, 194
paradoxical intervention in, 207-210
process issues, 206-207
as repressive therapy, 202
technical errors in, 207
therapeutic alliance in, 207
transference gratification in, 207
Feedback, 52, 151
interpersonal, 158
Fees, 58-59, 85
Feifel, H., 111
Fenichel, O., 65, 74
Fiester, A.R., 9
Figure 6.1, 131*t*
Folman, R., 10
Framo, J.L., 193
Frank, J.D., 33
Freud, A., 11
Freud, S., 11, 31, 111, 114
Fuller, D., ix
Fuller, M., 116

Gallows laugh, 24
Garfield, S.L., 8, 9, 172
Garza, A.C., 45
Gentry, W.D., 92
Genuineness, 2, 134
Glick, S.D., 193-94, 202, 211
Goldberg, C., 207
Gorney, J.E., 28
Gould, R.L., 110
Green, A., 152
Greenson, R.R., 34, 50, 74, 96
Groesbeck, C.J., 111
Group therapy, 171-92
adverse transference reaction in, 180-81

Group therapy (*cont.*)
antitherapeutic alliance, 179
casualty rate, 171
coleadership of, 186-91
composition, 177
and confidentiality, 173
contracts in, 173-77
countertransference in, 182-83
dropout rate, 171-72
ego-supportive, 173
evocative, 173
fees, 173-74
inadequate alliance in, 179-80
inappropriate group, 177-78
inappropriate placement in, 176
negative placement in, 176-77
norms in, 174, 178
physical contact in, 184
projective identification in, 185
reality factors in, 172-73
repressive, 173
rules, 174-75
Tavistock model of, 183
technical errors in, 184-86
transference gratification in, 183-84
Grunebaum, H., 195, 207
Gunderson, J., 152
Gurman, A.S., 194

Hadley, S.W., 164
Haley, J., 204
Havens, L.L., 33, 75, 139, 141
Heine, R.W., 9
Henry, J., 3
Here-and-now focus, 49, 52, 134
Homework, 216
Hospitalization, psychiatric, 136-38
of addicted persons, 138
involuntary, 136
Huffine, C., 9, 172
Hypnosis, 16

Identification, 52, 62
Impaired Physician Program, 127
Impasse
and antitherapeutic alliance, 18
and biological factors, 89-93
contract-related, 18, 42-60
controlled, 38
and countertransference, 18
countertransference-based, 101
creative solution of, 38
in couple and family therapy, 193-211
definition of, 8
diagnosis and management of, 8-41, 219-20
early, 8, 85-97
end-stage, 102-108
and ego strength, 18
in ego-supportive therapy, 155-70
family reaction to, 24-25
in group psychotherapy, 171-92
impending, 20
and inadequate therapeutic alliance, 18
and inappropriate contract for therapy, 18
and inappropriate therapist, 18
mid-stage, 97-102
and misdiagnosis, 18, 89
as nodal point, 35
positive aspects of, 35-40
process-related, 18, 61-83
reaction to, 24, 32-34
reality factors in, 18, 85-88
in repressive therapy, 128-54
resolution of, 25-32
secondary problems of, 23-25
as shared dilemma, 33
and stage of psychotherapy, 84-109
and therapist's life cycle, 110-27
therapist values and, 20, 64-65
transference-based, 18, 65-74, 141
transference gratification and, 18
and unclear therapeutic contract, 18
Impasse resolution, enlisting patient in, 25-26
Insight, 64, 72
Interpretation, 11, 14-15, 99, 141, 156, 166

Johansen, K.H., ix, 152
Johnson, V., 187
Jung, C.G., 117

Kadis, A.L., 53, 172, 176
Kardener, S.H., 116
Kardiner, A., 12
Kempthorne, G.C., 127
Kepecs, J.G., 22
Kernberg, O., 50, 126, 132, 141, 149
Kessler, D.R., 193-94, 202, 211
Kirescik, T.J., 42
Klerman, G., 89-90
Kniskern, D.P., 194
Krauft, C.C., 2, 114
Kurz, M., 8, 172

Lambert, M.J., 2, 129, 144
Langs, R.J., 44, 50, 82
Levinson, D.J., 110, 112
Lewis, J.M., ix, 3, 117
Lieberman, M.A., 2, 171
Liff, Z., ix, 35
Limit setting, 133, 141, 158
Lionells, M., 117
Little, R.E., 125
Little, R.R., 112
Lohr, N.E., 187
Lombillo, J.R., 42
Looney, J.G., 112
Lothstein, L.M., 171-72
Luborsky, L.B., 12

Malan, D.H., 184
Manipulation, 31
Mann, C.H, 117
Marsh, I.N., 116
Martin, P.A., 196
Masters, W.H., 187
Masterson, J., 151-52
Matthews-Simonton, S., 91
McCartney, J.L., 116
McGee, T.F., 187
Mecklin, L., Jr., 112
Meyer, V., 66
Miles, M.D., 2, 171
Minnesota Multiphasic Personality Inventory, 216
Mintz, E.E., 176, 219
Misdiagnosis, 62, 89
Mismatch, *see* Therapist, mismatch
Mitchell, K.M., 2, 114, 134
Modeling, 32
Mullahy, P., 139
Myerson, P., 141

Nadelson, T., 74
Narcissistic personality, 217
National Center for Health Statistics, 9
Nemetz, P., 111
Nemiah, J., 173
Neugarten, B.L., 110
New psychiatrist, 112
  typical mistakes of, 113
Nodal point, 5, 33-35, 40
Noncompliance, 10, 15-17, 40
  and context of treatment, 15
  therapist response to, 16

Objects
  introjected, 139-41
  persecuting, 141
One-way mirror, 26
Orgel, M., 42, 44, 60
Overall, B., 9

Paradoxical intervention, 207-210
Parataxic distortions, 167
Patients; *see also* Case vignettes
  paranoid, 139
  psychosis-prone, 145-48
  psychotic, 142-45
  as social outlets, 104-105
  as surrogate families, 105
  withdrawn, autistic, 144
Paul, G.L., 4
Pitts, F.N., 127
Pleasure principle, 214
Pope, K.S., 7, 68
Praecox gefuhl, 75
Premature closure, 45
Projection, 139-40
Projective identification, 152, 165
Psychiatrist
  new, 112
  late career, 118
  mid-career, 115
Psychoanalysis, 12, 50, 99, 138
Psychoanalytic psychotherapy, 50, 166

Psychological adaptive mechanisms, 129-32
Psychological testing, 27-28, 216
and borderline personality, 28
Psychologically triggered physical disorders, 91
Psychotherapy, *see* Therapy
Psychotherapist, *see* Therapist
Puryear, D.A., 85, 208

Rabinovitch, D., 145
Rabkin, J.G., 64, 148
Ravich, R.A., 196
Razin, A.M., 114
Reality testing, 142
Repetition compulsion, 65
Repression, 11, 74, 143
Repressive therapy, 51-52, 55, 128-54, 158
contracts in, 51-52
structuring of, 132-35
structuring environment in, 135-36
transference management in, 138-39
Rescue fantasies, 81
Resistance, 10-15, 40, 65
definition, 12
interpersonal, 11
intrapsychic, 11
superego, 12
therapist response to, 16
transference, 12-15
Rich, C.L., 127
Robbins, M., 138
Robertiello, R.C., 71
Rogers, C.R., 134
Rorschach Test, 28, 216
Rosenzweig, S.P., 10
Roth, N., 121
Roy v. *Hartogs*, 70
Rudestam, K.E.A., 9
Rush, A.J., 48
Rutherford, R.B., Jr., 60

Sager, C.J., 199
Saretsky, T., 125, 152, 217, 219
Schectman, F., 45
Schizophrenia, 114, 117
Schuman, B.N., 187
Schur, M., 73
Schwitzgebel, R.K., 42
Searles, H.F., 97
Secondary gain, 12
Secondary process, 158
Sexual exploitation, 70, 16
Shapiro, R.J., 10
Shaw, B.F., 48
Sherman, R.E., 42
Sign
borderline, 75
Havens', 75
Hendrick's, 75
Sullivan's, 75
Weiner's, 75
Simons, R.D., 60
Simonton,, O.C., 91
Simpson, N.H., 7
Singer, B.A., 12
Skirban, W., 60
Solomon, M., 194
Sparks, T.F., 91
Stalemates, minor, 123
Steidl, J., 145
Sternbach, R.A., 12
Stone, L., 67
Strupp, H.H., 64, 194
Sullivan, H.S., 139
Supervision, 23, 219

Talbott, C.D., 127
Taylor, B., 111
Termination, 10, 31, 102-108
fear of, 107
forced, 107
inappropriate, 102-105
patient unwillingness, 107
premature, 9-10, 85, 104, 171-72
therapist unwillingness, 105-107
threat of, 32
Thematic Apperception Test, 216
Therapist
aggressive impulses of, 151
attitude toward mental illness, 148
defensiveness, 26, 123

denial of illness by, 119
disability of, 126
emotionally deprived, 117
exhibitionism of, 124-25
feelings of, 26, 74-75, 107-108, 153
as go-between, 202
illness of, 122-25
impaired, 126
inappropriate, 9
isolated, 116
life cycle, 110-27
masochism of, 125
mismatch with patient, 61-65, 74
motivation for becoming a, 111, 112
narcissism of, 126, 175
narcissistic accretion of, 74, 118
narcissistic depletion of, 126
narcissistic injury or despair of, 38
narcissistic vulnerability of, 125
need to cure, 111
occupational hazards of, 117
omnipotent fantasies of, 175
personality variables of, 114
psychonoxious, 4
sadistic impulses of, 151
suicide of, 127
traumatic life events of, 122-27
untrained, 10

Therapy
combined, 172
definition of, 2
effectiveness of, 216
ego-supportive, 52, 98, 132, 155: contracts in, 52-54; structuring of, 157
errors in, 20, 22-23
evocative, 50, 54-55: contracts in, 54-55
existential, 33
harm by, 2, 6, 171, 194
interrupted, 108
limit-setting in, 133, 141, 158
mistakes in, 6
multiple, 30
orientation to, 49
outcomes of, 6
outcome measures, 2
overvalued, 64, 93-94
repressive, 50, 98
stages of, 84-109
supportive, 50
unrealistic goals for, 106
vacation from 25, 31-32

Tracking errors, 22
Transactional analysis, 66
Transfer of patient, 25, 29-30
Transference, 11-12, 30, 49, 55, 58, 65-74, 103, 120, 124, 172
erotic, 70
exploitation of, 70-71
gratification, 101
guilt, 72
interpretations, 30
management, 138: counterintrojective techniques, 141-42; counterprojective techniques, 139-41, 16*t*7; minimizing transference, 67, 98-99, 139
negative, 12, 132, 138
neurosis, 34-35, 54, 138: as impasse, 34
positive, 12, 132, 138
resistance, 97
Traumatic conditions, 11
Treatment, *see* Therapy
Trosman, H., 9
Truax, C.B., 2, 134

Ulanov, A.B., 71
Uncommunicativeness, 67

Vaginismus, 92
Vaillant, G.E., 129, 145, 157
Videotapes, 23
Voyeur, 15

Wangh, M., 213
Wechsler Adult Intelligence Scale, 28
Weiner, H., 91, 111
Weiner, M.F., 3, 7, 33, 44, 50, 75, 92, 124, 149, 153, 156, 165, 174, 177, 181, 184, 195, 197

Weinstock, S.J., 28
Whitaker, C.A., 207-209
Will, O.A, 63
Williams, R.B., Jr., 92
Wolpin, M., 9

Yalom, I.D., 2, 20, 171, 178, 187

Zetzel, E., 149
Zipkin v. *Freeman*, 70
Zuk, G., 193, 202